Universal Human Rights

A Comparative Research

'Allamah Muhammad Taqi Ja'fari

Translated by

Beytollah Naderlew

Edited by

Shahriar Fassih

Top Ten Award
International Network Inc.

2023

Published by: Top Ten Award International Network Inc.

Vancouver, BC **CANADA**
Email: Info@TopTenAward.Net
www.toptenaward.net

Ordering Information:
Quantity sales. Special discounts are available on quantity purchases by universities, schools, corporations, associations, and others. For details, contact the "Sales Department" at the above mentioned email address.

Imam Hussain (PBUH), 'Allamah Muhammad Taqi Ja'fari, 1st Edition.
ISBN: 978-1-990451-98-0   Paperback

In the Name of Allah,
the All-beneficent, the All-merciful

Among all of the weighty words uttered by man, two are literally of particularly profound depth – "right" and "duty."

M. T. Ja'fari

Universal Human Rights

A Comparative Research

M. T. Ja'fari

Translated by
Beytollah Naderlew

Edited by

Shahriar Fassih

Contents

Introduction

Among all of the weighty words uttered by man, two are literally of particularly profound depth – "right" and "duty."

If we regard right as man's sacred aspect, there is only one way to achieve it – duty. Moreover, if we see duty as being aligned one's path, the end of such a path will be no other than righteousness and the fulfillment of rights, which have always originated from God and poured down into all aspects of man's life. Therefore, we see "rights" as the beginning and also the end of duty. It is rights that wane man away from duties and guide him toward the domain of "becoming."

Thus, "rights" have been distant from man while being close to him as well; although they are separate from man, rights are intimately close to human nature – a fact that led to the beginning of the formation of a charter known as "rights" and a novel, elevated level which first originated from religion and spoke out through the divine words of God-sent prophets. Having established itself in the realm of history, it flourished and grew and eventually ended up in the hands of scientists who needed it to develop civilization. Therefore, as various social, economic and cultural aspects of humanity developed, "human rights" also took a more systematic, organized form. The relevant parts of human rights soon arose as well, and showed their necessities in man's mind, words, thoughts, and legacies.

Human rights were in fact man's belated outcry after Renaissance; the man was longing to find and return to his self. Unconsciously, he had decided to go back to his nature and seek out religion and his original self. Nonetheless, laws concerning human rights spread throughout the whole world but still failed to regain their religious aspect! Indeed, it was out of this very thought that the modern world and all of its appurtenance – good or evil – arose, and great philosophers such as Kant, Hegel and Voltaire each set out to presenting modern legal thoughts in the form of political and social rules for man. Kant made a particularly significant contribution; he is in fact regarded as the father of the United Nations. "Man's practical reason necessitates," he stated, "that nations move beyond their natural savage side – which leads to war – and makes a pledge for peace. Although the path toward forming a society of nations is a difficult one, it behooves us to put efforts into preserving sustainable global peace."

Meanwhile, Eastern nations were increasingly exploited and being deprived of even their slightest rights under the boots of colonizing nations. As ancient civilizations such as India, Mesopotamia, and Egypt were colonized, the only thing the oppressive colonizers were not taking into consideration was "human rights." Astoundingly, human rights have been intertwined and reiterated inside divine cultures and religions since the earliest of times.

As time passed and due to the events that gradually occurred throughout the world, colonization gave in to defeat and thanks to the awakening of men of reason and religion, return to religion found a clearer voice. Nevertheless, a comparative study of "human rights" and "divine rights" – which was absolutely necessary and should have been the first order on Eastern nations' agenda – never materialized. A charter known as Islamic human rights was never officially and actually compiled!

Time had decided to hand over this important duty to an able thinker who had a much more elevated point of view; he could shift the multi-aspect developments made by the West as well as the astounding humiliation suffered by the East with the mere interchanging of a few words – he called the West "the Eastern West" and the East "the Western East." As a matter of fact, "the universal human culture" – which was subsequently supported by many great pioneers and leading figures such as Tagore –was summing up East and West into something called "humanity," a series of elements continually witnessing the secret hidden within humanity.

The late scholar Muhammad Taghi Ja'fari began to ponder and draw his attention to human rights in the West in the 1960s; in parts of his comprehensive treatise of Rumi's *Masnavi*, there are discussions indicative of a critical point of view longing to find a way to open up a path that had been blocked. A few years later, when discussions about human rights were quite popular in many Islamic countries, he presented his theories under the title "A Comparative Study of the Universal Human Rights in the West and in Islam," which – for the first time – included new rights known as "Islamic human rights" as well as the human rights customary in the West. He spoke of and defended a subject that was unprecedented. Those who were supposed to notice that the compilation of such rights and the extraction of various materials from Islamic texts was the result of the Allameh's personal endeavors.

Those who considered the results of this research as peculiar and improbable and insisted that it was "innovative" were actually ignorant of the fact that through their statements of denial, refusal, and criticism, they were admitting that Muhammad Taghi Ja'fari had single-handedly undertaken the immense task of studying and compiling human rights from an Islamic point of view by means of his extensive endeavors. Indeed, he had dealt with the elements and contents of human rights with such legal accuracy that he could present his findings in domestic and international gatherings with the assurance of their concrete precision, thus strengthening Islamic human rights. In 1990, in the last decade of his life, having compiled an academic text, he was now ready to plead his cause to scholars and experts on legal matters.

In brief, this book is the vexillary of dialogs started by Muhammad Taghi Ja'fari, a man who insisted on the accuracy and firmness of his statements which were made by concrete and unquestionable intellectual and logical documents but left the case open for further research and discussion without the slightest prejudice.

We hereby feel obliged to thank Mr. Beytollah Naderlew as the translator, Mr. Shahriyar Fassih as the editor, Prof. S. M. A. Boutorabi and Mr. Mahmood Ahmadirad for their cooperation in the compilation of this book. We would also like to thank Mrs. Roya Azizi Mousavi for setting the computer layout.

The Allameh Ja'fari Institute

July 2014

A Brief History of Human Rights

God indeed deserves endless gratitude and encomium for creating man equipped with two significant forces – reason and conscience – and paying man tribute and respect by endowing him with the honor of knowledge, sense of duty, cognition of righteousness and respect and having him accept them in the realm of endeavors toward evolutionary life.

Moreover, may divine leaders be blessed infinitely for providing humanity with a comprehensible interpretation of progress based upon "righteousness" and "duty" to present man with an explanation and justification of progress in line with purposeful life for them.

Before turning to the central subject matters of the book, we will take into serious account the four premises mentioned below:

Premise I

The idea that all human individuals have many grounds for equality, harmony, and unity despite their egregious physical, mental, natural and cultural differences has a long history. This consequential theory has been warmly received by keen-sighted scholars and true reformists both in the Oriental and the Occidental communities both in the past and the present. Those who find themselves unable to touch the truth of this theory through personal probes and investigations could be benefited from the intellectual heritages of different cultures and nations – which are easily available in general libraries – and understand the theory above. We shall quote here an indispensable example of the hundreds of statements that demonstrate the universal principles of equality, harmony, and human unions:

Delicate philosophical ideas and exalted religious beliefs are widely reflected in legends along with superstitions and puerile impressions. Like coal mines, myths contain both massive portions of char and slim streaks of diamond at the same time. As a result, unless these myths are, from a mythological aspect, analyzed into their basic constitutive ideas, we will never discover the hidden treasures of human intellectual subtleties within the blind myths. Regardless of their recreational and lullaby-like aspect, indeed, what makes the study of these myths unavoidable for the researchers of history of philosophical ideas, those who manifest human universal conscience, anthropologists, sociologists, comparative theologians, ideologists and other scholars in human sciences and folklore

> *literature is the very reflection of these primordial treasures of intellectual and unconscious heritages of various nations in the myths.*[1]

If we take for serious the *"universal human conscience"* in this passage, we will instantly conclude that one basic factor or primordial faculty can harmonize all human individuals with each other and unite them in a universal legal system by their innumerable shared characteristics as human beings. To state the matter otherwise, if we could fathom human beings in terms of "conscience", "practical reason" and "human primordial nature (i.e., *al-fetra'*)", we will undoubtedly see that " delicate philosophical ideas and exalted religious beliefs", and in general terms, indissoluble streaks of diamond within the profusion of archaic stone coals and "the hidden treasures of human unending intellectual subtleties" are the very facts that even today are debated as the basis of the harmony of human unions with the same sense of factuality, novelty, and emergency. On the other hand, if we are to conceive human beings with the self-interested ideas and despotisms that they had, have and will continue to have, we will immediately find that no harmony and unity is conceivable among human beings not of yesterday, not in today and not in tomorrow, since the first outcome of these self-interested and despotic ideas is the propagation of the running principle of: "I am the end, and the other people are merely my means!" This is the very principle that has resulted in the eradication of "conscience", "practical reason", and most of all, the human pure "primordial nature" and the following conclusion has been obtained, for it is impossible to find two human beings who are harmonized and united with each other in an absolutely free and wholehearted fashion upon their concrete conditions "as they are".

Premise II

Contrary to the idea that the ratification of both universal declarations of human rights (Islamic and Western) by the authorities of both legal systems implies the end of all debates, investigations, and criticisms of the two legal systems, we should announce in a very straightforward manner that it is, in fact, the time to start an overall and foundational revision of both legal systems – the fulfillment of which would take a long period and is hinged upon truth-seeking and understanding the significance of demarcation of rights, obligations, and freedoms for human societies. Needless to say, ordinary human persons could not handle such an adventurous task; experienced and connoisseur anthropologists, who know every aspect of human existence and understand human norms, ramifications, lusts and interests and on whom is depended the happiness and prosperity of the society but their own personal happiness does not need the public

---

1 - Beier, Ullie, *The Origin of Life and Death: African Creation Myths.* (Originally in English)

understanding, are the ones who can undertake such a responsibility.

As you can see, in such conditions, ordinary people should have an unaccountable boldness to claim to be able to know every aspect of human existence within the both domains of "is-ness" and "ought-ness" – even in a determined historical era and in one society – and ordain the most realistic rights, obligations and freedoms for mankind. Accordingly, without being enchanted with "that's it, and there is no way out," we should use much more of our efforts to collect datum of both domains of "the human being as he or she is" and "the human being as he or she ought to be," and this is an essentially possible task. Having achieved this, we shall come to a necessary and sufficient investigation of human shared qualities and differences; it is only after handling these enterprises that we could proceed to provide a declaration of their rights, obligations, and freedoms.

Premise III

We have a clear exemplum that has frequently been used for the explanation of where a man stands in dealing with laws. Let us assume that we call upon the most professional engineers and architects for designing the plan of the most luxurious and magnificent palace of all human history, and they accept our request and prepare a perfect plan. After providing the best and strongest materials for the construction of the palace, when everything is ready for the project to go into operation and the experts ask us for the location of the plan, we take them to a volcanic hillside and tell them the place will be constructed on the top of this active volcano!! In such a situation, the experts will surely ask us, "Are there any ambulances of hospitals for the mentally deranged around here?"

Now this exemplum could be applied to the magnificent and impressive legal palaces of today that have all clearly been constructed on the top of the interior volcanoes of protagonists of indecency, despots and fanatic votaries of power – who unfortunately constitute the majority of people. Accordingly, we openly say that unless the interior volcanoes of the self-centered, self-interested and hedonist people are smothered by a true education upon exalted human principles and changed into fertile and cultivable lands for sowing the humanizing legal principles, it is impossible for such legal systems – and even their more developed versions – to have the capability to lead human societies to the sphere of "Intelligible Life"; particularly, with the disgusting discriminations that are seen in the application of these laws.

Premise IV

The fourth premise mainly belongs to the excavation of the basic grounds and roots of the universal idea of human rights. Generally speaking, the idea of human rights has originated from three basic grounds:

The First Ground: The Basic Principles of Natural Rights

Almost certainly, from the time humanity became aware of the shared mental and physical characteristics of his fellow human individuals and the necessity of social life, a man truly discovered the basic principles of his own natural rights (i.e., primordial rights). The building block of the basic principles of natural rights is the "protection and regulation of human life" in the two aspects mentioned below:

The First Aspect: A Purely Natural Life

The Second Aspect: Intelligible Life (i.e. the ideal form of life).

The first natural right of human beings to their purely natural life is the right of living, which has been recognized by all revealed religions and legal systems across the world.

On the other hand, the ideal life is the locus of four basic principles of the natural rights as follows: the right of respectability, the right to education, the right of committed freedom, and the right of legal equality.

The Second Ground: Revealed Religions

Since all divine religions have been revealed for the growth and perfection of human persons according to their primordial nature, God has already communicated the basic principles of primordial human rights through his holy messengers to the people. The people of Moses (PBUH), who are in fact followers of Abraham (PBUH), believe that:

> *Moses sees in his Sharia'h (Divine Law) the perennial law by which the universe moves forward. The sharia'h presented by Moses is a natural law.*[2]

As we shall see in the coming debates, the quintuple principles of human

---

2 - Bréhier, Émile, *The Religious and Philosophical Ideas of Philo of Alexandria* (*Études de philosophie antique*), 1955, translated by Muhammad Yusef Musa and Abdulhalim Najjar, pp. 29 (Arabic translation). It is noteworthy that natural and primordial rights in this context have the same resonance, as the primordial nature here signifies the very creation of human beings and their faculties and interests. Moreover, this is why we say that natural rights have a divine aspect, and when Earl Mino says, "The monarch and the peasantry left the scene in England by 1642 and a long course of unending challenges began and did not come to an end before 1668. James II (the son of Charles I who was executed in 1649) escaped to France while he still had the claim of divine right; nonetheless, it became clear in the same year that natural rights have defeated the divine rights!" (*The History of the Idea of Human Rights*). We could say that what is meant by "divine right" here is the same right that the deceased monarchs of the past claimed of their monarchies rather than the divine right in its true sense as is reflected in natural or primordial rights.

natural rights (the right of respectability, the right to education, the right of committed freedom, and the right of equality) are all substantiated in authentic Islamic texts and it is this very substantiation that will be clearly demonstrated in this book.

Revealed religions declare the acceptance and acting upon the principles of natural rights in intelligible life in the wake of free conscience and primordial human perfectionism rather than compulsion serving as the basis of human growth and perfection. And this is why acting upon the principles of natural rights and other righteously grounded rights which have their origin in the free and perfectionist conscience is not a public attitude. Although the protagonists of acting upon the principles of natural rights always constitute the minority of human societies, these crucial principles have never been totally uprooted from the life of nations. As we shall see, these principles could easily be traced in Islamic texts as primordial maxims, and moreover, Muslim thinkers have also reiterated upon them. For example, the following statements of Khajeh Nasir-e Tusi's are noteworthy:

> It should be taken into consideration that the goodness of human actions is either by nature or by convention, of which the former is the quality of actions and experiences of wise human persons throughout human history which also makes up the very basis of applied ethics.[3]

The Third Ground: The Responsiveness and Endorsement of Those of Developed Minds (the Elites)

It is needless to say that the idea of the emendation of human relations with their fellow humans – whether under the stimulus of understanding the necessity of the codification of a universal legal system for the global human society or for practical moves toward the articulation of the universal rights of human beings – has always preoccupied the developed minds of the human society. Since long times ago, true thinkers have grasped the vital necessity and the value of "justice," "liberty" and "peace" for human societies regardless of their race and nationality. It is precisely based upon these miscellaneous theoretical and practical moves that we see today some audible and constructive, however heterogeneous, things as "morality," "law" and "cultural factors" among the nations. That is to say, since very long times ago, semi-civilized societies have continuously witnessed the gradual exposure of the universal human face and its manifestations in human individual pleasures, hardships, and interests as the basis of natural human rights and the emergence of literary statements, moral maxims and legal articles in human societies.

For instance, in ancient African culture we can find some related matters in the latter spirit:

---

3 - Khaje Nasir-e Tusi, *Akhlaq-e Naseri ("Naserian Ethic")*. (Arabic translation).

1- In the myth of Maluzi, the hunter primitives are reproached by God for hunting the animals: "O' man, you have chosen a repulsive way of living your life, why do you kill these animals? These living beings are your brothers. Do not eat them, since you are all my children." (Myth 32)[4]

2- In a myth of the Yoruba people, the invalid and bedridden people, such as the sightless, hunchbacked, deaf, speechless, and paralyzed men are consecrated and respected since they are deemed to be the children of God. (Myths 64 and 65)[5]

3- In the myth of Kono, it is reiterated that whites and blacks are brothers and have the same mother and brother.

(Myth 26)[6]

This attitude reveals the brightest side of the human face that continues to emerge in human societies in various forms, as we mentioned before, and this can be seen, even though dispersedly, in most of the cultures, moral principles, and legal matters.

Cynic philosophers like Antisthenes and Diogenes believe that:

> It is due to their leaning toward rascalities, lusts and being enchanted with the glamour of mundane life that people have apprehensively pitched in to codify civil laws for themselves along with natural laws.[7]

As a matter of fact, the principles of natural law which all human beings should be benefited from residing in the minds of anthropologists and within those legal codes that the man has codified throughout the history, just like the water that has penetrated trees through their roots, trunks, boughs and Leafs.

Let us turn a sharp eye upon the following sentences:

> There is strong evidence that shows that the debate of nature versus convention has been popular among Athenians of 5th century B.C. and sometimes gone out and outer, always resulting in revolts against sovereign conventions and laws in the society under the guise of legal perfectionism. Among Greek literary classics that have dwelled upon this issue is **Antigone** by **Sophocles,** which probably represents the very first time that a man of letters has addressed the aporia of the human relationship with humanly ordained statutes and his obligations toward divine laws. In this book, Antigone – a woman who has broken the law and mourned for her brother in defiance of the existing traditions and thus been fined – says in response to **Kreon** in a poetical language, "Since these laws are neither coined by Zeus nor by the one who has seated on the divine throne beside goddesses,

---

4 - Beier, Ullie, The Origin of Life and Death: African Creation Myths.

5 - Ibid.

6 - Ibid.

7 - Bréhier, Émile, The Religious and Philosophical Ideas of Philo of Alexandria, p. 33. (Arabic translation).

and also because human statutes have not been enacted by justice, I do not imagine that you, as a mortal man, could nullify and neglect the heavenly primordial laws. These heavenly laws have not emerged today or yesterday. They do never die, and no single man knows when they have been brought into existence."

This idea – i.e. the discovery and exploration of nature through divine laws of the heavens and judging humanly ordained conventions with the true and the truth – after that became a formula for critiquing social misdeeds, and thus the idea of natural right changed into a touchstone for political evaluations of social norms. Similar recourses to the idea of natural right are also observable in Euripidean opuses, where he refuses to judge social deeds and ideas based upon racial concerns and family backgrounds and even based on bondsmen whose existence is essential and common in the Greek society. He says, "There is only one matter of shame in the case of bondsmen, and it is their having been labeled as slaves; otherwise, a bondsman is never of a lower quality than a freeman." Thus, they possess an exalted and noble spirit. He has also stated, "A nobleman is the one who is noble for nature."

The Athenian society of the 5th century B. C. was fully aware of its defects; thus, they submitted to criticism regarding conventions and statutes and replaced them with natural laws (rights).[8]

And generally speaking, Greeks of the 5th century B. C. held that natural laws are eternal and subsistent while human affairs are ephemeral and transitive; as a result, if we could discover the eternal laws of nature and harmonize human life with them, human life would somehow become logical and rational and less vicious. Human perfection does indeed require being in accord with subsistent laws of nature. The goal of this philosophy could be summarized as follows: seeking subsistence within the domain of transition, and unity within diversity.

After the emergence of this philosophy, some difficulty showed itself up regarding where does this subsistence stand in human life? The common and subsistent element which inheres deep inside human nature and makes her/his true who-ness against the surface identity – secondary nature – that has its origin in social habits, conventions, and statutes.[9]

As we have mentioned before, the primordial principles of natural rights (laws) of human beings have already been in noble minds and human laws and cultures in a seminal manner, and hereunder we shall point out some of them:

---

8 - Sabien, George, *History of Political Philosophy* (Vol. One).

9 - Ibid.

I) Zu-Qarnain

According to Allameh Seyyed Muhammad Hussein Tabatabaei in the thirteenth volume of his magnum opus *Almizan* ("*The Balance*," A Commentary of the Holy Quran), where he elaborates on the verse "*And they ask you about Zu-Qarnain. Say: I will recite to you an account of him,*" (The Cave 18: 83), Zu-Qarnain in this context refers to the ancient Iranian legendary emperor **Cyrus**. It is said that Cyrus (560 B. C.) issued a charter during his reign that veritably contains a considerable amount of human rights and freedom.[10]

Xenophanes praises Cyrus as, "He turned the hearts of peoples and nations to himself in as much as they all sought to be reigned by no one but him."

According to the above quoted words by Xenophanes, it seems tenable to say that Cyrus had been a just emperor who treated his people upon their freedoms and rights.

It is an almost unanimously endorsed view by wide range of historians that Cyrus had respected different nations' sacred beliefs.

II) The Principles of Essenism

Essenism represents a Hebrew Gnostic cult which has been founded upon the principles of egalitarianism, justice, pacifism and ....[11]

III) Stoics

Having Zeno of Elea as their philosophical leader, Stoics laid their anthropology in the 4th century B. C. upon some universal tenets that are briefly articulated as follows:

> *The highest principle of stoic politics and ethics reveals itself in the sense of communion and cooperation that not only should be applied to fellow countrymen but to all people around the globe .... Thus, Stoics must have historically been the pioneers of the idea of cosmopolitanism. The idea of the generic unity of humanity is one of the main sources of Roman laws regarding individual rights which is seen as the canon of nations and nature.*[12]

We shall now dwell upon the views of some of the most distinguished of the Stoics:

I) Marcus Aurelius (121-180AD), the Roman emperor and a stoic philosopher who has said:

---

10 - Pirnia, Hassan, *Ancient Persia* (Vol. 1), p. 447. (Originally in Persian).

11 - Montesquieu, Charles Louis de Secondat, *De L' esprit de Lois*. (Originally in French).

12 - Sarton, George, *The History of Science*. (Originally in English).

I have two homelands: one is Rome, the land of my emperorship; my second homeland is the cosmos, wherein my humanity becomes flourished. Goodness lies in simultaneously being useful for both homelands.... Beware, and do not forget that people are your brothers, so love them forever.[13]

Montesquieu has also once described stoicism in the following words:

Several intellectual schools have come and gone during the years passed. No ancient philosophical schools have been better and more meritorious for human prosperity than stoicism founded by Zeno of Elea, indeed.[14]

II) Cicero (43-106 AD) is the belief that:

The law is not based on doxastic knowledge, but there is an essentially subsistent primordial justice that originates in human conscience. (This idea has properly been articulated by Cicero): There is an original, intelligible and naturally consistent law that has seminally been there inside us in an eternal and indelible fashion.... And this is the very reason why another expositor should not be sought for. There is neither Roman nor Athenian nor today's nor tomorrow's law, but it is primordially the same for all nations and times forever.... Whoever does not obey this law is, in fact, escaping from himself and shutting his eyes to human nature. Thus, by doing so, he resigns himself to unbearable difficulties, though he imagines himself to have been relieved from other chagrins.[15]

III) Lucius Annaeus Seneca (c. 4 BC-AD 65) says of bondmen:

You call them slaves, while you should take them as your fellow humans. The one who you give the name of bondman has the same origin with you; he lives under the same heaven that you do and inhales the same air that you inhale. Like you live and die, so will he; in other words, he is equal to you in life and death.[16]

IV) Justinian the Great (AD 482-565)

Justinian issued his renowned Roman codes by the year 536 AD which reads:

On natural law, laws of nations and civil law: natural law has its origin in the traditions that have been infused to all living beings by the nature. This law is not restricted to homo sapiens, but it is in force for all living beings – including birds, mammals and aquatic organisms; this law is the tradition of reproduction and upbringing. Moreover, observations show that all living beings are primordially introduced to this tradition.

---

13 - Abusa'idi, Mahdi, *Human Rights and Its Evolutionary Course in the West*, p. 94.

14 - Montesquieu, Charles Louis de Secondat, *De L' esprit de Lois*.

15 - Del Vecchio, Giorgio, *Philosophie de Driot*.

16 - Abusa'idi, Mahdi, *Human Rights and Its Evolutionary Course in the West*, p. 95.

> a) *Civil law versus nations' law: there are some context-bounded codes that exclusively belong to a nation and are merely in force among the very nation alone (civil law), which is in contrary to those universal laws that stand upon common ground and have the same resonance for all nations (nations' universal laws). As a result, the Roman people have two ranges of codes of social and individual behaviors, one of which is confined to the Romans alone, but the second one covers all nations across the globe.*
>
> b) *It is needless to say that every country distinguishes its specific civil laws with its own name. As, for example, those who apply the name Athenian codes for the laws that have really been legislated by Solon and Dracon for Athenians have not gone wrong in doing so, the same applies to the Quirites and the civil law of Rome. Nevertheless, universal laws of nations are common rules among all peoples around the globe, since they represent their common needs and wishes that are thoroughly in harmony with natural laws....*[17]

With regard to the historical course of the idea of human rights, at this point of time (i.e., the second half of the sixth century AD), we should outline here the Islamic perspective on human rights, since no codified law representing universal human rights could be spotted at this point of time and the emergence of early Islamic sources (nearly 600 years *anno domini*). But since the universal declaration of human rights from an Islamic point of view is among the fundamental issues that this book is supposed to deal with, we will put it off for the last part of our historical studies to debate over universal human rights in the perspective of Islam, its legal premises, resources and privileges.

V) Magna Carta (The Great Charter)

> *Magna Carta – The Great Charter of England – that was signed and issued by King John in the year 1215 under the pressures of the feudal barons and bishops of England, has always been declared as a document granting some individual rights to average masses.*[18]

It should be taken into account that this charter does not stipulate the equality of other nations with the British, but in fact contains only some just and useful clauses for the people of England alone.

---

17 - Abdulaziz Fahmi, *On Justinian Codes*, pp. 6-7. (Arabic translation).

18 - Abusa'idi, Mahdi, *Human Rights and Its Evolutionary Course in the West*, p. 130. (Originally in Persian).

Nevertheless, its preamble denotes the appropriation of those just and functional clauses to all people who live in the kingdom of King John:

> *Addressing barons, bishops, abbots, sheriffs, Woodmen and other loyal subjects of his kingdom, King John announces that, for the health of his own soul and those of his ancestors and heirs, to the honour of God, the exaltation of the Holy Church, and the better ordering of his kingdom, he grants the free men of his kingdom a series of rights.*[19]

The last clause of *Magna Carta* (Clause 66) reads:

> *It is accordingly your wish and command that the English Church shall be free, and that men in our kingdom shall have and keep all these liberties, rights, and concessions, well and peaceably in their fulness and entirety for them and their heirs, of us and our heirs, in all things and all places for ever.*

VI) Thomas Aquinas (1374-1427)

> *As opposed to Greek philosophers and stoics, who took the natural laws to be the origin of law in general, he paid more attention to positive laws and having theorized it brought it into public focus…. However, in his view, the idea law has a universal, primordial and natural aspect and humanly ordained statutes are binding when they are not at odds with basic principles of justice.*[20]

VII) John Locke (1632-1704)

John Locke, whose ideas have had positive impacts on The American Declaration of Independence – which is seemingly penetrated with streaks of human rights – has said:

> *All human individuals are naturally in an equal position. In such a condition, all rights and concessions are so equally disseminated among the whole individuals that nobody would have a privilege to her/his fellow humans. Nothing is more self-evident than the fact that all human individuals are homogenous and have equal rights to be benefited from natural bounties. Natural liberty means being free from any bondage whatsoever and merely obeying the natural laws. Locke's point here is not to say that all human individuals are physically and intellectually equal; rather, his intention is to state that every individual represents an independent unity, and hence, he is essentially equal with other unities (individuals). Furthermore, every individual is also granted with particular rights just by virtue of his state of being human, not because of his physical power or social dignity.*[21]

19 - Ibid, p. 134.
20 - Ibid, pp. 116-136.
21 - Ibid, pp. 42-43.

Locke's ideas later left remarkable impact upon the American Declaration of Independence and its basic laws. It is said that Jefferson, who played an indispensable role in the preparation of the Declaration, was among the disciples of John Locke.[22] But since the people of the American society come from different ethnical origins and nations, it could be said that understanding the idea of human rights in contemporary times, has been easier for the American society than any other society. The Declaration reads:

> *We hold these truths to be self-evident, that all men are created equal, that they are endowed by their Creator with certain unalienable Rights, that among these are Life, Liberty and the pursuit of Happiness. — That to secure these rights, Governments are instituted among Men, deriving their just powers from the consent of the governed, — that whenever any form of Government becomes destructive of these ends, it is the Right of the People to alter or to abolish it, and to institute new Government, laying its foundation on such principles and organizing its powers in such form, as to them shall seem most likely to affect their Safety and Happiness. Prudence, indeed, will dictate that Governments long established should not be changed for light and transient causes; and accordingly, all experience hath shown that mankind are more disposed to suffer, while evils are sufferable than to right themselves by abolishing the forms to which they are accustomed. But when a long train of abuses and usurpations, pursuing invariably the same Object evinces a design to reduce them under absolute Despotism, it is their right, it is their duty, to throw off such Government, and to provide new Guards for their future security. — Such has been the patient sufferance of these Colonies; and such is now the necessity which constrains them to alter their former Systems of Government. The history of the present King of Great Britain is a history of repeated injuries and usurpations, all having in direct object the establishment of an absolute Tyranny over these States. To prove this, let Facts be submitted to a candid world....*
>
> *This declaration has been the basis for all latter codified bodies of basic laws... The opening of the Virginia Declaration of Rights – which is about human rights, equality, and freedom – has been endorsed by all legislated rights throughout the United States and particularly this principle that all power is vested in, and consequently derived from, the people.*
>
> *The main points of individual rights and freedoms implicated in early basic laws of United States are as follows:*

1. The freedom of expression and press and the freedom of religion and belief.
2. Being endowed with equal rights and concessions.
3. The right of possession (ownership) and the right of being benefited from natural bounties.

---

22 - Ibid, p. 179.

4. The right of society for those affairs that are connected with the public benefits.

5. That in all capital or criminal prosecutions a man has the right to demand the cause and nature of his accusation, to be confronted with the accusers and witnesses, to call for evidence in his favor, and to a speedy trial by an impartial jury of twelve men of his vicinage, without whose unanimous consent he cannot be found guilty;

6. Nor can anyone be compelled to give evidence against himself; that no man be deprived of his liberty, except by the law of the land or the judgment of his peers.

7. No heavy caution money should be claimed from those who have been found guilty.

8. No free individual would be imprisoned, or be deprived of her/ his properties and inalienable rights of a free life, but upon the legal judgment of a competent court.

9. Retroactivity in particular laws, in the cases that sharper penalties have been decided, is not allowed.23

VIII) Montesquieu (1689-1748)

Montesquieu's viewpoints on the classification of rights indicate that:

The laws that govern humanity originate in several kinds of rights:

1. *Natural rights.*

2. *Heavenly rights that represent the rights of religion.*

3. *Divine rights that guard the religion indeed.*

4. *Human rights, which are in other words one and the same as the Civilized man's Eight Deadly*

5. *Claude*

6. *; that is to say, as in every country the citizens have their civil rights as granted, every nation in the world also has an inalienable set of human rights concerning which every nation in the world represents an individual in human society.*

7. *Universal rights of public policy.*

8. *Areal rights of private policy which differ from one society to another.*

9. *The rights of victory. These rights come as the result of the fact that a nation, whether willingly or unwillingly, has invaded to other nation and defeated it.*

10. *Civil rights, which secure every individual's properties, life and legitimate freedoms from other individuals' incursions.*

---

23 - Ibid, pp. 181-184.

11. *Family rights or domestic rights. These rights have their roots in the fact that society has not been constituted from individuals, but in fact, families who need special sets of rights and a particular form of government to sustain their lives.[24]*

There are some noteworthy critical points on the classification of rights as depicted by Montesquieu that will not be discussed here, in particular on the rights of victory. Montesquieu characterizes the origin of this class of rights in the following words, "Those rights come as the result of the fact that a nation, whether willingly or unwillingly, has invaded another nation and defeated it."

The only human origin of these rights might be traced back to the state of "unwillingly being involved in the battle", for victory in a battle that has been triggered willingly and consciously by a nation under the plea of dominance and conquest would never make room for any rights whatsoever, since it is only the oppressed nation who has been invaded and slaughtered that is eligible to have the right to defend its life by any means and push the enemy out of its motherland. However, the fourth class of rights that Montesquieu regards as equal to civil rights has the ultimate value and magnificence.

IX) Thomas Paine (1737-1809)

Thomas Paine, the English-born American colonial writer, says:

Deep inside the nature of human individuals lies a sense that if left unawakened during their lifetime, it shall be buried with them in the grave. This sense is the very sense that pushes individuals to recognize and vindicate their natural rights and thus tear down the bondages of feigned necessity.

Paine repeatedly notices that freedom and happiness are crucial to human nature and, continually being threatened and for thwarting theses threats, humanity must recognize and reiterate their natural rights and strongly demand authorities to acknowledge and recognize them.[25]

According to Paine, political and social rights are the derivatives of natural rights. Humanity, by nature, has the right to secure himself from would-be dangers and be benefited from security as a naturally given bounty, and if left alone, man would not be able to provide himself with what naturally and truly belongs to him. Thus, humanity concludes the social contract so to secure human beings' survival through cooperation. However, Paine held that such a social contract should not violate individuals' natural rights because all basic laws of the society are born out of natural rights.[26]

24 - Montesquieu, Charles Louis de Secondat, *De L' esprit de Lois.*
25 - Abusa'idi, Mahdi, *Human Rights and Its Evolutionary Course in the West*, pp. 207-213. (Originally in Persian).
26 - Ibid.

X) Human Rights in French Constitutions

The Universal Declaration of the Rights of Man and Citizens (Déclaration des droits de l'Homme et du citoyen) issued on August 28, 1789, which is an inseparable part of the French constitution of 1791, comprises one preamble and 17 clauses. Of course, this declaration has been prepared according to England's declaration of rights of 1689 as well as the declaration of independence of 13 American colonies dated July 4th, 1776 and the constitution of United States of Northern America dated September 17th, 1787.[27]

French revolutionists appealed to the idea of natural rights, which regard all individuals equal in their rights and oppose concessions, to operationalize this significant doctrine.[28]

The Declaration of the Rights of Man and Citizens of 1791 has also addressed the issue of natural rights as inalienable rights.[29]

Déclaration des droits de l'Homme et du citoyen of 1791 reads:

"The people of society have a series of natural, sacred, unquestionable and definite right. Any ignorance of those in charge regarding the existence of these rights or their observance will be the single reason for the annihilation or misery of human societies."

The declaration goes on to state that the constitution guarantees the following as natural and civil rights for the people:

Article 1 — *Men are born and are to remain free and equal in rights. Social distinctions can be based only upon benefit for the community.*

Article 2 —*The aim of every political association is the preservation of the natural rights of man, which rights must not be prevented. These rights are freedom, property, security and resistance to oppression.*

Article 3 —*The fundamentals of sovereignty originate essentially from the Nation. No organization, or any individual either, may exercise any authority that does not expressly come from there.*

Article 4 —*Liberty consists in being able to do anything that does not harm other people. Thus, the exercise of the natural rights of each man has only those limits that that ensure to the other members of society the enjoyment of these same rights. These limits may be determined only by law.*

Article 5 — *The law has only the right to forbid those actions that are detrimental to society. Anything that is not forbidden by law may not be prevented, and*

---

27 - Ghasemzadeh, Murteza, *The French Constitution*, p. 24. (Originally in Persian).

28 - Ibid.

29 - Abusa'idi, Mahdi, *Human Rights and Its Evolutionary Course in the West*, p. 193.

no one is to be compelled to do what the law does not require.

Article 6 *— The law is the expression of the collective wishes of the public. All citizens have the right to contribute, personally or through their representatives, to the formation and compilation of the law.*

Article 7 *— No man can be accused, arrested or detained except in the cases determined by law, and according to the methods that the law has stipulated. Those who pursue, distribute, enforce, or cause to be enforced arbitrary orders must be punished; but any citizen summoned, or apprehended in accordance with the law, must obey immediately, for he will make himself guilty by resisting.*

Article 8 *— The law must introduce only punishments that are strictly and indisputably necessary; and no one may be punished except in accordance with a law instituted and published before the offense is committed, and legally applied.*

Article 9 *— Because every man is presumed innocent until he has been declared guilty if it should be considered necessary to arrest him, any force beyond the minimum necessary to arrest and imprison the person will be dealt with severely.*

Article 10 *— No one should be harassed for his opinions, even religious views, provided that the expression of such opinions does not cause a breach of the peace as established by law.*

Article 11 *— The free communication of thought and opinions is one of the most precious rights of man. Any citizen can, therefore, speak, write and publish freely; however, they are answerable for abuse of this freedom as determined by law.*

Article 12 *— Guaranteeing the rights of man and the citizen requires a public force. This force is therefore established for the benefit of all, and not for the particular use of those to whom it is entrusted.*

Article 13 *— For the maintenance of the public force, and for administrative expenses, a common tax is necessary. It must be spread in similar fashion among all citizens, in proportion to their capability.*

Article 14 *— All citizens have the right to verify for themselves, or through their representatives, the necessity for the public tax. They further have the right to grant the tax freely, to watch over how it is used, and to determine its amount, the basis for its assessment and of its collection, and its duration.*

Article 15 *— Society has the right to ask a public official for an explication of his management and supervision.*

Article 16 *— Any society in which the guarantee of rights is not ensured, nor a separation of powers is worked out, has no Constitution.*

Article 17 — *The right to ownership is an inviolable and sacred right, and no one may be deprived of it – unless, however, public necessity, legally investigated, clearly requires it, and just and prior compensation has been paid.*

> *The above are the articles of Déclaration des droits de l'Homme et du citoyen of 1789. Its principles of territorial sovereignty, liberty and equality have mainly been recognized in latter French constitutions.*
> *These principles made their ways into other territories and were recognized by their constitutions in the nineteenth century.*[30]

The constitution of 1795 consists of 377 main articles, 31 of which concern human rights and duties. This constitution begins as follows:

> *The French people proclaim in the presence of the Supreme Being the following declaration of citizens' rights and citizen.*[31]

In the second chapter (Articles 2-17) of the Constitution of 1848, some rights have been granted to individuals that could be of avail in the Universal Declaration of Human Rights from an occidental point of view.[32]

The Declaration of Human Rights and Man's Duties

The declaration of human rights and duties, which is at the heart of The Constitution of the Year III, has been arranged in two parts of rights and duties and comprises the below-mentioned clauses:

A) Rights

Article 1- The rights of man in society are liberty, equality, security, property.

Article 2- Liberty consists of the power to do that which does not injure the rights of others.

Article 3- Equality means that the law is the same for all, whether it protects or punishes.

Article 4- Security results from the cooperation of all to assure the rights of each.

Article 5- Property is the right to enjoy and to dispose of one's goods, income, and the fruit of one's labor and industry.

Article 6- The law is the general will expressed by the majority of the citizens or their representatives.

Article 7- That which is not forbidden by law cannot be prevented. No one can be constrained to do that which it does not ordain.

Article 8- No one can be summoned into court, accused, arrested, or

---

30 - Ghasemzadeh, Murteza, *The French Constitution*, p. 25-26.
31 - Abusa'idi, Mahdi, *Human Rights and Its Evolutionary Course in the West*, p.197.
32 - Ibid, p. 120.

detained except in the cases determined by law and according to the forms which it has prescribed.

Article 9- Those who incite, promote, sign, execute, or cause to be executed arbitrary acts are guilty and ought to be punished.

Article 10- Every severity which may not be necessary to secure the person of a prisoner ought to be severely repressed by law.

Article 11- No one can be tried until after he has been heard or legally summoned.

Article 12- The law ought to decree only such penalties as are strictly necessary and proportionate to the offense.

Article 13- All treatment which increases the penalty fixed by law is a crime.

Article 14- No law, whether civil or criminal, can have retroactive effect.

Article 15- Every man can contract his time and his services, but he cannot sell himself nor be sold; his person is not an alienable property.

Article 16- Every tax is established for the public utility; it ought to be apportioned among those liable for taxes, according to their means.

Article 17- Sovereignty resides essentially in the totality of the citizens.

Article 18- No individual or assembly of part of the citizens can assume the sovereignty.

Article 19- No one can, without legal delegation, exercise any authority or fill any public function.

Article 20- Each citizen has a legal right to participate directly or indirectly in the formation and the compilation of the law and also in the selection of the representatives of the people and the public functionaries.

Article 21- Public offices cannot become the property of those who hold them.

Article 22- Social guarantee cannot exist if the division of powers is not established if their limits are not fixed, and if the responsibility of the public functionaries is not assured.

B) Duties

Article 1- The declaration of rights contains the obligations of the legislators; the maintenance of society requires that those who compose it should both know and fulfill their duties.

Article 2- All the duties of man and citizen spring from these two principles graven by nature in every heart: Do not do to others anything which you would not want them to do to you. Moreover, do continually for others the good that you would wish to receive from them.

Article 3- The obligations of each person to society consist of defending it, serving it, living in submission to the laws, and respecting those who are the agents of them.

Article 4- No one is a good citizen unless he is a good son, good father, good brother, good friend, or a good husband.

Article 5- No one is a virtuous man unless he is unreservedly and religiously an observer of the laws.

Article 6- The one who violates the laws openly declares himself in a state of war with the society.

Article 7- The one who, without transgressing the laws, eludes them by stratagem or ingenuity wounds the interests of all; he makes himself unworthy of their good will and their esteem.

Article 8- It is upon the maintenance of property that the cultivation of the land, all the productions, all means of labor, and the whole social order rest.

Article 9- Every citizen owes his services to the fatherland and the maintenance of liberty, equality, and property whenever the law summons him to defend them.

***

The Constitution of 1946 comprises one preamble and 106 articles in 12 chapters. The ones that sanction this constitution, having endorsed the rights and duties that have been stipulated in the declaration of 1789, proclaim the following political-social-cultural concessions as the necessities of time:

✓ Every individual, regardless of ethnic group, religion or political beliefs, has sacred and unquestionable laws.

✓ The law guarantees women equal rights to those of men in all spheres.

✓ Any man persecuted in virtue of his actions for liberty may claim the right of asylum upon the territories of the Republic.

✓ Each person has the duty to work and the right to employment. No person may suffer prejudice in his work or employment by his origins, opinions or beliefs.

✓ All men may defend their rights and interests through union action and may belong to the union of their choice.

✓ The right to strike shall be exercised within the framework of the laws governing it.

✓ All workers shall, through the intermediary of their representatives, participate in the collective determination of their conditions of work and the management of the workplace.

✓ All property and all enterprises that have or that may acquire the character of a public service, or de facto monopoly shall become the property of society.

- ✓ The Nation shall provide the individual and the family with the conditions necessary to their development.

- ✓ It shall guarantee to all, notably to children, mothers, and elderly workers, protection of their health, material security, rest, and leisure. All people who, by their age, physical or mental condition, or economic situation, are incapable of work shall have the right to receive suitable means of existence from society.

- ✓ The Nation proclaims the solidarity and equality of all French people in bearing the burden resulting from national calamities.

- ✓ The Nation guarantees equal access for children and adults to instruction, vocational training, and culture. The provision of free, public and secular education at all levels is a duty of the State.

- ✓ The French Republic, faithful to its traditions, shall respect the rules of public international law. It shall undertake no war aimed at conquest, nor shall it ever employ force against the freedom of any people.

- ✓ Subject to reciprocity, France shall consent to the limitations upon its sovereignty necessary to the organisation and preservation of peace.

- ✓ France shall form with its overseas peoples a Union founded on equal rights and duties, without distinction of race or religion.

- ✓ The French Union shall be composed of nations and peoples who agree to pool or coordinate their resources and their efforts to develop their respective civilizations, increase their well-being, and ensure their security.

- ✓ Faithful to its traditional mission, France desires to guide the peoples under its responsibility towards the freedom to administer themselves and to manage their affairs democratically.

- ✓ Eschewing all systems of colonization founded upon arbitrary rule, it guarantees to all equal access to public office and the individual or collective exercise of the rights and freedoms proclaimed or confirmed herein.

- ✓ These were the principles included in the preamble to the 1946 constitution.

- ✓ As stated by some scholars on the constitution, the people of France have named the declaration above "a political Bible which expresses eternal rights." [33]

XI) Catherine, Late 19th Century German Thinker

After a thorough study of the concept and fundamentals of laws, Catherine states, "This issue is related to objective laws since subjective laws emerge from that and the foundation of laws must be sought for in the school

---

33 - Hassan al-Hassan, *al-Qanun al-Dastouri wal-Dastour fi Lobnan*, p. 56.

of natural laws – particularly natural laws in an objective sense. Thus conceived, natural laws naturally shall be consisted of a set of compulsory rules for humanity as a whole, without being mediated by some positive rules and principles – whether ordained by God or by human beings.

These laws have provided human beings with a set of rules for social life according to which it is required to pass everyone what belongs to them, and you should not do wrong toward your fellow humans.

The logical consequences of these two orders, without requiring any transcendent illumination or positive laws, are self-evident as follows: Do not commit murder, do not steal, do not accuse someone falsely, you should pay back your debt, you should pass what you have borrowed to it, owner, you should keep your word, and you should obey the rule of law.

As a result, natural laws in an objective sense not only are not merely subjective laws, but they represent a set of codes of real existence. These laws are natural and universal, and are credible in all countries and times, without being required to be mediated by a supreme will. Natural laws are not merely for making up the shortcomings of law; rather, they form the ground upon which the legal edifice is founded.

Natural laws are thus the necessary foundation for positive laws, without which no legal order would be secured, and no standard would be available for measuring humanly ordained social rules regarding justice. Without this sense of law, neither the rights of nations nor universal rights of man will be conceivable. Subsequently, natural laws are necessary for keeping the order of life and securing the social development of human societies.[34]

XII) François Gény (1861-1959)

François Gény, contemporary French jurist, states:

Natural laws lead us to the rules according to which one could human conducts... Social sciences, as the crowning achievement of the nineteenth century, have shown that human social and spiritual nature represents a teleological order that must be discovered from a scientific point of view. The law is a branch of social sciences.[35]

XIII) Giorgio Del Vecchio (1878-1970)

A millennium-old tradition of the philosophy of law witnesses the priority of natural laws to positive laws, the primordial principles of liberty and equality, the ideal of cosmopolitanism, and the inalienable right of a nation for civil disobedience. Consequently, the philosophy of law is not a futile practice, but it has its roots in a genuine human impulse that aims at an objective telos....

We could not merely restrict our study to positive laws. In doing so, we suppress the call of our conscience for scholarship on justice.[36]

---

34 - Javan, Moosa, *Fundamentals of Laws*, p. 137. (Originally in Persian).

35 - Ibid, pp. 140-142.

36 - Del Vecchio, Giorgio, *Philosophie de Driot*.

XIV) Claude Du Pasquier

The contemporary school of natural laws is less ambitious. This school reduces the idea of natural laws into a set of principles and rules of justice and common sense, the application of which has been assigned to positive laws. Its highest ideal is the primordial value of the human character, which has as its consequence the necessity of respecting the inalienable rights of life, freedom, and dignity of other people. The duty that is dictated by this principle is the necessity of compensating one's being wrongly mistreated. Moreover, social necessities require mutual obligations to be respected. In every state, the governing body should try to meet her charged duties with the ultimate impartiality, while the people must honestly obey the justly ordained laws of the state. Natural laws also call parents to be vigilant about their child-rearing and recommend that children should respect their fathers and mothers. Therefore, the proponents of natural laws accept that imperative rules could be adapted to practical necessities. Thus, natural laws have been as an objective (material) resource that nourishes formal sources as well.

XV) The Rise of Contemporary Approaches

As we have seen before, although the idea of natural law was overshadowed by the rise of legal positivism in the nineteenth century, it reemerged in legal thoughts very brightly. Having gone through its theological period during the medieval times and its philosophical period in the 17th and 18th centuries, the idea of natural law enters what Lefort has called it the scientific period.
Charmont regards Bouden's Individual Rights and the State (1891) as the dawn of the renaissance of natural laws or the renaissance of legal idealism. He then describes Leon Bourgeois and Bougle's social collaborationism as the return of spiritual sentiments into social theories.[37]

---

37 - Du Pasquier, Claude, *A la Philosophie du droit introduction a la Theorie*. (Originally in French). Moreover, some of the materials have been cited from the transcripts of the lectures of Academy of International law, 1927, Vol. 3, pp. 263-277.

Two Significant Issues Regarding

The Universal Declaration of Human Rights

Two issues must be taken into account concerning the Universal Declaration of Human Rights:

The First Issue concerns the human value of this declaration and its application and the question whether this declaration has taken a step in the course of the betterment of the human condition or not.

The Second Issue is concerned with the principle motive of the codification and ratification of this declaration.

The First Issue: Human Value in the Declaration and Its Application

This extremely significant issue should be seriously studied and debated without going to excesses. In this regard, three major theories have been developed:

The First Theory

Some theorists believe:

> *This declaration represents the most comprehensive and perfect document that has ever been drawn up in support of human rights and individual freedoms, and it is now ratified by nearly all nations around the globe. In other words, it is the Universal Declaration of Human Rights.*
> *This declaration outlines a synopsis of all declarations, religious and moral beliefs and theories that have been issued and developed even before Christ to secure human rights and happiness and is the outcome of indefatigable efforts that have been honestly made in this path during many centuries.*[38]

The writer of *Human Rights and Its Evolutionary Course in the West* has made sincere efforts in the study of the historical roots of the idea of human rights, and we were also benefited from it in the introduction to this book. But his stance on the Declaration of Human Rights, which he puts in the following words, is worthy to be revised: "This declaration outlines a synopsis of all declarations, religious and moral beliefs and theories that have been issued and developed even before Christ to secure human rights and happiness and is the outcome of indefatigable efforts that have been honestly made in this path during many centuries."

---

38 - Abusa'idi, Mahdi, *Human Rights and Its Evolutionary Course in the West*, p. 246.

With regard to the articles of human rights in the perspective of Islam – that we will study based on early and very authentic Islamic texts – the occidentally motivated Declaration of Human Rights could not be a synopsis of all declarations, religious and moral beliefs and theories that have ever been issued and developed to secure human rights and happiness and be the outcome of indefatigable efforts that have been honestly made in this path during many centuries, since – as Rumi has said – there is no doubt that:

> Severity and intolerance are the signs of crudity
> As long as you live an embryonic life, bloodsucking will be all you do...[39]

Furthermore, without being impressed by personal sentiments and attitudes, not only do all of the excellent articles of this declaration already exist in early authentic Islamic texts, but besides these articles, there are also legal observations concerning human beings and their global condition in Islamic resources that can be a privilege for Islamic law and jurisprudence and overcome the existing paradoxes in the Universal Declaration of Human Rights. We hope the day will come in the near future that all experts of human rights around the globe will revise and adjust the Universal Declaration of Human Rights according to the Islamic Universal Declaration of Human Rights.

Contrary to the first theory that was shortly discussed above, there is another theory that is mainly focused on the second issue – the principle motive of the codification and ratification of the Universal Declaration of Human Rights. We will first make a study of the overall outline of the theory itself, and then proceed to articulate our stance on both theories.

The Second Theory

This theory is related to the Third World conception of human rights. As Mr. Radhika Kumaraswamy says:

> The Third World remarkably neither had a major role in the codification of the Universal Declaration of Human Rights nor in its operationalization. Although the idea of human rights has backgrounds in all of the world's cultures, the theoretical origins of the human rights movement are undoubtedly Western. The codification of the major concepts of this movement – i.e. freedom, equality, social welfare, and free will – has been done according to the implications that they have already found in modern social movements of nationalism, socialism, and liberalism. These movements have all emerged in the West, but their political value systems came to power in all corners of the world.
> It is only these historical sources that have enforced cultural nationalists not to accept the movement of human rights as a universal norm. Accordingly,

---

39 - Rumi's *Masnavi*, Book 3.

human rights violations are justified in the Third-world countries appealing to the illegitimacy of some of its related values, and this issue has proven itself as a major crisis in the second half of the twentieth century.

The question is which path we should embark on to reconcile between the inherited traditions of human rights and the major developments in the non-Western world? Every reevaluation in this kind should inevitably begin in the light of history, which is both a universal experience and a synthetic process in the training and development of human rights. Now it is an urgent need for the Third World to take an insightful stance on the human rights case; however, this process must be a creative one rather than an absolute denial of the very concept of human rights. In other words, it must be a complementary process rather than an emaciating one.

The issue that this controversy has exposed the north and the south with is twofold:

First, there is the reconciliation of non-Western values with basic concepts of human rights.

The second issue concerns the coalescence of the experience of development with the norms and structures of human rights support.

One of the outlets of this predicament is not to take human rights as such the telos; rather, it should be seen as a process that demands particular taking of laws, politics and economics. In other words, the human being must be its central focus. The human rights movement should not be detached from its historical context in a thoughtless fashion. This work would result in its conceptual emaciation and add to its ambiguity.[40]

Kumaraswamy has analyzed the concept of human rights in a relatively competent way. If the reasons for the Third World's reluctance toward accepting the Universal Declaration of Human Rights is to be taken into serious consideration, we will see that this reluctance not only has its roots in the occidental origin of the declaration and essential difference between Western cultural signs and the cultural signs of the Third World countries, but also the most fundamental reasons for this disinclination toward the declaration lie in ideological differences existing between Third World countries, and particularly Islamic countries that have Islam as their religion, which denies some articles of the Universal Declaration of Human Rights as untrue upon its *Sophia Perennis* – as we will show at length in our comparative study of these two legal systems, Islamic and Western.

The Third Theory

The third theory states that the Universal Declaration of Human Rights is essentially valuable, for it represents a remarkable system and at least serves as the manifestation of an ideal. Furthermore, it has an interceptive function in north/south incursions and has been and will continue to be functional

---

40 - The 1988 UNESCO Message, a selection of articles for the 40th anniversary of UNESCO.

in the abstract culture[41] of developed countries, until when – having been revised and adjusted in accordance with cultural considerations – it proves to be functional and of avail for all countries, whether developed, developing or third countries.

The Second Issue: The Principle Motive of the Codification and Application of the Universal Declaration of Human Rights

Once again, there are three major theories regarding this issue:

The First Theory

This theory is the one that has been developed by the codifiers of Universal Declaration of Human Rights:

> *Whereas the recognition of the inherent dignity and the equal and inalienable rights of all members of the human family is the foundation of freedom, justice and peace in the world,*
>
> *Whereas disregard and contempt for human rights have resulted in barbarous acts which have outraged the conscience of humanity, and the advent of a world in which human beings shall enjoy freedom of speech and belief and freedom from fear and want has been proclaimed as the highest aspiration of the common people,*
>
> *Whereas it is essential, if man is not to be compelled to have recourse, as a last resort, to rebellion against tyranny and oppression, that human rights should be protected by the rule of law,*
>
> *Whereas it is essential to promote the development of friendly relations between nations,*
>
> *Whereas the peoples of the United Nations have in the Charter reaffirmed their faith in fundamental human rights, in the dignity and worth of the human person and the equal rights of men and women and had determined to promote social progress and better standards of life in larger freedom,*
>
> *Whereas member states have pledged themselves to achieve, in cooperation with the United Nations, the promotion of universal respect for and the observance of human rights and fundamental freedoms,*
>
> *Whereas a common understanding of these rights and freedoms is of the greatest importance for the full realization of this pledge,*
>
> *Now, therefore, the General Assembly proclaims this Universal Declaration of Human rights as a common standard of achievement for all peoples and all nations, to the end that every individual and every organ of society, keeping this Declaration constantly in mind, shall strive by education to promote respect for these rights and freedoms and by progressive measures, national and international, to secure their universal and effective recognition and*

---

41 - By abstract culture, we refer to a culture whose elements and foundations are formed by means of the abstraction and adjustment of a number of key issues or laws, which can lead to the elevation and evolution of man and the society.

observance, both among the peoples of member states themselves and also
among the peoples of territories under their jurisdiction.[42]

These motives – regardless of some highly significant cases that will be dealt with at length in our comparative debates on the two legal systems – could only be declared as worthy and valuable human motives if they are equally and none-prejudicially applicable to all nations as the second clause of the preamble proclaims them to be the highest aspiration of common people.

The Second Theory

On December 10, 1942, three years after World War II, a draft entitled "The Declaration of Human Rights" was ratified by the general assembly of the United Nations by 48 members of total 58 members; it had no opponents, although 8 members including Communist countries (the USSR, Belarus, Ukraine, Czechoslovakia, Yugoslavia, and Poland), South Africa and Saudi Arabia cast blank ballots for a variety of reasons. The positive voters for the draft were all either Western or Western-led countries.[43] Concerning the cast ballots, it becomes clear that this declaration has been issued in a Western spirit and is philosophical, ideologically and politically dependent on Western culture.

To study the story of the formation of the declaration up to its current state, it is necessary to go back to some years past and understand the roots.

In 1941, following Japan's invasion of Pearl Harbor, where the American marine base was located, America entered the war in favor of the Allies and against the Axis. During several conferences that were held by the heads of the Allies, such as the Dumbarton Oaks Conference in October 1944 and the San Francisco Conference of 1945, post-war issues were debated.

By that time, the United States of America, under the leadership of Franklin Roosevelt, was facing two major issues:

I) As the superpower of the victorious countries, and having suffered the less loss of life and property during the war, unlike the post-WWI years, the United States could not and did not want to be isolated again – especially due to the extreme weakness that had dominated European countries at that time, and also with the possibility of the spread of Communism and

---

42 - Preamble to the Universal Declaration of Human Rights.

43 - The countries that casted yes ballots include Afghanistan, Argentina, Australia, Belgium, Bolivia, Brazil, Burma, Canada, Chili, China, Columbia, Costa Rica, Cuba, Denmark, the Dominican Republic, Ecuador, Egypt, El Salvador, Ethiopia, France, Greece, Guatemala, Haiti, Iceland, India, Iran, Iraq, Lebanon, Liberia, Luxemburg, Mexico, Holland, New Zealand, Nicaragua, ⇾ Norway, Pakistan, Panama, Paraguay, Peru, the Philippines, Cambodia, Sweden, Syria, Turkey, the United Kingdom, the United States of America, Uruguay and Venezuela (*Yearbook on Human Rights*, 1949, p. 468)

the expansion of the dominance of the ideological scope of the USSR, the counterpart of the U.S., throughout Europe.

II) The United States, having experienced the fall of the international community – which was indeed a Wilsonian idea – gradually abandoned imaginary and idealistic ideas and turned to realist thinkers, but due to the dominant general atmosphere within the countries, there was no possibility for a sudden turn; therefore, in order to deceive the public opinions of the population of the world, philanthropic and democratic slogans had yet to be preserved.

The most debated issue of the time was the causes of the Second World War and the circumstances of preventing future wars. Idealists regarded totalitarian states like Germany and Italy as the triggering causes of the war and the violators of democratic rights of man; as a result, a dictator-style ruler would be able to bring the deaths of millions of human beings regardless of the will and destiny of human beings. The proposed Kantian solution for the *aporia* of war, which in their view could result in international peace and security, has been stated in the following words:

> Let the people decide on peace and war themselves; that is to say, with the revival of democratic states, we could be sure that the decision-makers shall precisely evaluate the backwashes of being involved in a war.[44]

This theory not only differed from Lenin's theory stating that economic competition of giant corporations of capitalist countries always triggers wars, but it was also different from the positions of realists or the followers of Machiavelli and Hobbes such as Niebuhr, Spiekman, Schumann, Morgenthau, and George Kennan, whose ideas overshadowed US policies in post-war years.[45]

It was in such conditions that Roosevelt proposed his thesis of protégées in the international scene. He proclaimed that it is the right of big countries as the big brothers of the human family to punish smaller countries that allegedly put in danger the global peace. He believed that four big countries including the United States, the United Kingdom, the USSR and the People's Republic of China must play the role of mandatory powers. In 1941 Roosevelt wrote:

> In the current chaotic state the world is in, it is not intelligible to stick to the idea of the reorganization of the international community, since the extent of the project results in oppositions and confusions ... There is no reason why the principle of tutorship in private affairs should not be applied to the international context. Tutorship is based on the principles of

---

44 - *Claude, Inis L.* Jr., *Swords into Plowshares: The Problems and Progress of International Organization*, New York: Random House, 1956, pp. 221-222.

45 - James E. *Dougherty*, Robert L. Pfaltzgraff, *Contending Theories of International Relations*, p. 68.

unselfish services. In all ages, there are numbers of children among nations of the world that need a tutor in their relations with their people and other nations, as many of big nations also need to be shown their places and to be guided toward goodness.[46]

On the other hand, small countries had to be involved in such a way that they would not feel ignored but still not have any part in the management of the international community. In this, regard Roosevelt states:

I am not against the formation of a global assembly, providing its management be passed to super powers.[47]

Accordingly, and for the reconciliation of opposing views, the United Nations was founded in its current form consisting of two main executive organs:

1- The Security Council, which was made up of five permanent members who were the victorious superpowers in the war and having "the right of veto"; no decision would be taken against their will in the council.

2- The General Assembly consisted of all allegedly independent countries, including superpowers, that have an equal right to vote on the issues discussed in the assembly, but it has no executive power and its decisions, therefore, do not amount to more than mere proposals. It was in such an assembly that the Universal Declaration of Human Rights was ratified.

In the San Francisco Conference, where the representatives of different states gathered to prepare the UN Charter, a number of delegates from various NGOs of the world as the representatives of millions of people around the globe insisted there that the Dumbarton Oaks proposals which insist on human rights as the highest ideal and ultimate goal of international community are not sufficient and thus need to be adjusted and protected by sanctions.[48] Accordingly, small countries in the conference insisted on the human rights issue to be taken in earnest; for instance, Panama proposed a declaration of human rights be included in the Charter. This proposal was opposed by four superpowers including the United States [49] since they were not willing to vest the new organization any authority on the issue of human rights; therefore, it was decided that the UN Commission on Human Rights was to prepare the UN Charter of Human Rights after its establishment.

Consequently, the San Francisco Conference left the Charter's articles on human rights ambiguous; some theorists, including Kelson, even hold that the members of the UN had claimed no commitment toward human rights

---

46 - Gaddis, John Lewis, *The United States and the Origins of Cold War*, 1972, p. 24.

47 - Ibid, p.25.

48 - Abusa'idi, Mahdi, *Human Rights and Its Evolutionary Course in the West*, pp. 248-249.

49 - Moghtader, Hooshang *The Developments of United Nations*, p. 192. (Originally in Persion).

by signing the UN Charter.[50] According to Inis Claude:

> *The privileges that have been granted to idealistic public opinions are nothing but verbal decorations; they are not a pattern for the establishment of an organization as the bulwark of ideals. The [global] pressures for introducing the UN as the universal authority on human rights only resulted in frequent references to the ideal of human rights promotion rather than practical steps toward the development of an international warranty for human rights observation.*[51]

The only thing that has been included in the Charter for the sake of small countries' satisfaction was what is explained in Article 68, which reads, "*The Economic and Social Council shall set up commissions in economic and social fields and for the promotion of human rights, and such other commissions as may be required for the performance of its functions.*" Although the mission of the Economic and Social Council was essentially tripartite: 1. preparing the declaration of human rights, 2. the articulation of conventions on human rights, and 3. the schematization of functional procedures, it succeeded only in preparing the declaration – and without the needed sanctions at that.

It can therefore be stated that those who ratified the Universal Declaration of Human Rights had no good will in the promotion of human rights and most probably still do not, either; this declaration has in fact merely been ratified under the influence of the dominant idealistic atmosphere over public opinions in Western countries and their consequent pressures in the San Francisco Conference without any sanctions.

Although the immediate approval of the Universal Declaration of Human Rights spurred public admiration and some scholars even declared it as the extremely significant achievement of United Nations, the simply achieved global consensus on the Declaration was not by accident, because the countries gathered in the General Assembly were well aware that the ratified declaration is not legally binding. To this very reason, the General Assembly defined it as a common ideal the actualization of which is desirable and according to Lady Eleanor Roosevelt, the head of the UN Commission on Human Rights at the time:

> *The Declaration is not a treaty or an international agreement, but an expression of inalienable rights of humanity, the fulfillment of which is desirable for all people around the globe.*[52]

To put the matter otherwise, the Declaration is a means for *deceiving* and *fooling* public opinions of the world and playing them around with its approval; something that has no practical value.

---

50 - Ibid, p. 198.

51 - Ibid, p. 200.

52 - *Claude, Inis L. Jr., Swords into Plowshares*: The Problems and Progress of International Organization, New York: Random House, 1956, p. 64.

The Third Theory

The third theory needs to be sketched regarding two issues:

The First Issue: It seems that the principle motive in establishing these universal rights is the understanding of the necessity of paying earnest attention to normative principles and dimensions of human life and reducing various sufferings brought about by destructive conflicts between human beings, particularly the sufferings and miseries that humanity has undergone during and after World War II. In our study of the basic motives of the establishment of this set of rights, we shall see that in addition to human general interest in being relieved from destructive conflicts, the primordial yearning of human beings for achieving freedom and sustainable peace was among the motives of codifiers of these rights and as it has been mentioned in the introduction, this set of rights logically aims at bringing peaceful relations between human beings. Regarding these basic motives, we could thus say that the Universal Declaration of Human Rights is remarkably intended to correct and adjust human relations and it is hoped that with some basic amendments in the articles along with the logical and humane interpretations of this legal system as well as the good will of the executive body in the indiscriminative performance of the Declaration, one of the highest of human ideals can become realized.

The Second Issue poses the question whether the establishment of these universal rights is a compulsory effect of conflicts between human beings or it has its origin in the understanding of the magnificence and valuable principles of human relationships. Regarding the motives that have been mentioned in the preamble, it could be said that the codifiers of this series of rights were focused on both issues; trying to uproot human conflicts and demonstrate the magnificence and value of human relations. But studying the matter more precisely and in a more comprehensive manner, we come to the conclusion that the basic ground of these rights, like every other special right, is preventing people from the violation of their fellow human beings' rights through revealing the excessive nature of human desires. Although this ground is a thoroughly logical reason and in one sense the only way to preventing human destructive conflicts, it should not be forgotten that if this is the main reason for the codification of these rights, it would be a matter of shame for humanity if the value of such declarations is reduced to a compulsory effect.

Interpretation in the Domain of Values:

The Prime Human Right

It would have been very appropriate if the preamble, which sketches the motives for the preparation of the Declaration, had been preceded by a thorough study of the human being nature so as to clarify who or what this "human being" is, and whom the declaration is about. Is he truly the very creature that prophets have described to us as a being of distinguished stature and primordial nobility who has been created by Divine Knowledge and is heading toward the highest goal only achievable through a competition in "goodness" and "perfection", unless man de-vests himself of this primordial status and rights and revolts against Divine Will? Or is the man the creature as defined by Hobbes and Machiavelli, *lupus* whose being is void of any primordial value? As they see it, in other words, human beings have no value bestowed to them by a supernatural Being, and thus are naturally selfish and deceiving beings whose only logic in a nutshell is, "I am the goal, others are means!"

In a conference on the relevance of occidental human rights for Asian and Oceanic countries held in Manila in June 1990, I presented the following points as parts of my lecture[53]:

1- The motives leading to the Universal Declaration of Human Rights, as sketched in its preamble, involve the necessity of the recognition of inalienable human rights so as to keep the man away from disregard and contempt and to realize freedom, justice and global peace upon inherited dignity of the human family and man's equal rights. It is needless to say that the realization of such human ideals unavoidably needs human inherited dignity to be demonstrated, while academic circles the globe not only have not taken a correct philosophical and scientific step toward the demonstration of human primordial stature but sadly, the theory of Leviathanism, on the one hand, and the project of the de-spiritualization of humanity due to cultural corruption and baseless analyses of the foundations of human history, i.e. the tripartite stages of excessive positivism, on the other hand, are becoming even more powerful as time goes on. Nevertheless, human beings from the point of view of Islam and other revealed religions – according to the revealed verse of the Holy Quran, *"And surely we have honored the children of Adam, and we carry them in the land and the sea, and we have given*

53 - See Ja'fari M. T., *The Message of Wisdom,* 2000, pp. 45-58. (Originally in Persian).

them of the good things, and we have made them excel by an appropriate excellence over most of those whom we have created" (The Night Journey 17:70) – has primordial dignity and great potential for intellectual and spiritual evolution. According to this view, recommending and ordering all human societies to observe human inherited dignity is totally logical.

This is why the Universal Declaration of Human Rights needs, first of all, to demonstrate primordial human status and save humanity from the swamp of Machiavellianism, Leviathanism, and utilitarianism and bring man back to his divine stature to be changed into a *global culture*.

2- As mentioned before, the Universal Declaration of Human Rights has been grounded on the ideal of peaceful coexistence with peace, justice, and freedom in human societies and no one would doubt on the ideality of these matters. But as it is needless to say that the mere indication of the necessity of these ideals never could bring about a world within which all individuals see themselves as the members of the same family, since such a claim must be dependent on the highest ground which is God in Islam; or at least for making all countries – including developed, developing and third world countries – commit to universal rights, there is no way but finding a generally accepted scientific ground.

3- Historical experiences have well shown that the codification of a competent legal system does not necessarily imply its actual application. This has mainly had two reasons: discrimination and social incompetence. Since the codification of a perfect legal system for a society in which the individuals have not been educationally prepared for the system is just like building a splendid palace on a volcanic mountain.

Thus, it is necessary that a series of common spiritual and moral principles be taught to all human societies so as to make them ready for the acceptance and application of universal rights. It is not in vain that Islam has laid such a stress on the moral education of humans to achieve the acceptance and application of rights.

4- The Universal Declaration of Human Rights has turned a blind eye to the virtue, and normative dignity of human beings and no concession has been recognized for virtuous and pious people in this declaration; Islam, on the other hand, regards this concession necessary for encouraging people toward intellectual and spiritual evolution and reaching proper social positions.

The concession that is given to virtuous people does not, however, violate other individuals' rights; as more sympathetic, intelligent and conscious individuals in all societies are taken to be more competent to hold some significant social positions, Islam has also indicated to this concession in a very straightforward fashion:

O you men! Surely we have created you of a male and a female, and made you tribes and families that you may know each other; surely the most honorable of you with Allah is the one among you most careful (of his duty); surely Allah is knowing, aware.

(The Chambers 49:13)

A Study of the Motives

For the Compilation of the Universal Declaration of Human Rights

The causes and motives for the codification of the articles of the Universal Declaration of Human Rights have been summed up here in seven cases. Since one of fundamental preliminaries here is the adequate knowledge of these articles, their background motives and evaluation, we see it necessary to have a debate on the motives sketched in the preamble:

1- Whereas recognition of the inherent dignity and of the equal and inalienable rights of all members of the human family is the foundation of freedom, justice and peace in the world…

That the hegemony of freedom, justice and peace in the world needs human primordial stature to be recognized is a self-evident fact that does not tolerate any doubt. However, its understanding is hinged upon the following issues to be taken into earnest consideration:

The First Issue poses the how one could demonstrate human inherent dignity. It was indeed up to the Declaration to have demonstrated this issue in the preamble, or at least to have assigned this duty to the scholars of human sciences like psychologists, philosophers, moralists, theologians, political and legal scientists and neutralist historians, since the Universal Declaration of Human Rights does not represent an ethnocentric system of legal codes that addresses human beings in terms of their cultural and religious differences. The addressees of this declaration are different nations and peoples of heterogeneous cultures, religions and historical backgrounds who are told, "You must accept and respect this set of rights disregarding your nationality, ethnicity, cultures, and historical backgrounds and above all your national privileges and powers." Consequently, it is not possible to convince people to shut their eyes to their religious, cultural and historical heritages.

It is for this very reason that continuous efforts should be made to inform the politicians of the necessity and value of such an intelligible rights and freedoms, because the sense of necessity of the codification of such a set of rights does in fact notify all legal, economic and political pioneers to be aware that, shoulder to shoulder with those rights securing the natural coexistence of human beings, human souls have rights for themselves as well that must be observed by governing bodies of human societies if they are to govern human beings rather than a bunch of spontaneous and unconscious things.

As a matter of fact, one of the biggest obstacles in the way of "mutual understanding" between nations is the disappearance of unity in human life's dimensions that has also resulted in the absence of this consecrated quality within the society itself – that is to say, separating the moral dimension of life from its legal dimension and setting this latter in turn apart from social dimension, which is itself thought to be detached from political dimension, and conceiving these four dimensions isolated from scientific the dimension and taking these latter five dimensions as totally distinguished and separated from the philosophical and ontological dimension of life and depicting all of these dimensions as isolated moments which have nothing to do with religion which has resulted in human self-alienation.

This compartmentalization has been declared to be desirable for a narrow scientific perspective, and thus has enervated and seared the sense of interdependence, integrations and unity in "Intelligible Life"[54]. Thus, we can say that to the same degree that analytic method of knowledge is significant in human life, the synthetic method is also necessarily as important and we could demonstrate by them – used in an integrated fashion – the basics of the unity of human souls and make them ready for the reception of universal rights.

Two immensely significant points that have been indicated above could be seen in the introduction that Robert Houghwout Jackson[55] has written to *Law in Islam*:

1- Islam has an integrated conception of human life while the most separatist form of understanding the phenomenon of *menschenleben* is essentially American:

> *American law has no concern over moral duties. In fact, an American citizen could act totally legal, while being a morally corrupted person. Thus, our legal system in America does not determine religious duties; rather, it deliberately neglects them.*[56]

Needless to say this conceptual separatism in understanding human being is not restricted to the United States of America; as a matter of fact, this legal separatism is almost visible in all Western and Eastern countries.

Jackson describes the unity of human life's dimensions in Islamic law in the following words:

54 - See Ja'fari, M. T. (2011), *Intelligible Life*, translated into English by Beytollah Naderlew and edited by Seema Arif, (Translator).

55 - Former US Attorney General (1940-1941).

56 - Lisbani, Herbert J., *Law in Islam*. (Originally in English).

On the contrary, in Islamic law, divine will is the source of laws; a will that has revealed itself to Prophet Muhammad (PBUH). This will regards all individual believers as the members of the same society, although they come from different tribes and live in various geographies. Here, it is religion that unifies the people, neither nationality nor geography. In this way, the state itself is submissive and amenable to the Holy Quran, and there remains thus no room for any other legislator, let alone any room for controversy and discord. The believer sees this world as a corridor which brings him to the other and better world, and the Quran provides a set of divine codes for individual and social conducts, in order to make the transition sounder and easier. It is impossible to separate Prophetic teachings from political and economic theories; the teachings instruct man how to conduct himself in social, economic, political and individual affairs....[57]

Regarding the necessity of harmony and unity in all human dimensions in "intelligible life", until this necessity has not been met, expecting a society constituted of intelligible individuals of a free conscience who recognize and observe their fellow individuals' rights seems impossible, let alone a global family constructed of different nations and countries with different cultures, religions and historical backgrounds who interact with each other in the spirit of fraternity.

2- Having satiated the legal needs of different societies around the globe, Islamic jurisprudence has succeeded in spurring pro-justice movements in many spots of the world. Jackson elaborates on this point as follows:

This religion – which is the youngest of all religions of the world – has brought about a legal system that satisfies the insatiable sense of many pro-justice movements in Asia, Africa and American continent .... It is the time not to see ourselves anymore as the only nation in the world who loves justice and understands it, since Islamic countries are pursuing it as an ultimate goal in their legal systems as well.[58]

As we have mentioned before, we never can force people to give up their special qualities and commit themselves to a universally valid set of codes and rights! Moreover, no one is allowed to object to the view that there is no case for psychological, philosophical, moral, political and economic debates of the law when sketching legal materials. Yes, this objection is baseless, since as we have mentioned above, universal rights are essentially different from particular rights of nations which have their origin in their cultural, economic, political, social and historical backgrounds and this implies a particular legal system whose formation does not demand the active participation of

---

57 - Ibid.
58 - Ibid.

the scholars of human sciences.

The presentation of these universal rights without laying the necessary grounds for unity in values, expectations, destinations and particularly in the Ultimate Telos of Life, if not totally useless, will in fact prove to be of little significance. Laying these grounds shall not be possible without dismantling normative judgments of theorists like Cesare Borgia, Machiavelli and Hobbes on humanity and human beings. Precisely speaking, true readiness of the international community for the reception of Universal Rights needs the Hobbesian formula of "Homo homoni lupus" – which results in "the senseless man in the senseless world" – to be dismantled by sufficient reasons. Being indifferent toward this highly significant task could result in the hijack of freedom and peace as the groundwork of Universal Rights by the proponents of devilish maxim of "I am the end and others are my means!" that has victimized millions of people throughout history and could take even more victims yet. This is the very destructive course that would agitate even the most optimistic of thinkers. Even Rumi, despite being one of the liveliest and most optimistic mystics of all centuries – since positive mysticism[59] requires optimism, speaks sadly when facing this harsh reality:

> O human beings who are putting great efforts into their lives!
> If you find that no one has any pity for you and takes no step to lessen your troubles,
> do what you must do yourselves rather than pinning your hopes upon others.
> Do you think the claims they make about humanity are sincere and heartfelt?
> Indeed not, for most people are like cannibals.
> Do not trust their benevolent appearance, for deep inside they harbor selfish monsters
> Beware that these "humans" are like devils set out to deceive you.
> Do you not realize that some of them kneel beside you like a butcher sits beside a sheep he is about to slaughter?
> Avoid setting up house in land provided for you by others; do your own thing,
> and be confident about what you do...[60]

In the same spirit, Alfred North Whitehead writes:

> Human nature is so complex that plans for society are to political leaders not worth even the price of a defect paper.[61]

The Second Issue: The expression "members of the human society" is loaded with a moral value, and while being the most constructive, useful and highest ideal of human relations through which individuals become the members of the same family, however, from the dawn of social

---

59 - See Ja'fari, M. T. (2008), *Positive Mysticism*, Allameh Ja'fari Institute, Tehran.

60 - Rumi's *Masnavi*, Book 2.

61 - Whitehead, Alfred North, *Adventures of Ideas*. (Originally in English).

life to the present time – except some few cases of divine leaders who have brought about inside individuals the sense of membership in one family through their eternal knowledge of the unknown spiritual regions of human soul – this ideal has not still found a true chance to be realized in the outside world.

It might be said that in the long course of human history, we have come across harmonious forms of life in societies that have not been led by divine leaders. The answer to such a statement is clear: the harmonious form of collective life has existed even in the age of slavery and most slaves, due to their ignorance of the primordial and inherited dignity and the status of humanity participated in collective social life affairs in a harmonious fashion with a shallow, baseless and feigned satisfaction. The very reason for this unconscious gregariousness is the intrinsic force of life that sustains people without restricting itself to higher positions and values (although the human mind essentially aims at higher positions and values.) Humanity has shown such potency for starting harmonious collective movements that, disregarding the philosophy and goal of those movements, their formal unity, displaying and demonstrating the formula all=1, deserves to be praised; sadly, however, after the disappearance of the motives for such effervescence, humanity returns to his previous stagnation, while human beings under the divine leadership of holy prophets touch the eternal truth of unity of humanity and see themselves the members of a large family that are fathered by the Lord. It is through such a sense of unity that man can be addressed using the contents included in the following verse by Rumi:

> What is all of this uproar?
> Are we all not companions and of the same kin and origin?[62]

If humanity does not succeed in this task, this will give rise to unconquerable obstacles on the path toward the realization of the spirit of fraternity and the global family of humanity, such as egotisms and self-centeredness that bring continuous wars – in fact, some shallow scholars have stated that "conflict and destruction are inherent in human nature!" – and different forms of slavery in the name of epicurean seekings of pleasure (hedonism) and utilitarianism.

Unfortunately, even in some articles of this Universal Declaration within which freedom is introduced as the highest ideal of humanity, it has not been taken into serious account that the dictation of freedom without giving a logical interpretation and justification – which could result in mental and spiritual growth – is itself one of the causes of human separations, let alone get people ready for reception of "spirit of fraternity" and membership in a family.

---

62 - Rumi's *Divan-e Shams.*

In our comparative studies of the articles of this Declaration, we shall debate at length the intellectual conditions of realization of individuals' membership in the human family and the spirit of fraternity, which are the basic motives of this declaration.

The Third Issue: Some of the basic elements of this declaration, such as "inherent dignity of humanity" and taking individuals to be "the members of a family," and even the peace and freedom as found deep inside the human self and conscience need human competence and potency for altruism [unselfish devotion to others] to be demonstrated. Although human beings have been persuaded by revealed religions and true scholars, and even by egotist hunters of power, to devote themselves to their fellow human beings and love them, and also despite the fact that no other concept has such an exalted position in human thought, reality shows however that humanity has not yet taken a strong step along the path of loving his fellow human beings. The only path that leads humanity to the pantheon of love is the way that is proposed by holy prophets. This path needs firstly human inherited dignity to be demonstrated for all individuals one by one so that everyone will be able to recognize their own existential value; to state the matter otherwise, they should recognize the human primordial stature to love their fellow humans for the sake of their humanity not on the basis of naïve and transient sensations.

The Fourth Issue: While human spiritual and mental growth is restricted to the borders of merely natural life and revolves around "the natural ego" and regards the orders of religions, moralists and theosophers concerning the necessity of intelligible adjustment of human desires, as baseless lullabies, not only these universal rights but every other set of highest rights are not incapable of taking humanity to his promised destination by means of these legal systems. The codification of such ideal rights for those human beings whose brains and souls are only preoccupied with the management of a merely natural life and growth within its borders is like building a splendid palace upon a volcano!

2- Whereas disregard and contempt for human rights have resulted in barbarous acts which have outraged the conscience of mankind, and the advent of a world in which human beings shall enjoy freedom of speech and belief and freedom from fear and want has been proclaimed as the highest aspiration of the common people…

The following issues could be addressed with regard to this motive:

a) As we have seen in our previous debates on the first motive, the inattention of social leaders and pedagogues to the necessity of the adjustment of human egotism and hedonism, which have always led to the disappearance of constructive loves from human societies and triggered destructive conflicts, has changed the members of a divine family to become, as Hobbes described it, hungry wolves in regard to each other. Thus, as long as this cause continues to be the effect, the fact that "disregard and contempt for human rights have resulted in barbarous acts" will also remain unchanged. Accordingly, it should be said that all essays written and activities done for the articulation of the universal rights of humanity is just like preserving the swamp that is the birthplace of malaria-carrying mosquitoes and settling for killing dozens of dying mosquitoes!

b) This motive introduces "freedom of speech and belief" and "freedom from fear and want" as the highest ideals of humanity. If the codifiers of the universal rights of man had an overall knowledge of human spiritual dimensions – whether in an individual sense of in a social sense – they would have evaluated these freedoms in a more logical fashion and introduced them as the highly significant issues in the course of life by virtue of their indispensable role in laying the social groundwork of purposeful life, since as we shall indicate in full length in our comparative debates, freedom of belief, freedom of speech and freedom of religion and so on and so forth, though being the sources of pleasure and happiness, logically appear to be mere means for arriving at an ultimate telos in life.

In order to prevent any potential misunderstandings, we insist, as we shall also insist in our coming debates, that the value of freedom does not lie in the ability to choose a path among many different existed paths, but the genuine value of freedom reveals itself in the chosen path. Is the one who chooses to deprive people of their freedom free? Criminals, despots and evil spirits of human history have all done their corruptions freely, since no action done by one who is being forced to do so is described as devilish. Nevertheless, in regard to to freedom from fear and want, it needs to be mentioned that something wrong has happened; in fact, there is an essential difference between what keeps something continuing to be and its end. Fear and want are obstacles inhibiting the continuation of human life, so their disappearance only means clearing what disturbs the natural course of life. Accordingly, no conscientious human being could say that the ultimate telos of life is this life minus fear and want.

3- Whereas it is essential, if man is not to be compelled to have recourse, as a last resort, to rebellion against tyranny and oppression, that human rights should be protected by the rule of law…

That the rule of law could secure human global rights seems to be totally right from a purely legal point of view, but if the United Nations could not demonstrate "human inherent dignity" through consistent reasons, which legal imperative can take on this?

It is for this very reason that since 1948, even after the approval of the Universal Declaration we have been witnessing racial, political, economic and social discriminations in their different forms; regional conflicts between two countries have frequently happened and still are happening; then it could be said that "humanity has always seen itself forced to revolt for sustaining in struggle for existence."

4- Whereas it is essential to promote the development of friendly relations between nations…

This motive is undoubtedly desirable in itself, but the United Nations needs to state how one nation could develop friendly relations with aggressive hunters of power.

5- Whereas the peoples of the United Nations have in the Charter reaffirmed their faith in fundamental human rights, in the dignity and worth of the human person and in the equal rights of men and women and have determined to promote social progress and better standards of life in larger freedom…

This motive, regardless of the conceptual complexity lying in "the equal rights of men and women" and the concepts of "equality" and "rights" that need to be defined in a very precise fashion, is very remarkable and essentially correct. Consequently, three issues should be taken into serious consideration in this regard:

a) "Equal rights of men and women," that shall be addressed in coming debates.

b) As we have mentioned in previous discussions, for demonstrating the inherent stature of human individuals – which is the effect of the recognition of "primordial dignity of humanity as a whole" – legal scientists could not do anything alone, but they need the hands of scholars of other branches of human sciences.

c) Although these motives per se are desirable for all nations around the globe, they nonetheless need a real belief in human values from those who are representing different nations in the UN.

6- Since Member States have pledged themselves to achieve, in cooperation with the United Nations, the promotion of universal respect for and observance of human rights and fundamental freedoms…

It would not be a baseless claim to say that the most valuable and constructive commitment that the state members of the UN could take on is pledging for the promotion of universal respect and observance of human rights and fundamental freedoms. There are two issues in this regard to be addressed, both of which have frequently been indicated previously as being the necessity of the demonstration of human primordial dignity and overcoming the political and social conflicts between state members that overshadow the fundamental issues of human rights.

7- A common understanding of these rights and freedoms is of the greatest importance for the full realisation of this pledge, now, therefore, the General Assembly proclaims this Universal Declaration of human rights as a common standard of achievement for all peoples and all nations, to the end that every individual and every organ of society, keeping this Declaration constantly in mind, shall strive by teaching and education to promote respect for these rights and freedoms and by progressive measures, national and international, to secure their universal and effective recognition and observance, both among the peoples of Member States themselves and among the peoples of territories under their jurisdiction.

This motive briefs all previous motives indicated in the preamble as follows:

> As long as human souls have not been bridged with each other, no common understanding would be conceivable at all.

History is, in its entirety, evidence to this point.

The Motive for Compiling

The Universal Islamic Declaration of Human Rights

The global face of a man, who owns universal rights, has been spotlighted in revealed religions, and as we shall see in the coming debates, in Islam it is accented in an unprecedented and absolutely clear manner. This very attitude emerges in the viewpoints expressed by Western intellectuals after Renaissance and finds various expressions in different societies, as, in the French Constitution of Year III (1795), 31 articles out of 371 in total directly address human rights issues. This constitution begins as follows:

> The French people proclaim, in the presence of the Supreme Being, the following declaration of citizens' rights and citizen.

One of the interesting points in this declaration is that it sanctions itself upon the two renowned principles of duty: 1. Do not do to others that which you would not have them do to you, and 2. Do continually for others the good that you would wish to receive from them.[63] The second principle recommends citizens to approach the highest human affairs in a transactional spirit as it invites them to do for others what they would wish to receive from them! This is to say that the good you receive from others is the compensation you would receive for your good deeds in dealing with them!! As a matter of fact, the true value of doing the good for others lies in the very act of goodness itself, as it is stated in the following verse of the Holy Quran:

> We only feed you for Allah's sake; we desire from you neither reward nor thanks. (The Time 76:9)

Although this verse has been revealed regarding the Holy Prophet's family, it nonetheless unveils the true value of good deeds which should not be sought for in rewards and thanks it addresses all human beings as a whole. Moreover, Rumi has also beautifully depicted this very inherent value of goodness in the following lines:

> If a flower does not open up with joy, what is it to do?
> If it does not let out fragrance, what is it for?
> If the glorious Moon shines out anything but goodness and beauty, what is it indeed to do?
> If the Sun is not to shine dazzling light upon this beautiful Earth, then what is it to do?

---

63 - Ghasemzadeh, Murteza, *The French Constitution*. (Originally in Persian).

Regarding Islam's serious attention to the global face of humanity and man's universal rights, it was up to Muslim interpreters and defenders of the Universal Declaration of Human Rights to have traced back the articles of *Declaration* to prophetic ideas on the global face of humanity and man's universal rights.

Whitehead, truly well-versed in the history of ideas and civilizations, has clearly indicated in his *Adventures of Ideas* that Hebrew Prophets have done great services to freedom and civilization. As we mentioned in the previous chapter, all of the items implied in the Declaration have already been articulated in Islamic texts.

Revealed religions have established their agendas on twelve equalities and triple unities of human beings which must be realized thoroughly in the context of "intelligible life" so that human individuals will be able to take part in the competition of goods and perfections by intelligible justice and freedom.

We shall see in our debates on triple human unities how human beings appealing to the primordial formula of "one for all in all for one"[64] ascend from the realm of quantities to the transcendent realm of quality. Let us take the following verse of the Holy Quran into precise consideration:

> For this reason did we prescribe to the children of Israel that whoever slays a soul, unless it is for manslaughter or mischief in the land, it is as though he slew all men; and whoever keeps it alive, it is as though he kept alive all men; and certainly our messengers came to them with clear arguments, but even after that many of them certainly act extravagantly in the land. (The Dinner Table 5:32)[65]

There are two highly significant quotations from the Holy Prophet (PBUH) in Islamic texts that directly address human global stature and man's universal rights.

The first narration reads as follows:

> All people are members of Allah's family, and their most blessed one with the Lord is the one who is most beneficial for the members of Allah's family.[66]

---

64 - Ja'fari, M. T, *A Translation and Interpretation of the Nahj ul-Balaghah*, Vol. 22, p. 81. (Originally in Persian).

65 - "Children of Israel" in this verse does not imply any racial consideration and Moses was the then prophet of all people around the globe after Abraham. All prophets have preached the same revealed truths – of course, in their own languages – within their mission's territory.

66 - Sheikh al-Horre al-Ameli, *Wasa'el al-Shi'ah*, Vol. 6, p. 510.

The second narration from the Holy Prophet Muhammad (PBUH) reads:

> *Everyone who hears the shout of a man for help and does not answer it, he is not, in fact, a Muslim.*[67]

It is needless to say that "man" in this context includes all human beings.

I wonder why Muslim researchers of the Universal Declaration of Human Rights have not pointed out the presence of its seminal themes in Islamic texts. As we shall see in our debates on the basic motives of the approval of the Universal Declaration, the major goal of holy prophets was to make people attentive to this *magnum Veritas* that they should communicate with each other in the spirit of fraternity and not only must everyone see themselves, members of the same whole, but they also need to accept that if they embark upon the path of intelligible life, their souls will be related to the divine soul in a way that sun rays are dependent upon the sun. No higher unity than this would be conceivable for humanity. Islam has also revealed the global face of humanity in other forms:

> *Say: o followers of the book! Come to an equitable proposition between us and you that we shall not serve any but Allah and (that) we shall not associate aught with him, and (that) some of us shall not take others for lords besides Allah; but if they turn back, then say: Bear witness that we are Muslims.*
>
> (The Family of Imran 3:64)

Regarding this holy verse and also the jurisprudential materials that shall be discussed in our coming comparative debates, it should be stated that the foundation of universal human rights must be sought for in Abrahamic religions, and especially, in Islam as the last of them. It might be objected that firstly, the addressee of this verse is only the followers of the book and not all human beings, and secondly, that God has briefed the whole idea in two articles of monotheism and tearing down all bondages from humanity and introduced them as the common word and truth for the people of the book and holy prophets.

The answer is that all articles are deducible from these two articles; this is to say that if humanity is to succeed in monotheism and relieve himself from bondages, he shall have to demonstrate his inherent dignity, and it is in fact through demonstrating the human primordial status that one shall be able to rationalize the necessity of freedom, peace, and respect for human social and individual rights, and after the necessity of human rights is revealed to all human beings, all people around the globe shall try to achieve them.

As a result, seeing the thirty articles of the occidentally-motivated Universal Declaration of Human Rights as something *totally other* is nowise justifiable. As we have already argued in the introduction to this book, the idea of reforming human relationships with man's fellow human beings – whether directly or indirectly – has ever existed in the enlightened minds,

---

67 - Ibid.

since an enlightened mind is primordially aware of the identity and the material and spiritual coordinates of humanity. Moreover, the man also knows that granting freedom and justice to his fellow human beings, even before relieving his fellow human beings from unbearable sufferings in social and individual life and making him happy, gives rise to eternal joy inside himself, which is an effect of paying his debt to humanity.

Divisions of Human Characters

In The Universal Islamic Declaration of Human Rights

About their characters, human beings are divided into six groups: [68]

The First Group are those who have not been evolved on their characters and have no epistemic and moral qualities – but what is necessary for living a merely natural life. This bunch of people could be appropriately classified as "Primitives."

The Second Group is those who have embarked upon the path of epistemic and moral evolution and achieved needed qualities for entering the realm of social life and peaceful coexistence.

The Third Group have gone ahead of the second group and recognized that this life and world could not be interpreted and justified without recourse to the world beyond it; while their mind and conscience order them to provide an intelligible interpretation and justification for this life and this world. To this very reason, they commit themselves to some duties to be able to be connected with the transcendent origin of existence.

The Fourth group believe in one of Abrahamic Religions such as Judaism, Christianity, Islam and Zoroastrianism[69], and are committed to their *Shari'ah*.

The Fifth Group: Muslims who while believing in all previous Abrahamic Religions have committed themselves to the religion that has been revealed to Muhammad, the son of Abdullah (SAW). This religion is called Islam according to Quranic verses and is an expression of Abraham's Religion which is the whole of Revealed Religions.

Note 1- Whereas the measure of dignity and value in abovementioned quintuple divisions of human characters is human growth and perfection, then the more peoples of these quintuple groups are grown and perfect, the more they shall be of value and dignity. It is for this very reason that those followers of the book who have more human features have been praised in the Holy Quran:

---

68 - Muslim theologians see division as definition.

69 - Providing, however, that this religion sees itself as an Abrahamic Religion.

And among the followers of the book there are some such that if you entrust one (of them) with a heap of wealth, he shall pay it back to you; and among them there are some such that if you entrust one (of them) with a dinar he shall not pay it back to you except so long as you remain firm in demanding it; this is because they say: there is not upon us in the matter of the unlearned people any way (to reproach), and they tell a lie against Allah while they know.

(The Family of Imran 3:75)

Moreover, according to Islamic jurisprudence, if some people from the followers of the book bring their case to Muslim judicial authorities and also take with themselves two groups of witnesses from the followers of the book one of whom are religiously committed and honest while the other one consists of unreligious, unjust and liar people, the first group is prior to the other, and this is not merely a devotional judgment, but it has its origin in a self-evident rational principle that tells discovering reality needs honest people. Furthermore, those people are elected to lead human societies and groups of individuals who are more honest, good and faithful to a human ideology, according to the judgments of human primordial nature, reason, and conscience, and this is not surely in the sense of discrimination and against the primordial principle of human equality as understood by the Universal Declaration of Human Rights. A frequently cited word by Imam Hussein (SAW) states this very point very brilliantly:

If you are not religious and do not fear from the Day of Judgment, at least you can be liberal-minded [faithful to primordial features of humanity and principles of conscience].[70]

This eternal Word clearly says that if some human beings do not believe in religion as a primordial source of dignity and value, at least by following humanly grounded principles in their life, they could be better than people who have no principle in life.

Note 2. the measure of dignity and value just articulated could be equally applied to all five abovementioned groups, and thus every human being who follows more human principles in her/his life is better than those who have not persuaded these principles although they regard themselves Muslim.

Explanatory Note: As mentioned before, Islam paves the ground for growth and perfection. The man only needs to equip himself with two primordial forces of reason and conscience so as to be able to embark upon the thorny path of growth and intellectual evolution:

---

70 - Abu Muhammad al-Hassan Ibn Ali Ibn al-Hussein bin Shu'ba al-Harrani, *Tuhaf ul-Ughul*, p. 114.

And that some of us are those who submit, and some of us are the deviators;
so whoever submits, these aim at the right way.

(The Spirits 72:14)

It is needless to say that Holy Prophet Muhammad has declared himself among those who submit to Divine Will. All enlightened souls like Ali (SAW), Malek Ashtar, Salman Farsi, Ammar, Oways Gharani and Prophet's Household have done so. Although there are some anthropoid savages that have also verbally declared themselves as Muslim like Yazid Ibn Mu'aviyah, Ibn Zyad, and so on and so forth. However, those none-Muslims who are faithful to primordial principles of human reason and conscience and have no claim of Islam are preferred to those who are only verbally Muslim.

The Sixth Group consists of those enlightened souls and minds that have been conferred with the eternal quality of Taghva (Divine Awe) which is insisted on in the following verse of the Holy Quran:

> *Surely the most honorable of you with Allah is the one among you most*
> *careful (of his duty).*

(The Chambers 49:13)

The Common Rights of Humanity in Islam

The previously discussed sextuple groups of human beings have the following rights in common:

I)   The Right to Life: All human beings, in every states and condition, always have the right to life.

II) The Right to Inherent Dignity: All human beings have inherent dignity and are essentially respectable.

III) The Right to Work and Activity: All human beings are eligible to have beneficial works and activities and to be paid for them.

IV) The Right to Education: All human individuals have the right to be educated by all legal means.

V)   The Right to Freedom: All human beings are equally eligible to be free in a *committed* fashion.

Since all of these rights shall be discussed at length in coming debates on human rights in the perspective of Islam, we will not address them here.

Every human being disregarding her/his place in the sextuple groups of humanity could ascend to the highest state of divine awe through embarking upon the path of mental growth and intellectual evolution and acting upon principles that are profitable for her/his individual life and society. As it is depicted in the following verse of the Holy Quran:

O you men! Surely we have created you of a male and a female, and made you tribes and families that you may know each other; surely the most honorable of you with Allah is the one among you most careful (of his duty); surely Allah is knowing, aware.

(The Chambers 49:13)

The addressees of this holy verse are all human beings who are eligible for abovementioned pentuple rights since all human individuals are members of the Lord's family and the most blessed ones with God are most beneficial ones for the family.[71]

However, these sextuple groups are distinguished on their intellectual growth and spiritual perfection. This is not merely a devotional issue, but since the dawn of human history up to the present time, people have always been classified according to their competences and individual qualities. Thus this competence based classification has provided the necessary impetus for talented and spiritually enlightened minds to take the lead of humanity and this, in turn, resulted in epoch-making achievements in human history. The obliviousness that Universal Declaration of Human Rights has shown toward this ultra-significant principle is deplorable. The absence of the principle of individual competence in the field of fundamental rights of humanity hollows the very concept of right from its genuine meaning and reduces it into mere means for securing peaceful coexistence between brutes.

The Necessity of the Divine Factor in Intellectual Evolution

We will need to address two fundamental issues in this discussion:

The First Issue:

The fact that humankind has been created for evolution and perfection is unanimously agreed upon by enlightened scholars, and no temperately-minded average individual would deny the primordial human sense of perfectionism. What silence this primordial sense of people is the following factors:

1- Being stuck in egotism and self-centeredness that hinders the natural activities of reason and conscience.

2- Formal differences of evolutions that mislead shallow-minded people.

3- Aggressive hunters of power who fail to make the wayfarers of the path of intellectual evolution means for their evil purposes. Whereas the true path of intellectual evolution and perfection could not be conceived by limited human knowledge, it seems natural the interpreter of evolution and the ways that lead humanity to it must inevitably be divine. This has also been demonstrated in its right that all human developments have in some way their origins in a religious sentiment. Moreover, it

---

71 - Al-Kulayni, Muhammad Ibn Yaqoub, *Usul al-Kafi*, Vol. 2, p. 166.

should be taken into earnest account that even modern humanist social developments have been benefited from religious sentiments although they pretend to be originated in irreligious ideals.

The Second Issue:

Abraham was the one who, after Noah, took the lead of primordial religion and laid the grounds of monotheism that is the fountainhead of great religions of Judaism, Christianity, and Islam. All revealed religions could represent Abraham's primordial religion if they purify themselves of superstitions, as the Holy Quran indicates:

1-

> *And who has a better religion than he who submits himself entirely to Allah? And he is the doer of good (to others) and follows the faith of Ibrahim, the upright one, and Allah took Ibrahim as a friend.*
> (The Women 4:125)

2-

> *Say: Surely, (as for) me, my Lord has guided me to the right path; (to) a most right religion, the faith of Ibrahim the upright one, and he was not of the polytheists.* (The Cattle 6:161)

3- The following verse indicates that all revealed religions could pace the right path if they act according to Abraham's primordial religion:

> *Surely those who believe, and those who are Jews, and the Christians, and the sabians, whoever believes in Allah and the last day and does good, they shall have their reward with their Lord, and there is no fear for them, nor shall they grieve.* (The Cow 2:62)

The theme of this verse has been repeated (such as The Dinner Table 5:69) and also reiterated (for instance, The Pilgrimage 22:17) in other parts of the Holy Quran.

4- Jews and Christians have been quoted in another verse (The Cow 2:135) as saying, "You must be either Jews or Christians to be on the guided path." The Jew says, "Be Jewish," whereas the Christian says, "Be Christian if you want to be guided." God, on the other hand, says that those who seek guidance and emancipation must follow Abraham's religion:

> *Say: Nay! (We follow) the religion of Ibrahim, the Hanif, and he was not one of the polytheists.*
>
> (The Cow 2:135)

5- Another verse says that the originality of Abraham's Divine Word should not be obscured by racial conflicts, diverse cultural names, geographical differences or claims. People are not to abandon the religion of Abraham in pursuit of mere names:

> *Ibrahim was neither a Jew nor a Christian, but he was (an) upright (man), a Muslim, and he was not one of the polytheists.*

(The Family of Imran 3:67)

6- Therefore,

> *Most surely the nearest of people to Ibrahim are those who followed him and this Prophet and those who believe and Allah is the guardian of the believers.*

(The Family of Imran 3:68)

Something like this has been quoted by Abbas Mahmud Al-Aghad from Saint Paul that reads:

> *Circumcising does not make a man Abraham's child. The truth is that the children of Abraham are those who pace on the path of faith and verily Abraham is our father and the Lord has made him the father of all nations.*[72]

7-

> *Say: O, followers of the book! Come to an equitable proposition between us and you that we shall not serve any but Allah and (that) we shall not associate aught with him, and (that) some of us shall not take others for lords besides Allah; but if they turn back, then say: Bear witness that we are Muslims.*

(The Family of Imran 3:64)

8-

> *Say: we believe in Allah and what has been revealed to us, and what was revealed to Ibrahim and Samuel and Isaac and Yaqoub and the tribes, and what was given to Moses and Jesus and to the prophets from their Lord; we do not make any distinction between any of them, and to him do we submit.*

(The Family of Imran 3:84)

9-

> *He has made plain to you of the religion what he enjoined upon Noah and that which we have revealed to you and that which we enjoined upon Ibrahim and Moses and Jesus that keep to obedience and be not divided therein; hard to the unbelievers is that which you call them to; Allah chooses for himself whom he pleases, and guides to Himself him who turns (to him), frequently.*

(Consultation 42:13)

---

72 - *Abraham: The Father of Prophets.* (Originally in Arabic).

Value Concerns and the Global Reception of Universal Declaration of Human Rights:

Definitions and Proofs

Prologue

The articles of the occidentally-motivated Universal Declaration of Human Rights have been declared as outlining the rights and duties of all human individuals in every human society; however, as we know, human societies have different ideologies, cultures, and living conditions and thus are governed according to various legal, moral and religious codes. As a result, it seems that these articles need to be defined and demonstrated in a way that they can be unanimously agreed upon by all societies and nations, or at least their definition and demonstration may reach a consensus able to discolor the existing conflicts on defining and demonstrating these articles between nations.

It might be said that when various judgments are being codified as legal articles, they need to be seen as definite codes that are essentially binding since any uncertainty around them shall render impossible the very existence of codified articles which help the judicial authorities to address legal problems. To this very reason, the task of the definition, interpretation of demonstration of the articles is assigned to books of philosophy of law.

Regarding the global character of human rights, the answer to this objection seems to be easy, since these rights are universal and have been codified for all human beings across the globe disregarding their ideological, cultural, historical, racial backgrounds and are thought to be globally binding for humanity as a whole. On the other hand, the binding factor in rights must be either the necessity of adherence to general policies of a civil society which address the citizens, that is to say, all individuals and parties who live within the territories of a country are legally obligated to observe the governing rules and rights in the country or religion which is one the most powerful of binding factors. Also, since the global rights indicated in the Universal Declaration are not backed by such a binding factor, they need to be defined, interpreted and demonstrated in a logical fashion for the global audience, except for a few cases that all human individuals are agreed upon.

But in codified laws of societies, the articles are not defined and interpreted, nor are the judgments demonstrated with sufficient reasons, because the citizens who are obligated to observe the codified laws and rights are at the same time certain that these legal articles have been enacted with a thorough knowledge of their material and spiritual interests by sincere and sympathetic authorities who are living themselves within the same territory and breathing in the same atmosphere. On the other hand, the global audience of the articles of the Universal Declaration of Human Rights has neither so far seen a sign of such a thorough knowledge of their needs nor witnessed any sympathetic sentiments from the ratifiers of these allegedly universal rights of man.

The necessity of researching on and demonstrating the value issues and judgments indicated in the Preamble and some articles of the *Declaration* has, for the most part, its origin in the doubts that have been cast by positivists on the possibility of scientific verifiability of value issues and judgments.

As we know, some publicly and sometimes academically praised figures in the contemporary Western world have doubted seriously on the very possibility of scientific verifiability of value issues and judgments. Here we shall outline some instances of them:

1- Those who declare the theory of the originality of power (i.e., "Leviathanism") as being a totally scientific theory and describe it regarding such scientific ideas as "natural selection" and "the survival of the fittest." This group has always dictated their theory to the public as the truth revealed by God! They sadly justify the egotisms and despotisms of aggressive hunters of power throughout human history regarding some inhumanly interpreted semi-scientific theories.

2- Those Freudians who have overstated on the dominant role of sexual instinct in all dimensions of human life and interpreted the activities motivated by sexual instinct as the moving cause of all developments throughout human history.

3- The idea that all individual, mental, physical, and social dimensions of human life are functions of economic factors.

4- The Malthusian theory of increase in population which argues that man, sooner or later, will run up against himself and that the population of humanity will eventually outstrip man's ability to supply himself with the necessities of life. This theory is based on the axiom that the population increases in a geometric ratio while the means of subsistence increases in an arithmetic ratio! This doctrine seems to suggest that we need to resort to war or any unethical means to stave off the explosion of population.

5- Scientific materialism that has brought the most grievous havoc upon the pantheon of human highest values, whereas no true scientific method would demonstrate materialism.

6- The Dominion of Machiavellianism, not only in politics but even in knowledge and philosophy in so far as we are witnessing it in contemporary Western philosophy in the form of excessive pragmatism.

These semi-scientific theories have grievously attracted many shallow minds. As we shall see in our coming debates, today the human sciences and philosophies that are in charge of debating on man "as he is" and "as he ought to be" within academia are not only at variance with each other on many points, but they also mostly reduce humanity into an "unconscious brute" or even into a mere machine with no sense of selfhood.

We will now address value judgments and issues that have been declared in the Preamble as the motives for the codification of the Universal Declaration of Human Rights.

Considering the illogical results commonly concluded from the humanities nowadays – which have effectively downgraded mankind to "the gears of an unconscious machine" – such issues neither have definite meaning in regard to nature or configuration nor do such issues and motives from a scientific point of view. All matters that are expelled from the realm of science as scientifically unverifiable issues by contemporary positivist human sciences are clearly verifiable through scientific methods indeed.

1- The Human Being [73]

Is the human being that has been alluded into an occidentally-oriented universal declaration of human rights indeed the same creature that has been created according to the blind rules of nature and after living a short purposeless life on earth and destructing its natural environment and struggling with its fellow creatures for limitless pleasure dies and disappears into nothingness? Or is man the creature that has been created, according to revealed religions, upon Divine Wisdom for a particular purpose?

The first view, according to which man is a creature whose values are merely restricted to natural dimensions and has no inherent perfection or dignity, is the very idea that has been stated by such philosophers as Thomas Hobbes stating man to be a selfish animal who wants to own the whole gamut of life, and in brief, a creature whose life spans around this maxim: "I am the end and others are my means;" accordingly, the inherent dignity of humanity is only a dream and life is nothing but struggle for existence and being benefited from worldly pleasures. According to this view, inviting people to cooperation for making the articles of the universal declaration of human rights more perceptible and acceptable is totally baseless. This leads us to the conclusion that the implementation of the articles indicated in the Declaration needs legal scholars to demonstrate the veracity of these articles in a very decisive fashion through sufficient logical reasons. Nonetheless, it is almost inconceivable that one is able to demonstrate upon scientific reasons for aggressive hunters of power that *human individuals are members of the same whole* and they must see themselves as the members of one family!

---

73 - This word has been repeated in three paragraphs of the Preamble, which outlines the motives of the codification of the Universal Declaration of Human Rights.

This is why you meet with aggressive reactions when you try to make room for the idea of human rights in current human discourses.

It is indeed a matter of surprise that, in the whole document, nothing has been stated on the majesty of virtue and moral commitment originated in divine awe, while without these two most exalted human qualities, the inherent dignity of humanity would be worthless.

2- *Human Inherent Dignity*[74]

There is no doubt that confessing to the inherent dignity of humanity is the necessary prerequisite of arriving at "justice", "peace" and "freedom", but as we have mentioned before, understanding this highly significant existential reality as a merely utopian ideal shall not help us to demonstrate its truth for disciples of Watson, Freud, Skinner, Machiavelli and Hobbes. There is a big task that should be implemented here, otherwise the whole grounds of human rights shall be conceived as demonstrated– the scientific demonstration of human inherent dignity, even in the face of so many scholars of humanities in the West who are mocking it as a dream. As a result, it was up to the codifiers of the Universal Declaration of Human Rights to have invited spiritually and mentally enlightened scholars both from the East and the West to ponder upon this immensely significant issue as a team and demonstrate its truth through logical reasons for the people across the globe.

Generally speaking, no other single issue within both Western and Islamic declarations of human rights is more vital than this very issue of inherent human dignity. Accordingly, the universal authorities on human rights needs to form a highly educated and spiritually illuminated team of scholars from all corners of the world comprised of anthropologists, psychologists – of course, not professional behavioral scientists – legal and moral scientists, religious authorities who believe in a holy scripture revealed by One God and equip them with all needed facilities so that they codify a true (and intelligible) declaration of human rights upon the basic rights of the right to life, the right to education, the right to committed freedom and the right to equality according to their enlightened reason and conscience.

The truth is that if the inherent dignity of humanity is not demonstrated through clear reasons, the ruining formula of "I am the end and the others are merely my means" shall so continue to trigger bloody conflicts between human beings. As we have already seen, Rumi – despite his positive approach to life and being a true optimist as a mystic did not tolerate the current state of human affairs and lamented:

---

74 - The idea of human inherent dignity has been reiterated upon in the last paragraph of the preamble and also in the first article of the Declaration.

O human beings who are putting great efforts into their lives!

If you find that no one has any pity for you and takes no step to lessen your troubles,

do what you must do yourselves rather than pinning your hopes upon others.

Do you think the claims they make about humanity are sincere and heartfelt?

Indeed not, for most people are like cannibals.

Do not trust their benevolent appearance, for deep inside they harbor selfish monsters

Beware that these "humans" are like devils set out to deceive you.

Do you not realize that some of them kneel beside you like a butcher sits beside a sheep he is about to slaughter?

Avoid setting up house in land provided for you by others; do your own thing, and be confident about what you do...[75]

The issue of the pessimism toward natural life, in which even the highest of educations have failed to bring about elevated human virtues, has also shocked many great scholars both in the East and the West. To understand this reality, it would suffice to take into serious consideration the following words by Alfred North Whitehead:

> *Human nature is so complex that plans for society are to political leaders not worth even the price of a defected paper.*[76]

3- The Members of the Human Family[77]

Needless to say, the expression "the members of the human family," like "human inherent dignity" also signifies a moral concept. Although the human relatedness of individuals as the members of the same family is one of the noblest ideals of humanity, since the dawn of human social life on the terrestrial globe up to the present time – except for those occasions that divine leaders and enlightened spirits have implanted the spirit of membership in the human family inside human individuals with their divine wisdom – it has nevertheless not found true occasion to be realized in the outside world. It might be said, however, that we come across harmonious lives in human history that has not been led by divine messengers. The answer is clear: harmonious forms of collective life have existed even in the age of slavery, and most of the slaves – due to their ignorance of the primordial and inherited dignity and status of humanity – participated in collective social life affairs in a harmonious fashion with a shallow, baseless and feigned satisfaction. The very reason for this unconscious gregariousness is the intrinsic force of life that sustains people without restricting itself to higher positions and values (although the human mind essentially aims at higher positions

---

75 - Rumi's *Masnavi*, Book 2.

76 - Whitehead, Alfred North, *Adventures of Ideas*.

77 - Preamble, first paragraph.

and values.) Humanity has shown such potency for starting harmonious collective movements that, disregarding the philosophy and goal of those movements, their formal unity deserves to be praised. Sadly, however, after the disappearance of motives of such effervescence, humanity returns to his previous stagnation, while human beings under the divine leadership of holy prophets touch the eternal truth of the unity of humanity and see themselves the members of a large family that are fathered by the Lord.

We all know that enlightened minds both in the East and the West have always made sincere efforts to untwist these intricacies though they have not yet met the target. To be sure, these efforts shall not yield the desirable result, and thus the intricacies shall remain twisted as they are, since expecting these efforts to be successful is like expecting a fish to be alive even when it is taken out of its living place in the sea or a lake, wrapped in a silky tissue and expected to sleep with narcotizing philosophical lullabies! That fish will die after a short while even disregarding what you have provided it with. This is also the case with human beings, whose primordial locus is the sea of Supreme Reality; if man loses touch with that, he shall not touch the realm of intelligibility and true life whether he lives in a luxurious palace, enjoy himself in the most spectacular yachts, or live a hermetic life in a small dwelling.

The formula that "all human beings are members of the same family and no one in this large family is better than the other as equal humans," is only acceptable in the divine logic of holy prophets, and of course not in the aggressive logic of hunters of pleasure and selfish hedonists. The universal authorities on human rights urgently need to secure man's connection with his creator and the realm of intelligibility if they are to implement fundamental human rights. It is for sure that today no religious conflicts would prevent humanity from touching his basic rights, as the needed ground has already been laid by cultural and philosophical discourses for mutual understanding on religion. Is it not possible now for us as humans to live peacefully with each other under the religion of father Abraham?

Every individual or society that denies this very possibility is either uninformed about the truth of the matter or does not want to leave his hedonistic and selfish position. We are certain to state, and clearly reiterate, that if humanity today does not submit to divinely conferred equalities, he shall not have any other way but living with anxiety in a natural state of war and under aggressive hunters of power.

4- Fraternity and Equality[78]

Fraternity and equality represent two of the highest of ideals of humanity which always fill the enlightened minds and spirits with the sense of eternal joy and security and push them toward making a better and intelligible

---

78 - The first article.

world. It could be said that no wise man would deny, as an indisputable truth, that human success in understanding and accepting the relation of fraternity and brotherhood between all human individuals is the very highest ideal of humanity in collective life, which has always been at the heart of holy prophets' mission and accounts for the ultimate goal of the enlightened minds' efforts for the betterment of human life. But the question is, do the aggressive hunters of power indeed taste the sweetness of this spirit through giving up their natural concessions?

As John Lewis Gaddis has quoted some officials of developed countries, "It is the right of big countries, as the big brothers of the human family, to punish smaller countries that allegedly put in danger the global peace."

He believes that five superpowers – the United Kingdom, the USSR, the People's Republic of China and France – must undertake the role of tutor. Franklin Roosevelt writes in a note of 1941 that:

> In the current chaotic state of the world, it is not intelligible to stick to the idea of the reorganization of the international community, since the extent of the project will result in oppositions and confusions ... There is no reason why the principle of tutorship in private affairs should not be applied in the international context. Tutorship is based on the principles of unselfish services. In all ages, there are some children among the nations of the world that need a tutor in their relations with their people and other nations, as many of big nations also need to be shown their places and to be guided toward goodness.

Roosevelt has also stated that:

> I am not against the formation of a global assembly, providing its management to be passed to super powers.

We shall now analyze these quotations:

I) *"It is the right of big countries, as the big brothers of the human family, to punish smaller countries that put in danger the global peace."*

The question that needs to be asked is: who has conferred this right upon the superpowers? Undoubtedly, this right has its origin in "power," that all legal activists and human conventions are seeking to adjust its grievous havocs and reinforce human relations. It is needless to say that power is the motive for dominion, selfishness, and egotism in the eyes of aggressive hunters of power, not the source of equality and fraternity between human individuals. Secondly, the best way to securing global peace and preventing worldwide wars is to stop selling arms to countries involved in war; this is to say, they must cease the sales of arms to them and also not let other countries provide their arms.

II) Moreover, it has been quoted that:

> *On the other hand, small countries should be involved in some way that, firstly, they would not think that they have been benched forever, and secondly, they must not be given any executive role in the management of international community [....] I am not against the formation of a global assembly, providing that its management is passed to super powers.*

We pray that there have been errors and mistakes in the translation or the quotations of the sentences above so that a renowned figure will not be attributed to such statements. These words are prescriptions of a Machiavellianism politician who is not informed by the essential ideals of human rights, fraternity and equality, and human inherent dignity. Do the enlightened minds and spirits who have been born into small countries and are intellectually more excellent than the thinkers of developed countries still need to follow the big brother countries that are more powerful? Were Jesus of Nazareth and Muhammad the Son of Abdullah who was born in Hejaz, an uncivilized wilderness in Saudi Arabia, not successful in leading humanity to the path of perfection and growth? Is it not so that small countries have contributed as much as the bigger countries into the development of human social life?

These words are wholly penetrated by the basic principles of Machiavellianism, which invites politicians to resort to unscrupulous and manipulative method in power equations. Roosevelt's idea of superpowers' right to tutorship is not actually consistent with highest ideals of fraternity and equality. I wonder why the codifiers of the Universal Declaration of Human Rights have not addressed the issue of "Big Brothers," which is obvious variance with great ideals of equality and fraternity that have been reiterated in the articles of the Declaration.

Even if we suppose that the idea of "Big Brothers" has its own logical reasons, these reasons must therefore be understood in terms of the highest of human sentiments rather than in a Leviathanistic fashion.

5- *Friendly Relations*[79]

There is no doubt that these relations have always been the sincere wish of enlightened minds and spirits throughout history. No one would deny the ideality of these relations if he has already felt how pleasant they are. Human spiritual unity is such an ideal that all human individuals confess to its ideality. Unfortunately, egotism, selfishness and self-alienation have rendered the global realization of these relations as impossible and Hobbesianism – stating that "human beings treat human beings like wolves" -- governs the human relations both in the individual and social levels.

---

79 - Preamble, fourth paragraph.

6- *Human Conscience*[80]

If we were supposed to underlie our considerations on "human conscience" with mainstream human discourse within the academia, we would have to take the subject of our considerations to be imaginary and nonsense. We don't know how to deal with the paradox that exists in Western discourse of human conscience in the sense that academic circles in the West are strongly denying the existence of human conscience upon allegedly scientific reasons while *human conscience* is indicated in the preamble of the occidentally-oriented Universal Declaration of Human Rights as a basic concept!

If the primordial call of human conscience was heard and respected by the men of power, not only would human history have changed its course very long time ago, but we would also now be able to cure many seemingly terminally ill sufferings of humanity. Is it reasonable, from a scientific point of view, to take "human conscience" as the source of human dignity and divinity, on the one hand, and to reduce the whole human existence and its related concepts into mere neurotic modes and phenomena on the other?

7- *Equal Rights*[81]

It is needless to say that the ideal of equal rights of humanity has always been an aspiration of the enlightened minds of human societies; sadly, however, as the actual course of events in past and present shows, like other human ideals, it has only been used as mere means in two ways -- either for the decoration of speeches and books or for deceiving shallow-minded people and covering brutalities.

8- *Freedom*[82]

Regarding the whole information available about human life and its spiritual and physical coordinates, we could justifiably claim that freedom sustains the desirability of life. Freedom is defined as human consciousness of positive and negative sides of the task done for the sake of what seems to be both physically and spiritually good for him.

Upon this definition – that is agreed upon by the majority of scholars of human sciences – we could precisely evaluate the freedoms that have been indicated in the *Declaration*.

Generally speaking, the hegemony of materialism in contemporary discourses of human life and its various dimensions finally gave rise to

---

80 - Preamble, second paragraph.

81 - Preamble, third paragraph.

82 - Preamble, the first, fifth and sixth paragraphs, and also Articles 1, 3, 13, the second clause of Article 16, Articles 18 and 19, clauses 1 and 2 of Article 20, Article 23, the second clause of Article 26, the first clause of Article 27 and Article 28.

the publicly desirable ideal of freedom as *unlimited will to desire*. Freedom in this sense is totally disconnected with the realm of values and allows human individuals to do what they would desire to do just providing it does not violate the natural rights of their fellow human individuals; thus, freedom in the sense of liberty (that leads human individuals to the realm of intelligible life) disappeared from human horizon. This was a lamentable defeat for humanity in the course of intellectual evolution. The promotion of eroticism in the name of freedom has deprived humanity of his unique quality of free will. It is indeed a matter of regret that the noble sense of freedom just mentioned has not been indicated in the Universal Declaration of Human Rights.

Another highly significant issue that needs to be addressed is that an occidentally-oriented declaration of universal rights of man is so penetrated with frequent references to human natural freedoms that there remains no place for human spiritual freedoms, other human freedoms and some social and collective rights to be indicated like the right of being free from want. It is noteworthy here to quote some key ideas of Whitehead's on freedom that could greatly help us to understand the issue in a very relevant fashion:

> *Now, in respect to the political factions of the ancient world, nothing has yet been settled. Every problem which Plato discusses is still alive today. Yet, there is a vast difference between modern and ancient theories, for we differ from the ancients on the one premise on which they were all now. Slavery was the presupposition of political theorists then. Freedom is the presupposition of political theorists now. In those days, the penetrability minds found a difficulty in reconciling their doctrine of slavery to certain plain facts of moral feeling and of sociological practice, and in these days our sociological speculations find difficulty in reconciling our doctrine of freedom to another group of plain facts. Yet, when all such qualifications have been made, freedom and equality constitute an inevitable presupposition for modern political thought with an admixture of subsequent lame qualification, while slavery was a corresponding presupposition for the ancients with their admixture of subsequent lame qualification.*[83]

9- *Peace*[84]

All moral, religious and rational reasons which demonstrate the significance and value of human life and insist on the necessity of its being protected and respected have also *logically* emphasized upon the significance and value of peace and the essentiality of its being defended and observed, since it is evident that wars and conflicts are ruining the causes of human life. On several occasions, the Holy Quran has invited people to live a peaceful life and laid strong stress on the vitality of peace for human life. However, some

---

83 - Whitehead, Alfred North, *Adventures of Ideas*.
84 - Preamble, first paragraph.

issues here need to be addressed:

A) Could we claim to have achieved peace by means of halting physical clashes while the motives for conflicts still exist in people's hearts?

B) Has a comprehensive and exclusive definition up to this time been proposed to humanity by true psychologists, sociologists and philosophers –not by those who see psychology, sociology and philosophy as their vocation indeed?

C) Can we claim to have woven peace between nations by storing atomic and biological bombs in our arsenals?

It is exactly based upon such issues that we may state that the United Nations needs, by resorting to Revealed Religions and constructive human cultures, firstly to set out to define humanity in clearly moral terms and invite human societies to make morality their prior source of regulation of their conducts, and then it will have the right to demand peace in its declarations.

10- Justice[85]

The common definition of justice, which is almost agreed upon by all scholars of human sciences, philosophers and religious authorities is as follows: an approved legally grounded conscious and free method. This definition also implies the ancient definition of justice as "putting everything in its own appropriate place." The most significant issue which must be addressed here is which criterion determines the legal ground upon which a method is declared as conscious and free and is defined as an extension of justice and the place which is seen as the appropriate place for a things, for all human individuals and societies have for themselves particular laws upon which some methods are being legitimized and things find their right places. Nevertheless, the Universal Declaration of Human Rights needs to explain the meaning of the "justice" it demands from all people around the globe. This is the very reason why the issue of human ideal morals originated in man's primordial nature and acting upon the principles of intellectual evolution reaffirms its necessity. Moreover, if we understand human freedom in an unlimited fashion and thus allow people to act unscrupulously, no truth as genuine justice shall emit light to man's soul, and he shall act merely upon natural spontaneity and principles of determinism. The justice which is necessary for the implementation of global rights of man would not be achieved without man's being equipped with human ideal morals.

11- People's Highest Aspiration[86]

The highest aspiration of common people has been indicated in the Preamble in the following words:

---

85 - Preamble, first paragraph.
86 - Preamble, second paragraph.

> *Whereas disregard and contempt for human rights have resulted in barbarous acts which have outraged the conscience of mankind, and the advent of a world in which human beings shall enjoy freedom of speech and belief and freedom from fear and want has been proclaimed as the highest aspiration of the common people…*

These words indicate that the global ideal of human rights is supposed to prevent barbarous acts that have outraged human conscience and also for the advent of a world in which human beings shall enjoy freedom of speech and belief and freedom from "fear" and "want". There is no doubt indeed that the halt of barbarous acts, the peace of human conscience, freedom of speech and opinion, and freedom from fear and want are all an evident necessity, but this necessity also shows that occidentally-motivated Universal Declaration of Human Rights leads humanity to a peaceful *natural life,* and this is in my view a self-evident truth agreed upon by all wise men. However, if we take these above-mentioned things as the highest aspiration of common people, we would make the very act of living in this world the ultimate telos of humanity. Undoubtedly, this view of human life is based on the idea of *"living life for the life itself"* which represents the basic philosophy of the animal history of humanity and thus is not an appropriate *weltanschauung* for the human history of humanity that begins when human beings decide to accept human necessities and competencies beyond determinism, hedonism, utilitarianism and egotism.

12- *Reason and Conscience*[87]

"Reason" and "Conscience," as indicated in the first article, are either for the demonstration of human values and dignity – which should have already been demonstrated in the preamble, not in an article, since conventionally speaking, dignity and value and their related issues do not belong to the realm of rights, but the latter could be their sources – or they are depicting human primordial nature. This is also an issue that must be addressed in the philosophy of rights (the preamble) rather than in articles.

There is no doubt that human beings have "reason," a mental power through which man distinguishes between right and wrong. There is of course so much to be debated on the essence, functions and limits of reason and its different appearances in practical and theoretical forms, that we shall nonetheless not deal with here.

It needs to be explained in full-length what conscience signifies in this context. Does it represent the very mental phenomena of consciousness and self-consciousness, which are dealt with in psychology? Or does it symbolize moral conscience with recourse to which the codifiers of the Universal Declaration are to persuade human beings to adhere and act upon the thirty articles indicated in declaration? If conscience in this context signifies the moral conscience that pushes humanity toward virtuous actions and keeps them away from evils, legal experts know for sure that it has lost its authentic power due to the sophistications of professional philosophers who have managed to reduce such a highly respected human spiritual compass into a merely mental phenomenon.

The revival of human moral conscience, and consequently, the implementation of the basic rights of peace, justice and freedom is necessarily hinged upon the renewal of theoretical discourse of conscience within human sciences. This is why we insists that in order to prove the necessity of peace, freedom, moral conscience and even a reason that, while being perfectly sound, can distinguish good from bad and also a wisdom that can moderate lusts and desires and prove the need for searching for the truth for man, such issues need to undergo study once again so as to prove the error made by people in the past by discarding such original ideas from humanity.

13- Life [88]

If we cast a sharp eye to the current state of biological and psychological discourses in the contemporary world, we shall see that excessive positivism and scientism have made many highly respected concepts like human life a victim of their baseless materialistic analyses. The deep well sunk by excessive scientism has buried many precious truths inside it and still continues to engulf the basic realities of the world. It was this excessive scientism that finally submerged the basic reality of human life into its deep well with the aid of aggressive hunters of power. Sa'adi has beautifully revealed the baselessness of such bumptious claims of egotists and deceivers in the following lines:

> The poor-minded person who sits by a candle in daylight,
> very soon you shall see him sitting in the darkness at night;
> the shallow rival who indulges himself in drinking
> never would think of his day of wanting

These self-deceivers would never think that a day will come when humanity will incessantly seek these truths (conscience, reason, freedom, justice, equality, fraternity, members of human family, universal respect, common understanding….) again as the last resort of human survival.

Now we can see how inconsiderately egotist and aggressive hunters of power have set the highest ideals of humanity on fire and buried their ashes in the deep well of carnal desires.

14- Opinion[89]

The question that should be asked of excessive proponents of scientism is,

88 - Preamble, seventh paragraph.
89 - Second article.

what indeed is "opinion"? Should everything in your view be grounded upon purely scientific premises in a positivistic sense, there would seem to remain no place for something like opinion. What does intuition mean? What are transcendent sensations? What signifies escalated sentiments? Consequently, many such existentially issues of immense significance will continue to be neglected with the hegemony of excessive scientism.

15- The Faith of the United Nations[90]

"Faith," like "opinion," needs to be banished from entering the realm of human life as believed by the proponents of excessive scientism, since these two concepts and many such highly respected concepts are not *commensurable* from a purely scientific point of view and with its materialistic indexes. This is the very root of the human annihilation that is the underlying concern of the Vancouver Declaration on Human Survival in the 21st Century issued by UNESCO[91]. This declaration reflects the deepest concerns over the grievous situation of the planet Earth and proposes general solutions for the problem, which are nonetheless not still sufficient. Here we shall discuss in full length the Vancouver Declaration, as it seems to be necessary for those who are concerned with the highly significant issue of human rights.

16- Global Respect

The concept of "global respect" has been mentioned in the preamble as:

> *"Whereas Member States have pledged themselves to achieve, in cooperation with the United Nations, the promotion of universal respect for and the observance of human rights and fundamental freedoms…"* [92]

It is obvious that requesting global respect for an issue without having clarified and elaborated upon the true cause of the issue concerned would fail to prove any more significance than an emotional request. Therefore, it is essential that the philosophy of the necessity of such universal respect be explained for the global population. Mere claims will not convince the population of the world to pay respect to universal human rights without having truly comprehended the aim and philosophy of the issue first, for respect is a mental phenomenon of potential merit, and if the United Nations fails to save merits and values from those who claim to be worshippers of science, it can never hope to expect such respect from people with

---

90 - Preamble, the fifth paragraph.

91 - In 1989, a conference was held in Vancouver to study the question whether man would be able to survive the twenty-first century or not. Muhammad Taghi Ja'fari has provided a critique of the declaration issued at the end of the conference in Vancouver in his book *The Human Genome*, which has also been translated into English. The critique is also available in the articles section of www.ostad-Jafari.com.

92 - Preamble, 6th paragraph.

diverse ideologies and cultures by means of begging for it. The Vancouver Declaration, which we have already discussed, has fully realized the significance of entering elevated human values into the domain of sciences and accepting their scientific merit and value. Obviously, without achieving such an essential step, no begging or political pressure of any kind will be of any avail – as has been so far.

17- *The Feeling of Common Understanding*

As stated in the seventh paragraph of the preamble:

> *"Whereas a common understanding of these rights is of the greatest importance for the full realization of this pledge,…"*

This statement is absolutely correct and logical. In other words, if all of the items included in the Declaration of Universal Human Rights are to be executed in full, it is essential to achieve a common understanding at a supreme level; however, it is quite concerning – and in fact makes such a common understanding quite remote from the minds of the global population, in particular the disadvantages and weak nations – how some societies have, throughout history, have seen those in charge of powerful societies as supporters of "endeavors toward self-survival even at the expense of the destruction of the weak" and claimed to have a common understanding with such brutal players of the arena of survival – who have even recently come to have taken a scientific look at the label "natural selection"? In brief, in order to achieve common understanding, sincere measures should be taken and baseless, evocative propaganda are to be avoided as far as possible.

18- *Barbarous Acts*

These two words have been mentioned in the second paragraph of the preamble:

> *"Whereas disregard and contempt for human rights have resulted in barbarous acts which have outraged the conscience of mankind…"*

Have thinkers of the humanities – in particular modern scholars of legal domains – come to realize that "the defeat of the weak by the strong" is an act of barbarianism, or do they still regard it as appropriate for the powerful to depend upon the issue of destruction, which can lead to any form of crime, as a means to "fulfill whatever our interests are?" In other words, have these thinkers managed to prove to theorists of political sciences, politicians and legal experts of various political systems that what selfish despots have done have been barbaric? As indicated by trends seen in political affairs, major human management and the performance of those truly in charge of human societies, the thinkers and pioneers of man's natural life in social and political aspects have still not succeeded in taking the immense human step that would prove that the likes of Genghis Khan, Attila, Napoleon, Hitler and Nero have committed barbaric acts throughout history; in fact, if one who believes in elevated values of life regards human beings from a pro-life aspect, one will cry out in protest:

> *What is all of this uproar?*
> *Are we all not companions and of the same kin and origin?*[93]

Equipped with a few so-called scientific and philosophical terms claiming that "You should not inhibit the natural flow of the originality of power," they have begun their raids upon humanitarian anthropologists and accused them of being ignorant of the general trend and flow of history, thus depriving them of making any remarks on humanity! Is it now not obvious who real knowledge belongs to? These indeed were the same who cried out, "Thinkers! Beware not to allow the principles of human values to be eliminated from the table of scientific theorems."

Nowadays, in order to promote human survival, we should put aside statements such as "Whatever I desire is my interest, and to my benefit and whatever I see as to my benefit, I will attain" and advocate instead this human sentence claiming that "I can attain entirely what I am entitled to, and the state and the society must also support this right of mine." If the former is not changed into the latter, despite the fact that the explosion of the planet Earth may be temporarily postponed, our planet will eventually fail to serve as a settlement for us.

Thus, we can explicitly state that if some societies, despite the fact that they are not directly involved in war or conflict, sell weapons to societies engaged in battle and lead to greater killings as to be acts of barbarianism. In other words, if a country does not even shoot a single bullet at anyone but provides arms for other societies which have the incentive to engage in conflict against one another – based on the statement, "My interests deem this" – such a country will unquestionably be committing the most savage and barbaric of acts.

19- Mutiny

As mentioned in the second paragraph of the preamble:

> *"Whereas disregard and contempt for human rights have resulted in barbarous acts which have outraged the conscience of mankind…"*

The concept of "outrage," along with "mutiny" and "rebellion" is regarded as an abdominal act and in conflict with a commitment toward human laws. As a result, it does not seem appropriate to use this term here, for if people of various societies around the world show resistance concerning insults in rights they see themselves as entitled to, that will not imply "mutiny."

---

93 - Rumi, *Divan-e Shams.*

The best interpretation possible is "resistance to attain one's rights," and one of the undoubted consequences, if rights continue to be ignored, may be conflict and resistance in any way possible until lives are saved from the oppressors.

20- Endeavor

The final statements of the preamble to the Universal Declaration of Human Rights, pointing out the motives for the compilation of these rights, state that:

> "… The General Assembly proclaims this Universal Declaration of Human Rights as a common standard of achievement for all peoples and all nations, to the end that every individual and every organ of society, keeping this Declaration constantly in mind, shall strive by teaching and education to promote respect for these rights and freedoms…"

As we have already mentioned, such terms contain ethical and value-based concepts, and if we use them in order to make a bunch of legal contents acceptable for people in societies in which such concepts are partially or totally disregarded of, people may reply accusingly, "Lecture yourself on such moral jargon, for we see no necessity or cause to observe or consider what you are talking about."

21- The Highest Limit of Growth and Development

As stated in Article 26, Clause 2:

> "Education shall be directed to the full development of the human personality…"

Moreover, Article 29 points out that, "Everyone has duties to the community in which alone the free and full development of his personality is possible."

The two articles quoted from above indicate that man's development and his free perfection is a matter of high significance as seen in the Universal Declaration of Human Rights. Since all God-sent religions and true schools of thought established by advocates of human moral ethics – and, in general, any human being with a true knowledge of mankind – are in agreement on this, will not go into further detail on this point. The more significant point, however, is how to interpret "development and perfection" and "freedom," which is unfortunately neglected. As we have frequently mentioned and reiterated, scholars and authorities on human rights and its philosophy must put the utmost emphasis on the interpretation, definition and clarification of these two supremely elevated truths – development and perfection – and thus save these universal rights from all ambiguity, stagnancy, limitation as well as any inconvenience or disturbance human beings may encounter. In any case, development and perfection may be interpreted in two different ways or both ways mentioned below:

1- By man's perfection and development, we are here referring to man's power to attain all of the aims it is possible for him to attain. On the other hand, development and perfection implying man's absolute power to attain whatever goal he may desire will depend on the fact whether the goal concerned is a human value or not. This is the very method used by the likes of Genghis Khan and Tamerlane, who always endeavored in conflict with man's true development and perfection and even humanity as a whole. Nonetheless, if the concept of power and aim falls into the domain of values and merits – i.e. if power implies one's mental domination over oneself, and aim indicates elevated human ideals which supreme human moral ethics call for – the definition above will be acceptable for development and perfection.

2- Development and perfection here imply mutual effects and influences between man and the universe created by God, Who provides His servants with development and perfection. There is no doubt that mutual effects and influences between man and the universe – which is dependent upon God – will not be possible without divine tendencies, the purification of the one's heart, adjusting one's deeds, beliefs and words in accordance with what God has assigned by means of His prophets as well as through man's common sense and pure consciences; nonetheless, the trend of fight and conflict for survival and the original essence regarded for seeking benefits and pleasures has not and still does not allow people in the world to enjoy the two terms mentioned above. Therefore, we can seriously and explicitly state that Western authorities on human rights as well as other researchers take development, perfection, and freedom into consideration regardless of the baseless imaginations expressed by some professional mercenaries of today's humanities, so that they may present the positive results of their endeavors in academic circles and centers of research. It seems that the first thing that must be done is for authorities on human rights to take these two issues – development and perfection and freedom – into serious and extensive consideration in their philosophical studies and also consider the items themselves in appropriate contexts, the best of which is the first item of human rights. Therefore, the first article will be as follows:

> *"All human beings are born free and equal in dignity and rights; no one has any advantage over another, except for greatnesses brought about by pure, sincere endeavors leading to the human development and perfection."*

It is only through providing developed men of merit and perfection over those who know nothing about life but food, sleep, anger and lusts that humanity can be saved from a shameful degradation to unconscious parts of a machine and thus prepare the grounds for survival upon Earth to become a possibility.

22- *Correctly Observing Moral and Ethical Requirements*

As stated in the second clause of Article 29:

> *"In the exercise of his human rights and freedoms, everyone shall be subject only to such limitations as are determined by law solely for the purpose of securing due recognition and respect for the rights and freedoms of others and of meeting the just requirements of morality, public order and the general welfare in a democratic society."*

Without the phrase "in a democratic society," "morality" could have been interpreted as equivalent to elevated human moral ethics – which we have already discussed in the previous section regarding full development – and thus regarded as correct; however, but the phrase "in a democratic society" makes the concept of "moral ethics" become vague, for, in a democratic society, the fulfillment of any free desires or wishes is only prohibited when it may provide disturbance or inconvenience for others, which makes the concept of elevated human moral issues somewhat vague. There is a great deal of experience showing that the democratic systems that have existed in human societies, in particular in the West, have degraded elevated human morals and ethical issues to the verge of destruction; in fact, any action committed based on legal approval and the principle of avoiding disturbance for others is similar to the smooth clockwork of the wheels of a machine.

Human Survival in the 21st Century

Introduction

Before our discussion on the declaration issued at the end of the Vancouver Conference, the following introduction will prove necessary:

Once again, the mysterious laws of human life have awakened the conscience of certain contemporary high-ranking scholars, calling their attention to the horrifying decadence of man's condition, spurred by his idolatry of wealth, power, hedonism, and egoism, and warning them about the gravity of the situation that is likely to annihilate the whole of humankind. It can be readily contended that the outcome of this conference was a serious warning to humanity, clearly enunciating: O men, rise, and correctly evaluate science, spiritualities, and values; moderate your urges for materialism, power, and hedonism, so that the 20th century would not mark the end of human existence of Earth. A few months ago, a group of prominent scientists attending a conference in Vancouver, Canada (held September 5-10, 1989) unanimously adopted a Declaration, which we shall study in this section.

Having read the declaration in detail, I have made certain points that occurred to me regarding its contents.

We all know that the dangerous divide created by certain writers between science and spirituality, values and transcendental norms, is one of the main sources of the problems relating to the cultural, political, legal, moral and religious realms and realities. This point is clearly tractable in this declaration. It is thus incumbent upon us to expound on the artificiality of this distinction. The majority of contemporary thinkers and philosophers, both Eastern and Western, share our views, for they all subscribe to the fact that our planet is now facing a critical situation. There is no doubt that one of the most basic causes leading to this dangerous situation lies in the distinction made by some thinkers between sciences and spiritual norms. Not long ago, some shallow-minded individuals enthusiastically proclaimed the introduction in this novel theory about human knowledge – "Yes, indeed," they claimed, "we have presented a new theory to the realm of human knowledge."[94] In this way, they paved the way for hedonists, egoists, and power-seekers, who in turn, assisted them in thoroughly convincing naive academics.

The most convincing reason for the invalidity of the distinction theory is

---

94 - As Rumi has said in Book 3 of *Masnavi*,

"A snake charmer has brought in a dragon,

Behold! What a rare hunt he has made indeed!"

the fact that the separation of sciences from values and spiritual norms have grafted a sense of futility onto human life. Whenever values and spiritual norms are branded as 'taboos,' life itself emerges as a taboo and becomes riddled with torture and pain.[95] That the audacity and contempt displayed by the egoists' *vis-à-vis* spirituality and lofty values have turned planet Earth into a 'hot engine' should take no one by surprise. Should such a thing not have happened, it would have been a matter of considerable surprise, since all scientific laws governing the universal order would have then been overruled.

We do not know whether these pseudo-scientists have ever found the opportunity to ask themselves if there is any better proof for the scientific validity of spirituality and values other than the fact that disregard for values and spirituality has become the most serious and unprecedented menace to human existence. The truth is that a great deal of negligence and senselessness is required for a man not to notice that fire can set him ablaze and that the causality that relates fire with burning does not, in fact, differentiate between cotton and man.

We should not overlook the fact that the argument about the threat to human existence inheres in the reality that the negligence of values and spirituality – the cornerstone of human dignity – must certainly result in the annihilation of man. If we were to retrospectively account for the applicability of the law of 'mutual conclusiveness' in human history, it would become evident that, thus far, millions of men, outstanding civilizations, and numerous individual rights have been betrayed by the simple negligence of values and spirituality. It would also become evident that power-seekers and egoists, rejecting the relevance of the 'musts' and the 'ifs' of everyday life, manipulated man's obliviousness to the experiences of past generations. They project themselves as ends while using others as means.

What if someone asks, 'What is wrong with the Earth becoming a burning engine?' He might be pointing out that the planet Earth, which used to be the ideal shelter for man, is now becoming the scene for the survival of the fittest, in which the strong deludes them into a futile life, and the weak succumb to pain and torture, and in which good and evil have lost all meaning. Then, so the argument might go, the Earth ought to be destroyed and, with it, the very life that has led Man to become a beast of burden. Though this rationalization is worth nothing, nonetheless it neither addresses the real issue nor does it justify the abandonment of the Earth to the egoists so that they can do whatever they wish, turning the very last page of human history.

The contention 'let all men be annihilated' is the very response forwarded by Einstein's colleague to the problem of the former. Einstein had warned

---

95 -Taboos are forbidden and disapproved acts that might spread in a society; at times they might even contradict logic and perceptions. In subsequent discussions, I will further elaborate on this issue.

that conflict could eventually culminate in the annihilation of all humanity. His colleague had, in turn, questioned Einstein's concern. Einstein finally argued that his colleague had been through tremendous suffering and had calculated and thought extensively but no avail; otherwise, he would not have responded as he did.[96]

If one concedes man's annihilation out of weakness in the face of egoism and selfishness, such a concession is nothing but suicide, betraying the will of man, of God, and of human history.

Now, let us consider the declaration issued at the Vancouver conference.

---

96 - I will elaborate on this story and its sources later on in this book.

The Declaration of the Conference

On Survival in The 21th Century, Vancouver

The survival of the planet has become of central and immediate concern. The present situation requires urgent measures in all sectors, scientific, cultural, economic and political, and a greater sensitization of all humanity. We must have a common enemy: any action that threatens balance within our environment or reduces our legacy to future generations. Today, this is the objective of the Vancouver Declaration on Survival.

I) *Mankind Confronting Survival*

Our planet is unstable, a burning engine undergoing constant change. Life on Earth began about 4 billion years ago and began developing and growing upon the ever-changing environment of the planet. The discovery of free energy in fossil fuels over 200 years ago enabled man to dominate the whole planet. In a matter of time that was inconceivably short, humanity has become virtually the most important factor leading to thoughtless changes and developments across whole continents. The consequences have been drastic and unique in the history of our species, for instance:

➢ Our population has risen from 1 billion to over 5 billion, with a current doubling time of 30-40 years;

➢ a comparable increase in the use of fossil fuels leading to global pollution, climate and sea-level change;

➢ an accelerating destruction of the habitat of life, initiating a massive and irreversible episode of mass extinction in the biosphere the basis of the Earth's ecosystem; and

➢ an unimaginable expenditure of resources and human ingenuity on war and preparation for war all licensed by a belief in inexhaustible resources of the planet, encouraged by political and economic systems that emphasize short-term profit as a benefit, and disregard the real cost of production.

The situation facing humanity involves the collapse of any balance between our species and the rest of life on the planet. Paradoxically, at the time when we stand at the threshold of degeneration of the ecosystem and degradation of the human quality of life, knowledge, and science are now in a position to provide both the human creativity and the technology needed to take remedial action and to rediscover the harmony between nature and humanity. Only the social and political will is lacking.

II) The Origins of the Problem

The origin of our present predicament lies fundamentally in certain developments in science that were essentially complete by the beginning of the century. Those developments, which are mathematically codified in a classical mechanical picture of the universe, gave human beings a power over nature that has, until recently, produced an ever-increasing, and seemingly boundless, the supply of material commodities. Swept up in the exploitation of this power, humankind has tended to shift values to those promoting the maximal realization of the material possibilities that this new power provides.

Suppressed, correspondingly, were the values associated with humanity. This omission of another human dimension is precisely in line with the 'scientific' conception of the universe as a machine, and of man as nothing but a cog within it.

Man's conception of himself is a principle determinant of his values; it fixes the conception of 'self' in the appraisal of self-interest. Thus, the ideological impoverishment associated with the view of man as a cog in a machine leads to the narrowing of values. However, scientific advances of the present century have shown this mechanical view of the universe to be untenable on purely scientific grounds.

Thus, the rational basis for the mechanical conception of man has been invalidated.

III) Alternative Visions

In contemporary science, the order, rigid mechanical picture of the universe has been replaced by concepts that permit a universe that is formed by a continual creative input that is not rigidly constrained by any mechanical laws. The man himself becomes an aspect of this creative impulse and is linked to the whole universe in an integral way that is not expressible within the older mechanistic framework. The 'self' thereby becomes converted from a deterministically controlled cog in a giant machine to an aspect of a free, creative impulse that is intrinsically and immediately tied to the universe as a whole.

Human values are, accordingly, in this new scientific view, enlarged into values consonant with those prevalent in earlier cultures. It is within the framework of the converging images of man provided by recent scientific and cultural developments that we look for visions of a future that would allow a man to survive in dignity and harmony with his environment.

The human species has reached limits in its use of the external world and also in its capacity to live in a changing social and cultural environment.

Man's developing perceptions in science suggest that he might be able to recapture lost beliefs and varieties of spiritual experience.

The present critical situation in humanity's occupancy of the planet requires new visions, rooted in a variety of cultures, in contemplating the future.

The perception of an organic macrocosm that recaptures the rhythms of life would allow a man to reintegrate himself with nature and understand his relationship in space and time to all life and the physical world.

Recognition that a human being is an aspect of the creative process that gives form to the universe enlarges man's image of himself and allows him to transcend the egoism that is the principle cause of disharmony among his fellows and between humanity and nature.

The overcoming of the fragmentation of the body-mind-spirit unity brought about by unbalanced emphases on any one over the others, allows a man to discover within himself the reflection of the cosmos and its supreme unifying principle.

Such visions change the conception of Man in nature and call for a radical transformation of models of development; the elimination of poverty, ignorance and misery; the end of the arms race; the introduction of new learning processes, educational systems and mental attitudes; the implementation of better forms of redistribution to ensure social equity; a new design for living, based on a reduction of waste; respect for biodiversity, socio-economic diversity, and cultural diversity that transcend outmoded concepts of sovereignty.

Science and technology are indispensable for the attainment of these goals, but they can succeed only through an integration of science and culture that leads to a sense of purpose, and an integrative approach designed to overcome the fragmentation that has led to a breakdown in cultural communication.

If we fail to redirect science and technology towards fundamental needs, the advances in informatics (hoarding of knowledge), biotechnology (patenting of life forms) and genetic engineering (mapping of the human genome) will lead to irreversible consequences detrimental to the future of human life.

We must recognize the reality of a multi-religious world and the need for the kind of tolerance that will enable religions, whatever their differences, to cooperate. This would contribute to meeting the requirements for human survival and the nurturing of the shared core values of human solidarity, human rights, and human dignity. This is the common heritage of mankind that is diverse in comparison to our perception of the transcendental significance of human existence, and from a new global conscience.

Critique and Evaluation

Was Man Destined to Worship the Triumvirate of Wealth, Power, and Evil and Become So Entangled?

Were we to gather all scientists past and present, from the East and the West, including those flowing any genre of doctrine and sets of beliefs, and to ask these men, 'Sirs, could man not opt for any solution other than the worship of this triumvirate that has immersed the whole of history in blood, hypocrisy, betrayal of rights, and selfishness?

✓ Could not Man choose any other path but the one that has led to the instability of our planet, turning it into a heat engine?' What would their answer be?

✓ Could man not act by honesty and serenity?

✓ Could he not qualify his life so that effort and hard work could emerge as merits?

✓ Could he choose for himself what he chooses for others?

✓ Could he abstain from the things that he asks others to abstain from?

✓ Could he not avoid lies, double standards, and duplicity?

✓ Can ways for man's rescue be improvised, or God forbid, must the Earth be left on its own so that the burnt cadavers of men fall prey to vultures if indeed vultures were to survive?

If a man has failed to take up any of these paths towards sensible life, it is not surprising that this beautiful shelter called Earth has turned into an arsenal, a scene for the survival of the fittest, and a heat engine. Now, let us explore each sentence in the Vancouver Declaration so as to evaluate both man's current situation on Earth and its underpinnings.

The Declaration states:

> *'Our planet is unstable, a constantly changing heat engine. Life appeared on its surface about four billion years ago, and developed in balance with an environment where sudden unpredictable change is the norm. The discovery, over 200 years ago, of free energy locked in fossil fuels has given mankind the power to dominate the whole planetary surface. In an unbelievably short span of time, unplanned and almost mindlessly, our species has become by far the largest factor for change on the planet. The consequences have been drastic and unique in the history of our species.'*

We must take this fundamental point into consideration that the undesirable, unpleasant consequences of selfishnesses, opportunist manipulations and waywardnesses are not products of our era alone. In other words, such disasters and calamities have not arisen in our time; in fact, this evil tree has always been making man swallow its venomous fruits. However, the phenomena that will arise in our era as a result of such selfishnesses, opportunist manipulations and waywardnesses will prove to be immense and irreparable, such as the destruction of the tree of life. Moreover, the climax in excited lusts for power may even lead, in its most intense form, to the annihilation of the planet itself as well.

I recall bringing up the issue once with a caring man of delicate human emotions who had spent his life justly thinking of defending intelligible freedoms and rights of human beings. Claiming that human identity and its elevated values and merits had been demolished in the world, he said, "Now that the Earth has become an arsenal, a place of lusts and pleasures, a nest of nihilism and campaign against all aspects of human greatness, it might as well be destroyed as fast as possible. "In addition, once Einstein said to a famous person, "If World War III were to start, the entire world might be annihilated." His response was, "Why do you care so much about the annihilation of mankind?!" As Einstein stated, "I imagined he had said this out of the fact that human life has lost its true identity and the only thing that has remained of elevated human values is a mere word rather than out of pessimism and anti-human attitudes."

Therefore, the claim made in the Declaration in regard to the lack of time is not something new; there has always been lacking time for the deliverance of man's natural and spiritual life. Moreover, as the casualties and consequences of the void of identity – most significantly, nihilism – are extremely catastrophic, all human beings must accept the basic principle that "Time is short" at all times and in every period of history. On the other hand, some authorities may say that although there has continually been insufficient time for saving mankind in all aspects of his life, and delay in such cases has been an undesirable issue throughout history, why has it received such immense emphasis in our era? The answer is that nowadays, it is not only the weak and the deprived class who face the danger of destruction – in fact, the powerful and the powerless, rich and poor, those in the palaces and those in the slums, the rulers and the ruled are all endangered. As a result, the outcries, symposiums, congresses, books and all other endeavors all point out that all classes of human beings will be deprived of survival, not only the weak and the destitute.

Furthermore, the Declaration warns us that any hesitation or delay in the establishment of economic and cultural peace in the world will make us have no choice but to pay an even higher price for survival. In any case, we must state that if the originality of human identity and human values had received their due attention and the outcries of caring, pious scholars and authorities – who indeed cared for man – had been heard by despotic rulers and consequently, serious measures had been taken in order to avoid paying a much heavier price and human values and human identity had not been trampled upon, man's generations would not be in the state they are today. Nonetheless, we hope that the outcries and warnings regarding human survival and movements toward "intelligible life" and observing man's rights and committed freedoms will meet serious decisions and actions. Nevertheless, some authorities believe this to be naive claim that has been previously made as well. One cannot expect, they believe, that despotic rulers and opportunist, greedy men of power will be swayed from their perennial goals as a result of such outcries and uproars; in other words, they are unlikely to abandon their secondary nature, the motto of which is, "I am the end, and others are the means to that end."

The Declaration states that, "We must recognize the reality of a multi-religious world and the need for the kind of tolerance that will enable religions, whatever their differences, to cooperate together."

Such a suggestion, which has been presented as an effort to create greater mutual understanding among human beings, is a fine one, but if we suppose that the religions existing in the world, in addition to their common areas, also have irresolvable contradictions – which is so – what should be done then? Can one of these religions be preferred to another for no good reason and despite the contradictory features they have? Or, can we state that all of the issues which lead to conflict and argument between religious leaders must be eliminated and only the common areas are to be taken into consideration? Even if that were possible, how would these areas of common beliefs be determined?

We are not sure whether such declarations will truly bring about effects in human societies – in particular in societies of immense power – or not. Nonetheless, we know for certain that if these declarations lead to impact, there will undoubtedly be enormous upheaval in the history of humanity.

What Should Be Done?

Having studied the contents of the declaration stated at the Vancouver Symposium on human survival in the 21st century, and considering the extremely vast scope of sciences, values and spiritual issues on one hand and man's constructive power and will on the other, we may conclude that the most fundamental (in fact, one of the most fundamental) ways to save man – who is, according to this declaration and other declarations issued nowadays endangered – is for authorities and scholars on science, philosophy and values in general (including moral ethics, aesthetics, religions, and any other spiritual issue relevant) to collaborate and thus rediscover and once again establish and prove harmony and continuity in sciences, spiritual affairs and values and present them to the public in a way understandable and acceptable for all.

Moreover, we hope that respectable scholars and authorities will have read this book, provide us with their ideas and views on the contents of this book along with the relevant reasons as much as possible, as an effort to further the basic cause of man's survival and the immense commitment they have toward their fellow human beings. We hope that, with God's blessings, we may take a step to the best we can to settle this basic issue of mankind's.

As an introduction to our studies here, we must first point out parts of the Vancouver Declaration which clearly state errors made by persons who have separated sciences from spiritual culture and human values. Then, we shall discuss parts of the declaration which explicitly offer solutions for the chaos and man's exposure to destruction, providing coordination between and linking the two issues mentioned.

1- The following parts of the declaration point out that the reason why man is in danger of annihilation lies in the separation of spiritual culture and human values from sciences:

a) *The sentences mentioned below state explicitly that scientific advances that began at the beginning of the twentieth century made developed societies manipulate and take advantage of values to the benefit of their materialistic use; as a result, values were suppressed. As we read in the Vancouver Declaration:*

> *The origin of our present predicament lies fundamentally in certain developments in science that were essentially complete by the beginning of the century. Those developments, which are mathematically codified in a classical mechanical picture of the universe, gave to human beings a power over nature that has, until recently, produced an ever-increasing, and seemingly boundless, the supply of material commodities. Swept up in the exploitation of this power, humankind has tended to shift its values to those promoting the maximal realization of the material possibilities that this new power provides. Suppressed correspondingly, were the values associated with dimensions of the human potential that had been the foundations of earlier cultures.*

b) *The impoverishment of the conception of man caused by this omission of other human dimensions is precisely in line with the "scientific" conception of the universe as a machine, and of man as nothing but a cog within it.*

c) *If we fail to redirect science and technology towards fundamental needs, the advances in informatics (hoarding of knowledge), biotechnology (patenting of life forms) and genetic engineering (mapping of the human genome) will lead to irreversible consequences detrimental to the future of human life.*

d) *Man's conception of himself is a principal determinant of his values; it fixes the conception of "self" in the appraisal of self-interest. Thus, the ideological impoverishment associated with the view of man as a cog in the machine leads to the narrowing of values.*

There is no need for elaboration on the sentences above, for they clearly depict that the perilous state man is in nowadays has been brought about by the separation of sciences from spiritual culture and human values.

2- The following sentences of the Declaration, on the other hand, provide solutions to resolve the danger man faces today; these solutions lie in creating a link between sciences and values:

a) *Paradoxically, at the time when we stand at the threshold of the degeneration of the ecosystem and the degradation of the human quality of life, knowledge, and science are now in a position to provide both the human creativity and the technology needed to take remedial action and to rediscover the harmony between nature and humanity. Only the social and political will is lacking.*

b) *However, scientific advances of the present century have shown this mechanical view of the universe to be untenable on purely scientific grounds. Thus the rational basis for the mechanical conception of man has been invalidated.*

c) *In contemporary science, the older rigid mechanical picture of the universe is replaced by concepts that permit a universe that is formed by a continual creative input that is not rigidly constrained by any mechanical law. Human values become, accordingly, in this new scientific view, enlarged into values consonant with those prevalent in earlier cultures.*

d) *The human species has reached limits in its use of the external world and also limits its capacity to live in a changing social and cultural environment. Man's developing perceptions in science suggest that he might recapture lost beliefs and varieties of spiritual experience.*

e) *The present critical situation in humanity's occupancy of the planet requires new visions, rooted in a variety of cultures, in contemplating the future.*

In this declaration, there is another point which is worthy of careful attention:

The perception of an organic macrocosm that recaptures the rhythms of life would allow a man to reintegrate himself with nature and understand his relationship in space and time to all life and the physical world.

The Motives for the Islamic

Declaration of Human Universal Rights

O you men! Surely we have created you of a male and a female, and made you tribes and families that you may know each other; surely the most honorable of you with Allah is the one among you most careful (of his duty); surely Allah is knowing, aware.

(The Chambers 49: 13)

The following outlines what have been mentioned in the preamble to the Universal Islamic Declaration of Human Rights; I have also included my glosses on them:

1- The belief in God, the Beneficent and Merciful, the Creator, the Sustainer, the Sovereign, the sole Guide of mankind and the Source of all Law who made the man his vicegerent on the planet earth and commissioned him to fulfill Divine Will on the terrestrial globe.

2- The belief in the wisdom of Divine guidance brought by the Prophets, whose mission found its culmination in the final Divine message that was conveyed by the Prophet Muhammad (Peace be upon him) to all mankind. Indeed, he was the Prophet who proclaimed the idea of universal equality of human beings and said that all human beings are equal with God and no one has any privilege to the other unless in being truly committed to divine obligations. It was the Holy Prophet (PBUH) who removed all discriminations and conflicts by announcing that all human beings are the members of the same family and have been created by Divine Breath.

3- The belief in monotheism, which is the building block of Islam, the quintessence of all revealed religions around the globe. Monotheism here signifies believing in one God, not associating aught with Him and never taking other human being as someone's lord – the belief that made the genuine foundation of human primordial dignity which makes man eligible for inalienable rights to education, committed freedom, equality and fraternity; indeed, this is the belief that signifies human deliverance from all bondages and slaveries.

4- Fulfilling an *eternal shari'ah* (i.e., Divine Law) which secures all domains of human life, that is in fact Islam, which addresses humanity in a very moderate (intelligible) language and invites the believers to act upon the primordial principles of intelligibility and sobriety.

5- Emphasizing the role that Islam has played in human civilization and the Islamic *Ummah*, i.e. the people of Islam (which in fact translates as "submission to God") which comprises all human individuals across the world as the children of God. Islam is a religion of intelligibility and integration and has managed to bridge this world to the other world and reconcile science with faith and vice versa.[97]

6- The common ground of human efforts for the revival of basic rights of humanity that simultaneously represent the highest ideals of an honorable human life, which is consistent with Islamic Shari'ah.

7- The belief in the necessity of a divine source for justifying and securing unto humanity who is well equipped with positive knowledge of his primordial rights in along his path toward the highest civilization of history, which is indeed the ultimate goal of all Holy Prophets' prophecy.

8- The human rights, which have been decreed by the Divine Law and are a part of the religion of Muslims, aim at conferring dignity and honor of mankind and are designed to eliminate oppression and injustice. By virtue of their Divine source and sanction, these rights can neither be curtailed, abrogated or disregarded by authorities, assemblies or other institutions, nor can they be surrendered or alienated. Therefore, the observance of these rights and freedoms are regarded in Islam as equal to worship, and negligence toward them is a mistake. Every person, whether individually or in social settings (i.e., within the Islamic society) is responsible for being committed to these decrees.

Due to the motives mentioned in the preamble, all member states in the Islamic Conference are obligated to observe and protect all articles indicated in the declaration of the universal Islamic human rights.

A Study of Universal Human Rights in the Era of the Emergence of Islam

When Muhammad ibn Abdullah (PBUH) was appointed as the last prophet of God in the late 6th century, the fundamentals of the most comprehensive life plan for mankind in various aspects such as ethics, economics, politics, art, management, jurisprudence and law was presented to people all across the world. As we will see in our discussions on the preamble, explanations and interpretations of Islamic human rights, all of the articles and items included in human rights already exist in the basic sources of Islam, albeit not in a specific, compiled form but rather existing in miscellaneous and scattered areas. Furthermore, we must have this significant point in mind that by "basic sources" here we do not imply the decrees presented by jurisprudents – that may be subject to criticism that jurisprudential scholars have presented such *fatwas* on the basis of their own subjective comprehension. In fact, we are referring to the Holy Book, the *Sunnah*,

---

97 - See Ja'fari, M. T. *Science and Religion in Intelligible Life*. (Originally in Persian).

man's common sense and consultation, which are the pillars of Islamic jurisprudence and legal domains.

Why did Muslims not present Islamic human rights across all human societies until contemporary times (i.e. from 1948, when the Universal Declaration of Human Rights was ratified up to 1978, when Islamic nations decided to compile universal human rights)? This question, which is unquestionably of significance, can be logically dealt with as follows:

Universal human rights were not compiled and presented from an Islamic point of view up to the present time does not lie in the fact that such rights were not included in the religion of Islam; when Western nations and societies compiled and presented the Declaration of Universal Human Rights, Islamic jurisprudential scholars also decided to set about preparing a declaration of universal human rights from an Islamic point of view. As we have already mentioned, all basic Islamic sources and references as well as the essence of justice in Muslims' mutual coexistence with other peoples and nations interacting with them very clearly show that not only does Islam fundamentally include all of the articles of human rights, but it also has the advantage of having concrete proofs and documentation justifying each item. The reason why these universal rights were not presented prior to the Declaration of Universal Human Rights published in the West lies in the fact that the tendency of various nations and peoples around the world toward becoming the inhabitants of a town is a new phenomenon, and the greater the contact and interactions, the better the endeavors and compilations made toward the achievement of unified, common laws.

On the other hand, we are all aware of the fact that tyrants and despots in Islamic societies have avoided executing true Islamic rights in order to protect, continue and strengthen their own rule. On the other hand, how could these wrongdoers have ever allowed man's true universal rights be followed and realized seriously in all societies?

The two following highly significant truths can be concluded from the discussions we have made so far:

1- The supernatural factor is of essence when it comes to man's true development and growth.

2- All righteous religions revealed by God are consequences and effects of the religion propagated by the Holy Prophet Abraham.

Therefore, it is essential for all human cultural elements as well as all of man's economic, political, legal, ethical, and artistic ideas take into consideration the importance of the realization of elevated human ideals of Abraham's religion, for the authorities leading today's civilized societies know Abraham and regarded their religions and nations as originating from Abraham's. As a result, the contents of the Declaration of Universal Human Rights as seen in Islam must not only be in no contradiction with Islam – which is nowadays an expression of Abraham's religion – but also be in absolute accordance and agreement with it as well.

The Common Principles Underlying the Motives

For the Idea of the Codification of Universal Human Rights

Although none of the occidentally-motivated and Islamic universal declarations of human rights have directly stipulated the following quintuple basic rights as the fundamental principles, and they are initially debated in an ordered fashion in this book, they have nonetheless been alluded to in preambles and some articles of the declarations in a general and disordered manner and with some differences that shall be mentioned in the following debates.

The Quintuple Basic Rights

Both legal systems are in one mind that human beings essentially need some basic rights and obligations which secure their natural and ideal (intelligible) lives. The quintuple basic rights are as follow:

1- The Right to Life; both legal systems have unanimously stipulated that every effort should be made by the state and the society to protect and secure this basic right in the face of possible violations.

2- The Right to Inherent Dignity; both systems have declared humanity to be a creature of primordial stature.

3- The Right to Education; according to both legal systems, the state, and the society are obligated to educate the citizens.

4- The Right to Freedom; both systems have declared freedom to be a basic human right and commissioned the state and the society to prepare the ground for it. Although according to Islam the right to freedom is legitimate insofar as it is not in confliction with social and individual obligations, no one is allowed to violate other peoples' rights resorting to his rights to freedom, life, inherent dignity and other rights and he is not even allowed to endanger his own life with recourse to these rights. Islam forbids everything that would be in conflict with other citizens' rights or social obligations or individual duties toward the Divine. This shall be debated in full length in coming discussions.

5- The Right to Equality both in rights and laws.

The Fundamental Differences and Privileges

The Universal Islamic Declaration of Human Rights – as we have already seen in our debate on the eightfold point included in its preamble – is a religiously informed legal document. It seems that a religiously informed legal system in the 21st century, the age of technological and intellectual breakthroughs, might appear totally to be odd to many people and to mainstream disciplinary legal and human scientists in particular. It is obviously understandable that it is almost impossible for mainstream disciplinary legal thinkers to accept that a religiously informed declaration of basic human rights could be of avail in terms of human ideals that have been indicated in an occidentally-oriented universal declaration of human rights; the question we need to pose here is, however, what has made it so difficult for some people and thinkers to encounter the reality? Undoubtedly, this issue has primarily originated from the dominated misinterpretations of religion, and we agree in our own right that if religion is what has been depicted in the recent Western interpretations (misinterpretations in fact), not only can a religiously motivated legal system not be regarded as competent for regulating peoples' legal relations, in fact even no religiously informed moral and cultural system can be qualified for addressing the issues of human life, since religion, as recently understood in the West, is merely a limited spiritual relation between man and God which has no serious connection with any other aspects of human life. On the other hand, religion from an Islamic point of view – which represents the primordial perspective of *Abrahamism* – is accounting for all fundamental quadruple existential relations: man's relation to himself, man's relation with God, man's relation with the world, and man's relation to his fellow human beings in both domains of *"is-ness"* and *"ought-ness"*.

Thus conceived, religion could not be indifferent toward "law," "politics," "economy," "art," "morality" and in brief, all domains and aspects of human life. The fact that Islam has united all natural and ideal dimensions of human life in a transcendentally intelligible unity is evident by itself and agreed upon by all Islamologists. However, we shall quote here as an example a non-Muslim jurist:

As Robert Houghwout Jackson, former United States Attorney General (1940-1941), has stated:

> *The existing obstacles discouraged the people to show their interest in Islamic laws. For paying our debts to Arab culture, we contented ourselves with preparing surprising reports on their laws [....] In the eye of an American, law and religion are essentially in conflict with each other. In the West, even in those countries which do not strongly believe in the separation of religious and civil affairs, the legal system is seen as a totally secular phenomenon within which current circumstances play a major role [....] Thus, our law in America does not determine religious duties; rather,*

it deliberately neglects them indeed. The law in the US has limited contact with moral obligations. In fact, an American citizen could act totally by legal issues, while being a morally corrupted person. On the contrary, in Islamic law divine will is the source of laws; a will that has revealed itself to Prophet Muhammad (SWA). This will regard all individual believers as members of the same society, although they may come from different tribes and live in various geographies. Here it is a religion that unifies the people, neither nationality nor geography. In this way, the state itself is submissive and amenable to the Holy Quran; therefore, there remains no room for any other legislator, let alone room for controversy and discord. The believer sees this world as a corridor which brings him to the other and better world, and the Quran provides a set of divine codes for individual and social conducts, so to make the transition sounder and easier. It is impossible to separate Prophetic teachings from political and economic theories; the teachings instruct man how to conduct himself in social, economic, political and individual affairs...[98]

The Advantage of the Religious Nature of Human Rights in Islam over Western Human Rights

1- Religiously grounded Islamic legal system is essentially dependent on Divine Will; that is to say, it is indeed Almighty God that has willed these rights and duties for his servants. It is needless to say that believing in this essential dependence of rights and duties upon the Divine Will persuades every conscientious human being to be more alert toward his duties as their observance results in the intellectual and spiritual evolution and consequently in the nearness of God, which in itself constitute the very *Ultimate Telos of Life*; this is a major advantage that no other legal or political system has but Islam. A conscientious human being whose consciousness has remained immune from modern intellectual and spiritual narcotizations shall find the religious and moral obligations determined by Divine Will wholly consistent with his common sense and conscience. It is for sure that such an advantage could not be found in any humanly ordained legal codes that are restricted to natural human demands.

2- The sanction of religiously grounded codes lies in the very perfectionist primordial nature of humanity and the executive in charge of surveillance will only prepare the necessary objective and subjective circumstances for the better understanding of the codes.

3- It is obvious that grounding universal human rights on cultural values of a particular region shall thwart their universality; on the other hand, if we ground universal human rights on *Abrahamism* – Abraham's primordial religion, which is the ancestor of all revealed monotheistic religions of

---

98 - Lisbani, J., Herbert, *Law in Islam*. (Originally in English).

the world – they shall be better understood and operationalized. Of course, there is also an issue that must be addressed here: which revealed religion represents Abraham's primordial religion in the purest form? This conflict could easily be changed to an opportunity for more mutual understanding through reading in earnest the *Old Testament*, the *New Testament* and the *Holy Quran* for discovering the common primordial and intelligible grounds.[99]

4- As we have already seen, both the occidentally-oriented and Islamic declarations of human rights strongly insist in their preambles and articles on human inherent dignity, fraternity, and equality. If we pay serious attention to them in a comparative spirit, we shall immediately see that they are neither philosophically nor primordially, conscientiously, scientifically comparable on the issues mentioned above. We shall now outline once again the grounds of these issues in Islam.

Islam regards all human beings equal and united in the following matters:

✓ Equality in the Creator (all human beings have been created by One God Whose attributes are totally perfect).

✓ Equality in Providence that is the source of their creation.

✓ Equality in being created by the same *prime material* (Soil).

✓ Equality in their First Parents Adam and Eve.

✓ Equality in their essential nature.

✓ Equality in the Ultimate Telos of Life that all human beings are equally eligible to achieve, which consists of nearness to God through exposing oneself to Divine Perfection.

✓ Equality in the path: Intelligible Life.

✓ Equality in inherent human dignity.

✓ Equality in primordial aptitude for intelligibility.

✓ Equality in Ideal Unity of Humanity which reveals itself in the formula: *"one for all in all for one."*

✓ Equality in *Conatus* as the basis of all human activities in both natural and intelligible lives.

✓ Equality in rights and duties.

✓ Equality in transcendental unities.

✓ Equality in the inclination to form social groups (sociality).

---

99 - This is the proposal I suggested to the Islamic Society of Philosophy and Theosophy in 1985 during a session with Hans Kung and several other German scholars, who received my proposal very warmly but very sadly it has not been pursued later.

5- Human rights systems arising from purely materialistic civilizations, and also those civilizations which regard spiritual matters as issues which are merely ornaments and luxurious decorations in life that need to be sidelined, are not able to account for human primordial desire for perfection, while Islam, equipped with the above-mentioned twelve equalities and triple unities, can, in fact, guide man along the hazardous path of perfection.

6- As we have already seen in our discussions on the quintuple basic principles of human rights in Islam as well as in our interpretations of the articles and the comparisons we have made with Western human rights, the principles presented in the Islamic view of the law are in fact richer that all other man-made legal systems that have arisen so far. In other words, inherent dignity, education, equality and committed freedom, which are indeed elevated truths, can only be achieved through the humancentric agenda of Islam.

Who Is Responsible for the Exercise of Human Rights?

I) *The Addressees of the UN Declaration*

The UN Declaration of Human Rights assigns the protection and execution of human rights to the following people and organs:

a) People of the United Nations (Preamble § 5): "Whereas the peoples of the United Nations have in the Charter reaffirmed their faith in the fundamental human rights, in the dignity and worth of the human person and in the equal rights of men and women and have determined to promote social progress and better standards of life in larger freedom,"

b) All People and All Nations (Preamble § 8): "Now, therefore, the General Assembly proclaims this Universal Declaration of Human Rights as a common standard of achievement for all peoples and all nations, to the end that every individual and every organization of society, keeping this Declaration constantly in mind, shall strive by teaching and education to promote respect for these rights and freedoms and by progressive measures, national and international, to secure their universal and effective recognition and observance, both among the peoples of Member States themselves and among the peoples of territories under their jurisdiction."

c) The United Nations (Preamble § 6): "Whereas Member States have pledged themselves to achieve, in cooperation with the United Nations, the promotion of universal respect for and observance of human rights and fundamental freedoms."

d) Member States (Preamble § 6).

E) Every Organ of Society (Preamble § 8).

Regarding the organizations and groups of people who are addressed by the UN Declaration of Human Rights and the factor of *Common Understanding* (Preamble § 7), it seems that the codifiers of the UN Declaration were well aware of the fact that when a legal system is designed for all people around the globe all people, groups and international organs are responsible for its observance and execution. To put the matter otherwise, all individuals and member states are responsible to work collectively upon a common understanding for the implementation of the highest ideals of humanity. The common understanding in this context reveals the very moral orientation of the idea of human rights.

II) The Addressees of the Islamic Declaration

A) Islamic states – whether those who are members of the Islamic Conference or independent states – are all responsible to justly and properly execute all of the articles indicated in the Universal Islamic Declaration of Human Rights. Every state that heedlessly tramples these universally valid rights of man shall be interpellated by the Islamic Conference and the people.

B) Every human individual who can defend and carry into execution these rights is responsible for defending and executing them whether individually or collectively.

C) When the state fails to implement these inalienable rights, the citizens are themselves accountable to do the task. The individual's executive role has not been mentioned so colorfully in the UN Declaration, while in Islam these rights are depicted as *Heavenly Rules* decreed by Divine Will which could not be curtailed, abrogated or disregarded, and all human institutions and individuals are entitled to struggle for their implementation. For example, Islam orders people not to submit to sufferings and abjectness, as shown in the following verse of the Holy Quran:

> **Surely (as for) those whom the angels cause to die while they are unjust to their souls, they shall say: in what state were you? They shall say: We were weak in the earth. They shall say: Was not Allah's earth spacious so that you should have migrated therein? So these it is whose abode is hell, and it is an evil resort.**
>
> (The Women 4:97)

The Universal Declaration of Human Rights in Islam: Who Are the Addressees?

It might be said that whereas the Islamic Declaration of Human Rights is a religiously-grounded document, it could not be acceptable and applicable for non-believers. Nonetheless, although it is estimated that 1.2 to 1.57 billion Muslims populate the world [in other words, about 20% of an estimated 2009 world population of 6.8 billion], Muslims are still regarded as a minority in the world, so an Islamic Declaration would not be globally binding.

In response to this objection, we could say that human rights and duties are divided into three kinds:

1- The natural rights and duties of human beings which are documented to the primordial human *nature*. These primordial rights comprise the right to life, the right to education, the right to inherent dignity, the right to equality and the right to committed freedom. It is needless to say that these very rights have also been indicated in other expressions in the occidentally-motivated UN Declaration as natural human rights.

2- The rights and duties which are meaningful only within the borders of a particular national and cultural territory and on a special form of life. In this case, Islam not only does not impose any rights and duties to nations and cultures but according to the verses of the Holy Koran and jurisprudential principles, other nations and cultures are in fact free to preserve the traditions that underlie their form of life. Of course, this ideological liberalism does not necessarily mean that Islam recognizes all forms of life as legitimate; lifestyles are legitimate as far as they are not in conflict with human conscience and common sense. There are some clear reasons for this issue:

I) Some verses of the Holy Quran, such as the following, which reads:

> *Say: O followers of the book! Come to an equitable proposition between us and you that we shall not serve any but Allah and (that) we shall not associate aught with him, and (that) some of us shall not take others for lords besides Allah; but if they turn back, then say: Bear witness that we are Muslims.*
>
> (The Family of Imran 3:64)

It is needless to say that inviting to "equitable proposition" in this context signifies peaceful coexistence according to monotheism, which implies not associating aught with the Lord. For certain, this equitable proposition along with the primordial rights and duties of man could bring humanity a peaceful coexistence even without people ever having to give up their intelligible national and cultural traditions. Another verse of the Holy Quran reads:

> *Allah does not forbid you respecting those who have not made war against you on account of (your) religion, and have not driven you forth from your homes, that you show them kindness and deal with them justly; surely Allah loves the doers of justice.*
>
> (That Which Examines 60:8)

As a maxim, it is agreed upon by scholars that goodness is primarily a matter of morality and justice is essentially a legal issue.

II) Addressing Malek, the ruler of Egypt, Imam Ali (PBUH) writes in a state correspondence:

> *Inform your heart with love, benevolence and mercy to your people, and do not behave with them like a bloodsucking predator lying in ambush to hunt them, since they are from two groups: either your religious brother or your fellow in kind.*[100]

---

100 - *Nahj ul-Balagha*, Letter 53.

It is obvious that there is no mercy and benevolence for people higher than helping them to reach their primordial and natural rights.

III) The maxim of commitment, which reads:

Commit all those who are not followers of the same faith as you to what they are committed to themselves.

This maxim states that Muslims must respect and observe those rights and duties that non-Muslims are committed to. This has been applied in the second clause of Article 29 of the UN Declaration.

3- Those legal codes that have been instituted by egotist and aggressive hunters of power to exploit people in the name of rights and duties! Undoubtedly, every humancentric school needs to struggle for reforming these codes and replacing them with more humanly ones, as Islam fought against idolatry and many inhuman traditions which were seen as legal in the age of Arabian Ignorance.

The Dilemma of Legality versus Globality!

In some articles of the Universal Islamic Declaration of Human Rights, the stipulated rights and duties have been conditionally accepted upon their accordance with the canonic rules of Islamic Shari'ah. To this very reason, some believe that this conditionality causes the articles of the Universal Islamic Declaration to lose their *globality*. To deal with this objection, we shall first study the stipulated rights and freedoms in the UN Declaration, that are conditioned in a particular way to serve a certain purpose; subsequently, we will debate in detail all of the articles and clauses in the Islamic Declaration that are conditioned to Shari'ah laws.

1- The second clause of Article 29 reads:

> *"In the exercise of his rights and freedoms, everyone shall be subject only to such limitations as are determined by law solely for the purpose of securing due recognition and respect for the rights and freedoms of others and of meeting the just requirements of morality, public order and general welfare in a democratic society."*

It is needless to say that "democratic" in this context does not signify Western democracy since there are many countries across the globe that do not live according to Western democracy and believe that they could be happy if the aggressive hunters of power leave them alone with their lifestyle.

2- The third clause of Article 29 reads:

> *"These rights and freedoms may in no case be exercised contrary to the purposes and principles of the United Nations."*

3- Article 30 states:

> *"Nothing in this Declaration may be interpreted as implying for any State, group or person any right to engage in any activity or to perform any act aimed at the destruction of any of the rights and freedoms set forth herein."*

Thus, all of the rights and duties in the UN Declaration are conditioned to:

I) Recognition and respect for rights and freedoms of the others.

II) Meeting the just requirements of morality.

III) Public order and the general welfare in a democratic society.

IV) The principles of the United Nations.

V) "Nothing in this Declaration may be interpreted as implying for any State, group or person any right to engage in any activity or to perform any act aimed at the destruction of any of the rights and freedoms set forth herein."

4- The first clause of Article 13 reads:

"Everyone has the right to freedom of movement and residence within the borders of each State."

Although no condition has been stipulated in this clause, it is nonetheless evident that this right is conditional upon one's not being subjected to a legal prosecution; surely, one's residence in a place should not bother or violate other peoples' rights.

5- The second clause of Article 13 states:

"Everyone has the right to leave any country, including his own, and to return to his country."

This clause is right on the condition that the one is not under legal prosecution and thus prohibited to leave the country.

6- Article 14 comprises two clauses, the first of which is conditioned upon the second clause and the first clause reads:

"Everyone has the right to seek and to enjoy in other countries asylum from persecution."

The second clause states,

"This right may not be invoked in the case of prosecutions genuinely arising from non-political crimes or acts contrary to the purposes and principles of the United Nations."

Generally speaking, the execution of all of the articles on human rights is totally conditioned upon their not being in conflict with the governing legal codes of the society.

The Conditionality of Rights and Freedoms in Islam

Now we shall proceed to interpret all of the articles of the Universal Islamic Declaration of Human Rights that have been made conditional upon being by canonic rules of Islamic Sharia'h. After studying and interpreting these articles, we shall see that there is no single article in the Universal Islamic Declaration that has lost its global nature due to its being conditioned upon the canonic rules of Islamic Sharia'h. These conditions not only do not localize the rights, duties, and freedoms stipulated in the Universal Islamic Declaration but in fact, complement their human and evolutionary aspects:

1- Clause I of Article 1 reads,

"Human life is sacred and inviolable, and every effort shall be made to protect it. In particular, no one shall be exposed to injury or death, except under the authority of the Law."

112 Universal Human Rights

It is needless to say that the death sentence is confined to those cases in which the convict has murdered one or for corruption on earth, both of which endanger human life in general or ideal life. Thus, it is the convict himself that has expelled his life from the sphere of values and protection, and it is indeed the individual himself that has willingly ruined his life.

Those who critique the death sentence on the basis of naïve sentiments do not understand that if their sentiments were, in fact, human and genuine, they would have had to be aroused for the sacred lives of people, and thus they would have understood that their fanatic and baseless sentiments toward the murderer and the corrupt person undermine the very value and dignity of human life.

On the other hand, as it has been mentioned in the textbooks of Islamic jurisprudence, and we have also debated in this book, it is not so that every murderer is to be sentenced to the death penalty in all conditions and under all circumstances; rather, the murderer should first be determined to have been in a good state of mental health at the time of crime. Otherwise, the death penalty leaves the table. Secondly, blood ransom is confined to those cases in which the avenger of blood does not forgive the murderer or does not accept to be compensated by blood-money. It is obvious that in many cases, forgiveness or blood-money prevents blood-ransom. Thus, the legal and jurisprudential condition of the issue is not merely devotional, but regarding the value and dignity of life, it is in fact wholly intelligible, of course, only for those who are conscious of the value and dignity of life. Undoubtedly, such an overvaluation of life makes people regard human life as a serious issue and not only delivers human beings from the bondage of "alienation from each other" but also relieves them from undermining malady of "self-alienation."

2- Clause II of Article 1 reads,

"Abortion is prohibited except for a Shari'ah-prescribed reason."

This could be seen as the devotional and theoretical basis of the impermissibility of abortion in Islam. Since the right to life is one of the basic, and inalienable rights of man and the fetus have life right from the time that sperm enters the uterus, abortion has therefore been prohibited in Islam except when the mother's life is in danger. This is the most logical condition ever proposed for the foetal right to life.

3- Clause I of Article 3 states,

"In the event of the use of force and case of armed conflict, it is not permissible to kill non-belligerents such as old men, women, and children. The wounded and the sick shall have the right to medical treatment; furthermore, prisoners of war shall have the right to be fed, sheltered and clothed. It is prohibited to mutilate dead bodies. It is a duty to exchange prisoners of war and to arrange visits or reunions of the families separated

by the circumstances of war.

Making the exchange of prisoners of war and reunions of separated families conditional upon duty, which implies in this context jurisprudential consultation, is totally intelligible since the exchange of prisoners, and the reunion of separated families are matters of national security and must be supervised by authorities.

4- Clause II of Article 3 reads,

> *"It is prohibited to fell trees, to damage crops or livestock, and to destroy the enemy's civilian buildings and installations by shelling, blasting or*
>
> *any other means [unless for a Shari'ah-prescribed reason]."*

Civilian buildings and installations could be used by the enemy as shields; thus, the prescription of Shari'ah is needed.

5- Article 4:

> *"It is not permitted without a legitimate reason to arrest an individual, or restrict his freedom; moreover, to exile or to punish people without a Shari'ah reason is not prescribed."*

The authority of Shari'ah in this article is totally logical and is not merely a matter of devotion since all nations and peoples of the world limit the freedom of the one who misuses his freedom and violates other people's freedoms; it is also the case with expatriation and other punishment.

6- Clause III of Article 9 reads,

> *"Everyone shall have the right to privacy in the conduct of his private affairs, in his home, among his family, concerning his property and his relationships. It is not permitted to spy on him, to place him under surveillance or to besmirch his good name. The State shall protect him from arbitrary interference according to the rules of Shari'ah."*

Making the protection of this right conditional upon the rules of Shari'ah is stating that this right is legitimate insofar as it is not in conflict with other people's freedoms and rights. Thus, this right shall be abrogated when one's house has become the center of corruption or people's necessities have been cornered in the name of personal properties, or reputation has been misused against other peoples.

7- Clause IV of Article 9 states,

> *"A private residence is inviolable in all cases. It will not be entered without permission from its inhabitants or in any unlawful manner, nor shall it be demolished or confiscated and its dwellers evicted unless for a Shari'ah prescribed reason."*

As mentioned in the previous clause, the condition of being by Shari'ah laws states that the right is protected insofar as it is not against and in confliction with other people's rights and freedoms. By the same token, one who is under heavy debts is not permitted to own a luxury house; thus, Shari'ah laws permit the creditors to expropriate the house. Moreover, if it is confirmed that a house has been bought by illegitimate money, it shall be confiscated.

8- Clause II of Article 11 states,

> *"The fathers and those who are in charge of position and duties of a father have the right to decide the appropriate education for their children in the light of moral values and Islamic Shari'ah laws."*

The necessity of a morally conditioned education for children not only is not objected by anyone, but it represents the very magnificence of the Islamic legal system that has enriched the rights with the highest of human ideals, and in doing so, it oriented human life toward an overly refined goal. This is also the case with making Islamic Shari'ah law the educational framework for children. This condition, as we have already seen, is nothing but observing the highly human principles in life – which is certainly the gate of eternity.

9- Clause I, Article 13:

> *"The promotion of good and the prevention of evil is an obligatory practice upon everyone who has the capability and sufficient rational reasons for their success including the state and the society. The state is more obligated toward this duty since it has much more capability. Every human being can cooperate with other individuals and groups in implementing this right, and all these rights and duties must be carried into execution according to Islamic Shari'ah laws and the state and society are obligated to make the grounds ready for the implementation of these rights and duties."*

It is needless to say that Shari'ah laws in this regard are not also devotional since everyone who is to promote good needs to have enough knowledge of the goodness rather than merely sees it a purely religious obligation.

10- Article 15:

> *"Everyone is entitled to freely express their opinion, providing it is not against Shari'ah laws."*

This condition is one of the most logical conditions without which the society might be exposed to moral corruption. It is the lack of this necessary condition in the Universal Declaration of Human Rights that makes it paradoxical since in the preamble it strongly insists on the observance of inherent human dignity and subsequently in articles 18 and 19 declare the unconditioned (unprincipled) freedom of expression and opinion the universal right of all human beings.

11- Article 16:

> *"Everyone shall have the right to enjoy the fruits of his scientific, literary, artistic or technical labour of which he is the author; and he shall have the right to the protection of his moral and material interests stemming from that place, provided it is not contrary to the principles of the Shari'ah."*

This condition also takes the good of the author and society into prime consideration; that is to say, the author should not produce harmful things for society, like authoring immoral, inhuman and sacrilegious books or producing products that are damaging to social health such as narcotic drugs, gambling devices, etc.

12- As stated in Article 20:

> *"Every man shall have the right, within the framework of the Shari'ah, to have free movement and to select his place of residence whether within or outside his country and if persecuted, is entitled to seek asylum in another country. The country of refuge shall be obliged to provide protection to the asylum-seeker until his safety has been attained unless asylum is motivated by committing an act regarded by the Shari'ah as a crime.*

The conditionality of the right to freedom of residence and asylum upon Shari'ah principles is restricted to the possible misuses and is thus a wholly rational condition. Islamic Shari'ah has not addressed this issue in a devotional fashion.

13- Article 21:

> *"Work is a right guaranteed by the State and the Society for each person with the capability to work. Everyone shall be free to choose the work that suits him best and which serves his interests as well as those of the society. The employee shall have the right to enjoy safety and security as well as all other social guarantees. He may not be assigned work beyond his capacity, nor shall he be subjected to compulsion or exploited or harmed in any way. He shall be entitled – without any discrimination between males and females – to fair wages for his work without delay, as well as to the holidays' allowances and promotions which he deserves. On his part, he shall be required to be dedicated and meticulous in his work. Should workers and employers disagree on any matter, the State shall intervene to settle the dispute and have the grievances redressed, the rights confirmed and justice enforced without bias upon Islamic Shari'ah laws."*

As a result, Islamic Shari'ah serves here as the absolute guarantee of justice and indiscrimination, which reveals its very social relevance.

14- As stated in Clause II, Article 23:

> *"No penalty or punishment is permissible unless under the authority of Islamic Shari'ah principles."*

"Shari'ah Principles" in this context underlines the necessity of the observance of individual rights. As any crime needs credible reasons to be proved, punishment must also be documented to intelligibly grounded principles, in accordance with Shari'ah laws.

15- Clause I, Article 24:

> "*Confiscation and seizure of property are prohibited except for a necessity dictated by Shari'ah law.*"

This condition has already been explicated discussing clause III and IV.

16- Clause I, Article 25 states:

> "*Everyone shall have the right to earn a legitimate living without monopolization, deceit or causing harm to oneself or others. Usury (riba) is explicitly prohibited.*"

"Legitimate living" in this context clearly implies those livings that are harmful to individuals and the society, like drug trafficking, cornering or usury, which are prohibited based on the principles of Islamic Shari'ah. As a result, we could not find a form of living in Islamic jurisprudence that would have been prohibited without any reason acceptable for common sense. As it has been related by Hassan ibn Ali ibn Shu'ba,

> "*Any form of living that is prohibited in Islam is either physically harmful or spiritually harmful.*"[101]

17- Clause II, Article 27:

> "*Everyone shall have the right to participate, directly or indirectly, in the administration of his country's public affairs. He shall also have the right to assume public office by the provisions of Shari'ah.*"

In this case, it is also clear that assuming public office in society could be either upon a proper ground or according to an improper ground, like giving public offices to unprofessional and uncommitted people, which is harmful to the society. Similarly, trusting an individual with sabouteral public offices could be certainly damaging for the community.

18- As stated in Clause I, Article 29:

> "*All the rights and freedoms stipulated in this Declaration are subject to the Islamic Shari'ah.*"

Reading the articles of the Universal Islamic Declaration of Human Rights with enough attention demonstrates that all of these articles are almost needless of further explication and interpretation for all nations and peoples as they address human primordial natures and in such cases as prohibition of usury, abortion and some controversial family issues a global consensus could be achieved through scientific demonstrations. We have tried in

---

101 - Abu Muhammad al-Hassan Ibn Ali bin al-Hussein Ibn Shu'ba al-Harrani, *Tuhaf al-Ughul ("The Masterpieces of the Mind")*, pp. 332-333.

this book to take a step toward such a global consensus regarding human rights through undertaking a comparative study of the Islamic and Western concepts of the idea.

19- Article 30 has stated that:

> *"The Islamic Shari'ah is the only source of reference for the explanation or clarification of any of the articles of this Declaration."*

This could be better understood in the light of my explanation of the clause I of Article 29.

The Cairo Conference on Human Rights in Islam

In the Cairo conference on human rights in Islam held after the OIC Tehran meeting in 1989, the then agreed Islamic Charter (Covenant and document) of Human Rights underwent serious modifications that we shall discuss in full length in this book. The two below-mentioned modifications have liquidated its legal and binding characters and reduced it into a bunch of moral prescriptions. These two modifications are as follows:

1- The word *"al-wathighah"* – which means "covenant or document" and in modern terminology it would be properly rendered to "charter" – in Article 26 has been replaced by "Declaration." It is needless to say that this literal modification has been intended to discolor the presence and role of Islamic Shari'ah Law in Muslims' everyday life, while *"al-wathighah"* in this context simultaneously has both binding and practical connotations.[102]

2- The Cairo Conference of Islamic Countries has not even contented itself with this, but has even removed Article 28 of the Tehran Charter, that obligated and commissioned the member states to implement the articles stipulated in the covenant; sadly, they did not even accept the proposal of Iranian delegates to add that, "member state shall be obligated to implement these articles as much as their ability allows". The following is the report made by Iranian delegates in the Cairo Conference:

> *Article 28 was removed. This was the most controversial article of the declaration. It had obligated the member states to make the needed preparations for the implementation of articles of the declaration. Egypt suggested that if it is not in conflict with their constitutions, the member states were to be obligated to the implementation of the articles. Malaysia and Indonesia, having already insisted on this issue in the Tehran Meeting, strongly supported Egypt's proposal. Iran's view was that making the implementation of the declaration conditional upon its conformity with member states constitutions would reduce its value to none. Accordingly, Iran proposed that the "conformity condition" should be replaced with "if it is possible;" that is to say, the Member States were obliged to implement the articles as far their ability allowed. Malaysia and Indonesia vetoed this proposal as well. Iran suggested again that Article 28 be removed from the declaration. Malaysia and Indonesia accepted this proposal on the condition that it would be stipulated in the declaration that it is essentially*

---

102 - Although we have frequently used the word "declaration" in this book, what we in fact mean by it here is "charter" and "covenant."

prescriptive and not binding. Finally, the Cairo Islamic Declaration of Human Rights comprising 25 articles, which had already ratified by the political committee, has eventually been approved by the Conference of Ministers.[103]

Many well-informed Muslim scholars of the time had already predicted this tragic destiny for the Islamic Charter of Human Rights in Cairo. Verily, it was not surprising that such an extremely significant Islamic covenant on human rights to have been reduced to a bunch of moral prescriptions without any practical sanctions, since the silliest men on the earth shall immediately claim that if the provisions of Islamic Shari'ah that outline the path of "Intelligible Life" had the occasion to be implemented on the global scale, they would have very long ago cleared away the wares of egotists and Machiavellian aggressive hunters of power through the Islamic twelve equities and triple unities. I was told that some member states in that conference said, "Does the Universal Declaration of Human Rights any practical sanction that you want the Universal Islamic Declaration of Human Rights to have sanction!!"

It is a matter of regret that a jurist of Muslim origin is wholly uninformed of the principles of Islamic jurisprudence that state that everything that is provisioned as a legal code in Islam and is ratified by just jurisprudents is regarded as an extension of limits ordained by the Lord. As the Holy Quran states:

These are the limits of Allah, so do not exceed them and whoever exceeds the limits of Allah these it is that are the unjust.

(The Cow 2:229)

Has it been due to the absence of a global legal system in Islam that some prevented from the codification and approval of an Islamic declaration of human rights? This is a malicious accusation that shall not be tolerated by Islam, Muslims and the history of the legal life of Muslim societies. Are the legal materials that have been debated in this book and could be used in developing a global system of human rights indeed baseless? Do they merely embody our intellectual and spiritual aspirations, or do they represent the legal ideas inspired by Islamic authentic texts? The truth is that we have authorized textual basis for these materials.

In the past it was said that:

Muslims have themselves covered up the primordial truth of Islam.

Today it must be said that:

Today Muslim despots live fearful of Islam.

This is totally natural, as Islamic human rights movement has – as its first target – to uproot as the source of evil acts against inherent human dignity.

If the Universal Declaration of Human Rights has no practical sanction,

103 - Iranian delegates' report on the Cairo Conference, p. 4.

upon which bases are human rights being used as means of pressure and intimidation against nations around the globe?

Had Muslim authorities who had gathered in Cairo depleting their mental energies and the public treasury of the Muslims to codify universally credible rights for man upon provisions designated by Islamic Shari'ah better not study carefully, for a few moments, the preamble of the UN Declaration so as to see how seriously the implementation of the articles stipulated in it has been recommended in a purely legal language? The preamble to the UN Declaration reads:

> *Whereas it is essential, if man is not to be compelled to have recourse, as a last resort, to rebellion against tyranny and oppression, that human rights should be protected by the rule of law,*
> *Whereas the Member States have pledged themselves to achieve, in cooperation with the United Nations, the promotion of universal respect for and observance of human rights and fundamental freedoms,*

Alas, this issue why the participants in the conference who were representing Muslim countries refused to approve Article 28 and even some of them explicitly proposed the declaration to be proclaimed as merely a descriptive statement shall remain unanswered forever! That is to say; the Declaration embodies good-willed advice, not the primordial provisions, duties, rights and freedoms! Why have these anti-Islamic figures represented Muslims in that conference as Muslim jurists and decided Muslims' legal and even political destiny?

Thus, it could be said that no conference has ever been seen in the long course of history that been held for regulating a legal system for a large nation (on the scale of Muslim nations) according to their religious provisions and aspirations but surprisingly ended up adopting policies just contrary to the ultimate goal of the nation that they representing it. As stated in the Holy Quran:

Does he not know that Allah does see?

(The Clinging Clot 96: 14)

However, we shall discuss and investigate in this book the modifications that have been imposed upon the Tehran Charter of Human Rights in the Cairo Conference.

As our debates in this book turn around the quintuple basic rights, we have rearranged both the Universal Islamic Declaration of Human Rights and the UN Declaration.

Although the right to life is the most basic of all human rights, it has been stipulated in the second article of the Universal Islamic Declaration of Human Rights while it is indicated in the third article of the UN Declaration. Thus, these legal systems need to be rearranged according to a more integrated legal system.

By 1990, the OIC held its Nineteenth Islamic Conference of Foreign Ministers (focusing on peace, independence, and development) in Cairo with the approval of *The Universal Declaration of Human Rights in Islam* discussed and finalized in Tehran meeting of 1989 on the agenda. Unfortunately, the Tehran Charter underwent serious modifications in Cairo that shall be debated in this book.

The Tehran Charter of 1989	The Cairo Declaration of 1990
Article 2: I, II, III.	Article 1: I, II, III, IV.
Article 18: I, II.	Article 2: I, II.
Article 3: I, II.	Article 3: I, II.
Article 21.	Article 4.
Article removed	Article 5 (Added)
Clause removed	Clause on animal rights
Article 1: I, II.	Article 6: I, II, III, IV.
Article 6: I, II.	Article 7: I, II.
Article 4.	Article 8.
Article 19: I, II, III.	Article 9: I, II, III, IV.
Clause removed.	Clause added.
Article 5: I, II.	Article 10: I, II.
Article 7: I, II, III.	Article 11: I, II, III.
Article 10: I, II.	Article 12: I, II.
Article 23: I, II, III, IV.	Article 13: I, II, III.
Article 12: I, II.	Article 14: I, II.
Article 23.	Article 15.
Article 17.	Article 16.
Article 8	Article 17.
Article 9	Article 18.
Article 11	Article 19: I, II, III.
Article 13	Article 20
Article 14	Article 21
Article removed	Article 22, I
Article 20: I, II, III.	Article 23: I, II, III.
Article 16: I, II.	Article 24: I, II.
Article 15	Article 25: I, II.
Article 22	Article 26
Article 25: I, II.	Article 27: I, II.
Article 24: I, II.	Article 28: I, II.
Article 26	Article 29: I, II.
Article 27	Article 30
Clause removed	Clause: I, II.
Article 30	Article 31
Clause removed	Clause: I, II.

The Universal Declaration of Human Rights in Islam

1- *The Right to Life*

Article 1:

I) Life is a God-given gift, and the right to life is guaranteed to every human being. It is the duty of individuals, societies, and states to protect this right from any violation, and it is also prohibited to take away life except for a Shari'ah prescribed reason.

II) It is forbidden to resort to such means that may result in the genocidal annihilation of humanity.

III) The preservation of human life throughout the term of time willed by God is a duty prescribed by Shari'ah.

IV) Those oppressed people whose life and dignity have been threatened by natural forces or by the oppressors shall be obligated to protect their life and dignity against the threats by any legal means they can. Anyone who does not stand up for the fulfillment of this obligation would have indeed helped natural forces and oppressors in weakening himself and shall be among those about whom as the Holy Quran has stated:

> *The angels cause to die while they are unjust to their souls, they shall say: In what state were you? They shall say: We were weak in the earth. They shall say: Was not Allah's earth spacious so that you should have migrated therein? So these it is whose abode is hell, and it is an evil resort.* (The Women 4:97)[104]

Needless to say, migration is merely one of the means to drive oneself away from the threats of cruelty and oppression.

V) Abortion is forbidden except for a Shari'ah prescribed reason.

Article 2:

I) Everyone shall have the right to live in a clean environment, away from vice and moral corruption, an environment that would foster their self-development; it is incumbent upon the State and society, in general, to

---

104 - This clause has been replaced by another in the Cairo Declaration: "Safety from bodily harm is a guaranteed right. It is the duty of the state to safeguard it, and it is prohibited to breach it without a Shari'a-prescribed reason." It is wrongly claimed that this clause has been neglected in the Tehran Charter while it has already been stipulated in the second clause of Articles 2 and 4.

afford that right.[105]

II) Everyone shall have the right to medical and social care, and to all public amenities provided by society and the State within the limits of their available resources.

Note: The State shall ensure the right of the individual to a decent living which will enable him to meet all of his requirements and those of his dependents, including food, clothing, housing, education, medical care, and all other basic needs. [106]

Article 3:

I) In the eruption of war and case of armed conflict, it is not permissible to kill non-belligerents such as senior man, women, and children. The wounded and the sick shall have the right to medical treatment; furthermore, prisoners of war shall have the right to be fed, sheltered and clothed. It is prohibited to mutilate dead bodies. It is prescribed to exchange prisoners of war and to arrange visits or reunions of the families separated by the circumstances of war.[107]

---

105 - We have brought this again as clause IV of Article 6 in the Right to Dignity, since this clause is related with the basic right to dignity.

106 - This clause can be analyzed as follows:

I) The Right to Dignity (The state shall ensure the right of the individual to a decent living which will enable him to meet all is requirements and those of his dependents)

II) The Right to Life (food, clothing, housing, education, medical care)

III) Other Rights (other basic needs).

107 - This clause can be analyzed as follows:

I) - The Right to Life: (In the eruption of war and in case of armed conflict, it is not permissible to kill non-belligerents...)

II) - The Right to Freedom: (It is a duty to exchange prisoners of war and to arrange visits or reunions of the families separated by the circumstances of war.)

III) - The Right to Life and its derivatives: (It is prohibited to fell trees, to damage crops or livestock, and to destroy the enemy's civilian buildings and installations by shelling, blasting or any other means).

In the Cairo Declaration, "eruption of war" has been replaced by "the use of force". This replacement does not seem to be correct, since the use of force is conceptually more extensive than war and may not to include the corresponding collateral damages.

 The Cairo Declaration does also proclaim it a duty to exchange the prisoners of war and to arrange visits or reunions of the families separated by the circumstances of war while the Tehran Charter had declared it a prescribed task. Since the circumstances of war vary, the prescriptive language in this case seems to be more intelligible than the imperative one. Prescription in this context is more consistent with the essentially context-bounded provisions of Islamic jurisprudence indeed.

II) It is prohibited to fell trees, to damage crops or livestock, and to destroy the enemy's civilian buildings and installations by shelling, blasting or any other means – except for cases designated or decreed permissible by the Shari'ah.

Article 4:

It is not permitted without a legitimate reason to arrest an individual, or restrict his freedom, to exile or to punish him. It is not permitted to subject him to physical or psychological torture or any form of humiliation, cruelty or indignity. Nor is it permitted to subject an individual to medical or scientific experimentation without his consent or at the risk of his health or of his life. It is also not permitted to promulgate emergency laws that would provide executive authority for such actions.[108]

Article 5:

Everyone shall have the right to live in a clean environment, whether in urban or rural districts, an environment that would foster his self-development and it is incumbent upon the State and society, in general, to afford that right.

Note: Whereas all living beings – including human beings and also other creatures, even if they have no use for humanity and only if they are not baneful – are equally eligible to right to life, it is a duty of the owner of animal to afford all its requirements (food, lodging, medical care and other necessary supplies of life); otherwise, the animal shall be expropriated by the state officials responsible for animal affairs.[109]

---

108 - This article can be analyzed as follows:

I) - The Right to Committed Freedom: (It is not permitted without legitimate reason to arrest an individual, or restrict his freedom, to exile or to punish him)

II) - The Right to Life (It is not permitted to subject him to physical or psychological torture or to any form of humiliation, cruelty or indignity. Nor is it permitted to subject an individual to medical or scientific experimentation without his consent or at the risk of his health or of his life. Moreover, it is not permitted to promulgate emergency laws that would provide executive authority for such actions).

III) - The Right to Dignity (It is inappropriate to expose man to subjections leading to cruelty or degradation, or actions in conflict with human dignity.)

109 - We have already driven and codified animal rights from an Islamic point of view in 32 articles based upon original Islamic resources in see M. T. Ja'fari, *A Translation and Interpretation of the Nahj ul-Balaghah*, Vol. 12, pp. 159-164. Also see M. T. Ja'fari, *Legal Inquiries* (2014). (Originally in Persian).

2- *The Right to Dignity*

Article 6

I) All human beings form one family whose members are united by submission to God and descent from Adam. All men are equal regarding basic human dignity and basic obligations and responsibilities, without any discrimination on the grounds of race, color, region[110], language, sex, religious belief, political affiliation, social status or other considerations. True faith is the guarantee for enhancing such dignity along the path to human perfection. No one shall be allowed to abrogate this inherent dignity from a human individual except due to felony, treason, corruption or polytheism, since the one who associates aught with the Supreme Being – the source of all human values, goodness and perfection – or denies his omnipresent existence has in fact betrayed himself, and if he is a socially influential figure, he would also be betraying to his society, and the one who is disloyal to his society has surely abrogated his inherent dignity, unless he would have been intellectually and conscientiously weakened.[111] Moreover, all human individuals are equally eligible to the primordial right of inherent dignity regardless of their political ties and social class.

II) The abrogation of one's right to inherent dignity due to the above-mentioned reasons shall not also abrogate his right to life unless he faces his verdict issued by Islamic Shari'ah authorities; for instance, when someone commits murder, although he has himself abrogated his right to dignity by homicide – since he has deprived someone of his basic right to life by killing a human being – the murderer's right to life is nonetheless preserved before the execution of his verdict and no one shall deprive him of food, housing, clothing, and medical treatment.

III) All human individuals are the members of Allah's family and their most blessed one with the Lord, is the one who is most beneficial for the members of Allah's family. Verily no one is superior to the other, unless upon *Divine Awe* (acquired existential nobility by being more

---

110 - This word has been removed from the Cairo Declaration under the plea of its semantic similarity with "race." This modification does not seem intelligible regarding the denotative differences of the two words, as "region" in this context connotes geographical districts like continent or countries, and in this sense it is semantically more limited than race – people from the same racial origin may live in different parts of the world.

111 - The intellectual and conscientious weakness of an average mind in understanding divine unity appears to be impossible, since human primordial nature is indeed in charge of understanding the divine unity of the Lord and it would hardly be contaminated to the degree that it might fail to touch this basic reality. Moreover, the essential baseness of felony and corruption in the human society is intuitively understood by enlightened conscience and common sense.

committed to divine obligations) which all ideal human values are related to. Moreover, good opinions and acts in the quadruple relations (man's relations with himself, man's relations with God, man's relations with the world, and man's relations with his fellow human beings) are guarantees of this existential nobility in the path of Intelligible Life.

IV) Every human being has the right to live in a morally clean environment that would foster his self-development, and it is incumbent upon the State and society, in general, to afford that right.

Article 7

I) The woman is equal to the man in human dignity, and has rights to enjoy as well as duties to perform; she has her civil entity and financial independence, and the right to retain her name and lineage.

II) The husband is responsible for the support and welfare of the family.

Article 8

Just as in life, as well as after death, the sanctity of a person's body shall be inviolable. It is the obligation of believers to see that a deceased person's body is handled with due solemnity.

Article 9

I)   Everyone shall have the right to live in security for himself, his religion, his dependents, his honor and his property.

II) Any form of religious privilege arises from its documentation in a religion revealed by God. All monotheistic beliefs including Judaism, Christianity, Islam, Zoroastrianism and Sabaism shall be protected by the rule of law. None-revealed beliefs[112] are not eligible to this right, even though their right to life and dignity will be intact as long as they do not deviate from these rights themselves. Thus, the advocates of such fake beliefs are not allowed to broadcast and propagate their beliefs if they are harmful to the spiritual aspects and mentalities of the society.

III) Everyone shall have the right to privacy in the conduct of his private affairs, in his home, among his family, concerning his property and his relationships. It is not permitted to spy on him, to place him under surveillance or to besmirch his good name. The State shall protect him from arbitrary interference.

IV) A private residence is inviolable in all cases. It will not be entered without permission from its inhabitants or in any unlawful manner, nor shall it be demolished or confiscated and its dwellers evicted except upon Shari'ah prescribed reason.

---

112 - Article 19 describes the non-revealed beliefs' position in the Muslim society.

Note: Whereas the execution of the latter clause has been assigned to Shari'ah authorities, it is incumbent upon the Muslim Judge to decide with the ultimate caution.

Article 10

I) The family is the foundation of society, and marriage is the basis of its formation. Men and women have the right to marriage, and no restrictions stemming from race, color or nationality shall prevent them from enjoying this right.

II) Society and the State shall remove all obstacles to marriage and shall facilitate the marital procedure. They shall ensure family protection and welfare.

3- *The Right to Education*

Article 11

 I) As of the moment of birth, every child has rights due from the parents, society and the state to be accorded proper nursing, education, and material, hygienic and moral care. Both the fetus and the mother must be protected and accorded special care.

II) Parents and those in such like capacity have the right to choose the type of education they desire for their children, provided they take into consideration the interest and future of the children in accordance with ethical values and the principles of the Shari'ah.

III) Both parents are entitled to certain rights from their children, and relatives are entitled to rights from their kin, by the tenets of the Shari'ah.

Article 12

I) The question for knowledge is an obligation, and the provision of education is a duty of society and the State. The State shall ensure the availability of ways and means to acquire education and shall guarantee educational diversity in the interest of society so as to enable man to be acquainted with the religion of Islam and the facts of the Universe for the benefit of humanity. This right is called "the right to intellectual enlightenment."

II) Every human being has the right to receive both religious and worldly education from the various institutions of, education and guidance, including the family, the school, the university, the media, etc., and in such an integrated and balanced manner as to develop his personality, strengthen his faith in God and promote his respect for and defense of both rights and obligations. This right is called is called "the right to educational enlightenment."

Article 13

I)   Everyone shall have the right to advocate what is right, propagate what is good, and warn against what is wrong and evil, whether individually or collectively, according to the norms of Islamic Shari'ah.[113] This duty is obligatory upon everyone who has the capability and sufficient rational reasons for his success including the state and the society. The state is more obligated toward this duty since it has many capabilities. Every human being can cooperate with other individuals and groups in implementing this right, and all these rights and duties must be carried into execution according to Islamic Shari'ah laws and the state and society are obligated to make the ground ready for implementation of these rights and duties.

II) Information is a vital necessity to society. It may not be exploited or misused in such a way as may violate sanctities and the dignity of Prophets, undermine moral and ethical values or disintegrate, corrupt or harm society or weaken its faith.

III) It is not permitted to arouse nationalistic or doctrinal hatred or to do anything that may be an incitement to any form or racial discrimination.[114]

4- *The Right to Committed Freedom*

Article 14

I)   Human beings are born free, and no one has the right to enslave, humiliate, oppress or exploit them, and there can be no subjugation but to God the Most-High.

II) Colonialism of all types, being one of the evilest forms of enslavement, is

---

113 - The second clause of Article 23 of the Tehran Charter states, "Everyone shall have the right to advocate what is right, and propagate what is good, and warn against what is wrong and evil, whether individually or collectively, according to the norms of Islamic Shari'ah, and it is incumbent upon the state and the society to afford these rights and duties."

This clause in the Cairo Declaration has been grievously modified; it reads, "Everyone shall have the right to advocate what is right, and propagate what is good, and warn against what is wrong and evil, whether individually or collectively, according to the norms of Islamic Shari'ah."

Unfortunately, this extremely significant Islamic duty has sorely been underestimated by removing the words that articulate indispensible roles of the state and society in fulfilling this duty. No explanation has been provided regarding what is meant by observing others' rights and duties. Is this applicable to all cases, even those which are in conflict with the human society and Islamic societies?

114 - As the first clause of this article was more relevant with the right to committed freedom, we moved it to its appropriate place.

totally prohibited. Peoples suffering from colonialism have the full right to freedom and self-determination. It is the duty of all States and peoples to support the struggle of colonized peoples for the liquidation of all forms of colonialism and occupation, and all States and peoples have the right to preserve their independent identity and exercise control over their wealth and natural resources.

Article 15

Everyone shall have the right to express his opinion freely in such manner as would not be contrary to the principles of the Shari'ah.

Article 16

Everyone shall have the right to enjoy the fruits of his scientific, literary, artistic or technical production and the right to protect the moral and material interests stemming from that place, provided that such production is not contrary to the principles of Shari'ah.

Article 17

Every human being is eligible to be benefited from his right to citizenship, and no one shall be deprived of their citizenship.[115]

Article 18

Every human being has the right to enjoy his legal capacity regarding both an obligation and commitment, and should this capacity be lost or impaired; he shall be represented by his guardian.

Article 19

I)   Islam is the religion of unspoiled nature. It is prohibited to exercise any form of compulsion on man or to exploit his poverty or ignorance to convert him to another religion or atheism.

II) It is incumbent upon the state and society to obliterate heresies and baseless ideas from Muslim societies, and if possible, from non-Muslim communities through intellectual debates and rational advice. If the followers of fake and unfounded beliefs give up their deviated thoughts, the society will be guided toward the path toward evolution. If they neglect the logic, wisdom and other justifications provided to them, the state is to safeguard the sound mentalities and spiritualities of the people in fashion in line with Islamic and humane principles. This duty,

---

115 - Being the eighth article of Tehran Charter this article has been removed from Cairo Declaration, since there is no such concept as citizenship in Islam. We have delineated the Islamic sense of this term in the article 20 of this declaration.

if fulfilled, could result in the spiritual and intellectual evolution of the society.

III) The coexistence of believers of unorthodox views with Muslims is a matter that shall be decided by the Islamic Judge who is the guardian of Islamic Shari'ah Law according to the exigencies of time and emerging issues.

Article 20

I) Every man shall have the right, within the framework of Shari'ah, to free movement and to select his place of residence whether inside or outside his country and if persecuted, is entitled to seek asylum in another country. The country of refuge shall ensure his protection until he reaches safety unless asylum is motivated by an act which Shari'ah regards as a crime.

II) No non-Muslim is permitted to cross the Sacred Shrine of Mecca unless having acquired the permission of the Leader of Believers.

III) Non-Muslims are not permitted to dwell in Mecca.

Article 21

Work is a right guaranteed by the State and Society for each person able to work. Everyone shall be free to choose the work that suits him best and which serves his interests and those of society. The employee shall have the right to safety and security as well as to all other social guarantees. He may neither be assigned work beyond his capacity nor be subjected to compulsion or exploited or harmed in any way – without any discrimination between males and females – except upon a specific reason prescribed by Shari'ah.

Article 22

I) Employees shall be entitled to fair wages for work without delay although they may have been unaware of his service's *just value* either due to his ignorance or because of compulsion. As the Holy Quran states:

> *Therefore give full measure and weight and do not diminish to men their things.*   (The Heights 7:85)

The necessity of paying just value applies to both services and goods, as applicable to all cases in which the employee or the owner of goods are either aware or unaware of the just value of their services and goods.

II) All workers are entitled to demand fair wages for their work and services, and it is incumbent upon the state to help them in attaining their right. The employee shall have the right to the holidays' allowances and promotions which he deserves. For his part, he shall be required to be dedicated and meticulous in his work. Should workers and employers disagree on any matter, the State shall intervene to settle the dispute and have the grievances redressed, the rights confirmed and justice enforced without bias.

III) The employee shall be entitled to be provided with his expenses by his employer at the time of disability, senility, and gestation (for female employees) and should the employer prove to be unable to assure this right, the state shall be obliged to undertake the duty.

Article 23

Liability is, in essence, personal.

I) There shall be no crime or punishment except as provided for in the Shari'ah.

II) A defendant is innocent until his guilt is proven in a fair trial in which he shall be given all the guarantees of defense.

Article 24

I)   Everyone shall have the right to own property acquired in a legitimate way and shall be entitled to the rights of ownership, without prejudice to oneself, others or society in general. Expropriation is not permissible except for the requirements of public interest and upon payment of immediate and fair compensation.

II) Confiscation and seizure of property are prohibited except for a necessity dictated by law.

Article 25

I)   Everyone shall have the right to legitimate gains without monopolization, deceit or harm to oneself or others.

II) Usury (Riba) is prohibited.

Article 26

Taking hostages under any form or for any purpose is expressly forbidden.

Article 27

I) Authority is a trust and abuse, or malicious exploitation thereof is prohibited so that fundamental human rights may be guaranteed. If Muslim authority is at the hands of Holy Prophets and Immaculate Imams, they shall not be interpellated due to their Divine Immaculateness; otherwise, the interpellation shall necessarily be done according to the provisions of Islamic Shari'ah Law. Interpellation is not a   penal device, but it serves as means of transparency in a democratic sense. Since authority is a *dignitate homenis,* it shall be conferred upon those who are just and more adherent to the principles of conscience.

II) Everyone shall have the right to participate, directly or indirectly, in the administration of his country's public affairs. He shall also have the right to assume public office by the provisions of Shari'ah.

5- *The Right to Equality*

Article 28

I)   All individuals are equal before the law, without distinction between the ruler and the ruled.

II) The right to resort to justice is guaranteed to everyone.[116]

III) Everyone who lives in the Islamic society is not to cause turmoil in the society and everyone who lives in a non-Islamic society is not to corrupt the society, regardless of his race, color, language, religion – providing that it is not based on heresies and unprincipled beliefs – nationality, and social class shall be entitled to be benefitted from all freedoms and rights stipulated in the Universal Declaration of Human Rights in Islam.

Article 29

Every human being has an equal right to establish societies for charity activities, and all individuals are entitled to found associations for social and political consultations, providing they do not trample on the constitution and governing provisions of the society. Should there be any legal deficiencies, they shall need to consult and cooperate with the authorities in a peaceful manner.

Article 30

I)   All the rights and freedoms stipulated in this Declaration are subject to the Islamic Shari'ah.

II) In non-Islamic societies, people shall need to commit themselves to their native rights and duties. This is the commitment maxim which reads:

> *Commit all those who are not followers of the same religion as you to what they are committed to themselves.*

Article 31

The Islamic Shari'ah is the only source of reference for the explanation or clarification of any of the articles of this Declaration.

Note1. Whereas some of the articles stipulated in this Declaration may be matters of dispute between jurisprudents, Muslim states shall be obliged to establish an organization for the proximity of Islamic schools of jurisprudence.

Note 2. Continuous comparisons shall be made between Islamic and Western concepts of human rights.

---

116 - This article, along with its two clauses, and also Article 24 along with its four clauses in the Tehran Charter were reduced into one article (Article 19) in the Cairo Declaration. Although the two articles have the same origin, they are essentially different; thus, this reduction does not seem intelligible.

Article 32

Islamic states – whether member states of the Organization of Islamic Conference or independent states – shall be obliged to afford all rights and duties stipulated in this Declaration.

Note 1. It shall be obligatory upon member states to establish an organization to observe the process of implementation of articles of declaration in Islamic societies and each member shall have at least one representative of that organization. Every member state shall need to have a national organization to observe the process of execution of articles in the country.

Note 2. The articles stipulated in this Declaration, having Ben researched and articulated by the jurists and ratified by just jurisprudents and authorities of Islamic countries, shall be regarded among the *Limits Ordained by God* and nobody shall be allowed to transgress them. As stated in the Holy Quran:

> *These are the limits of Allah, so do not exceed them and whoever exceeds the limits of Allah these are the unjust.*

(The Cow 2:229)

The Universal Declaration of Human Rights

Article 1

All human beings are born free and equal in dignity and rights. They are endowed with reason and conscience and should act towards one another in a spirit of brotherhood.

Article 2

1- Everyone is entitled to all the rights and freedoms outlined in this Declaration, without distinction of any kind, such as race, color, sex, language, religion, political or another opinion, national or social origin, property, birth or another status.

2- Furthermore, no distinction shall be made on the political, jurisdictional or international status of the country or territory to which a person belongs, whether it be independent, trust, non-self-governing or under any other limitation of sovereignty.

Article 3

Everyone has the right to life, liberty, and security of person.

Article 4

No one shall be held in slavery or servitude; slavery and the slave trade shall be prohibited in all their forms.

Article 5

No one shall be subjected to torture or cruel, inhuman or degrading treatment or punishment.

Article 6

Everyone has the right to recognition everywhere as a person before the law.

Article 7

All are equal before the law and are entitled without any discrimination to equal protection of the law. All are entitled to equal protection against any discrimination in violation of this Declaration and any incitement to such discrimination.

Article 8

Everyone has the right to an effective remedy by the competent national tribunals for acts violating the fundamental rights granted him by the constitution or by law.

Article 9

No one shall be subjected to arbitrary arrest, detention or exile.

Article 10

Everyone is entitled in full equality to a fair and public hearing by an independent and impartial tribunal, in the determination of his rights and obligations and any criminal charge against him.

Article 11

1- Everyone charged with a penal offense has the right to be presumed innocent until proved guilty according to the law in a public trial at which he has had all the guarantees necessary for his defense.

2- No one shall be held guilty of any penal offense on account of any act or omission which did not constitute a penal offense, under the national or international law, at the time when it was committed. Nor shall a heavier penalty be imposed than the one that was applicable at the time the penal offense was committed.

Article 12

No one shall be subjected to arbitrary interference with his privacy, family, home or correspondence, nor to attacks upon his honor and reputation. Everyone has the right to the protection of the law against such interference or attacks.

Article 13

1- Everyone has the right to freedom of movement and residence within the borders of each State.

2- Everyone has the right to leave any country, including his own, and to return to his country.

Article 14

1- Everyone has the right to seek and to enjoy in other countries asylum from persecution.

2- This right may not be invoked in the case of prosecutions genuinely arising from non-political crimes or acts contrary to the purposes and principles of the United Nations.

Article 15

1- Everyone has the right to a nationality.

2- No one shall be arbitrarily deprived of his nationality nor denied the right to change his nationality.

Article 16

1- Men and women of full age, without any limitation due to race, nationality or religion, have the right to marry and to found a family. They are entitled to equal rights as to marriage, during the marriage and at its dissolution.

2- Marriage shall be entered into only with the free and full consent of the intending spouses.

3- The family is the natural and fundamental group unit of society and is entitled to protection by society and the State.

Article 17

1- Everyone has the right to own property alone as well as in association with others.

2- No one shall be arbitrarily deprived of his property.

Article 18

Everyone has the right to freedom of thought, conscience, and religion; this right includes freedom to change his religion or belief, and freedom, either alone or in community with others and in public or private, to manifest his religion or belief in teaching, practice, worship and observance.

Article 19

Everyone has the right to freedom of opinion and expression; this right includes freedom to hold opinions without interference and to seek, receive and impart information and ideas through any media and regardless of frontiers.

Article 20

1- Everyone has the right to freedom of peaceful assembly and association.

2- No one may be compelled to belong to an association.

Article 21

1- Everyone has the right to take part in the government of his country, directly or through freely chosen representatives.

2- Everyone has the right of equal access to public service in his country.

3- The will of the people shall be the basis of the authority of government; this will shall be expressed in periodic and genuine elections which shall be by universal and equal suffrage and shall be held by secret vote or by equivalent free voting procedures.

Article 22

Everyone, as a member of society, has the right to social security and is entitled to realization, through national effort and international cooperation and by the organization and resources of each State, of the economic, social and cultural rights indispensable for his dignity and the free development of his personality.

Article 23

1- Everyone has the right to work, to free choice of employment, to just and favorable conditions of work and to protection against unemployment.

2- Everyone, without any discrimination, has the right to equal pay for equal work.

3- Everyone who works has the right to just and favourable remuneration ensuring for himself and his family an existence worthy of human dignity, and supplemented, if necessary, by other means of social protection.

4- Everyone has the right to form and to join trade unions for the protection of his interests.

Article 24

Everyone has the right to rest and leisure, including reasonable limitation of working hours and periodic holidays with pay.

Article 25

1- Everyone has the right to a standard of living adequate for the health and well-being of himself and of his family, including food, clothing, housing and medical care and necessary social services, and the right to security in the event of unemployment, sickness, disability, widowhood, old age or other lack of livelihood in circumstances beyond his control.

2- Motherhood and childhood are entitled to special care and assistance. All children, whether born in or out of wedlock, shall enjoy the same social protection.

Article 26

1- Everyone has the right to education. Education shall be free, at least in the elementary and fundamental stages. Elementary education shall be compulsory. Technical and professional education shall be made available, and higher education shall be equally accessible to all of merit.

2- Education shall be directed to the full development of the human personality and the strengthening of respect for human rights and fundamental freedoms. It shall promote understanding, tolerance, and friendship among all nations, racial or religious groups, and shall further the activities of the United Nations for the maintenance of peace.

3- Parents have a prior right to choose the kind of education that shall be given to their children.

Article 27

1- Everyone has the right freely to participate in the cultural life of the community, to enjoy the arts and to share in scientific advancement and its benefits.

2- Everyone has the right to the protection of the moral and material interests resulting from any scientific, literary or artistic production of which he is the author.

Article 28

Everyone is entitled to a social and international order in which the rights and freedoms outlined in this Declaration can be fully realized.

Article 29

1- Everyone has duties to the community in which alone the free and full development of his personality is possible.

2- In the exercise of his rights and freedoms, everyone shall be subject only to such limitations as are determined by law solely for the purpose of securing due recognition and respect for the rights and freedoms of others and of meeting the just requirements of morality, public order and the general welfare in a democratic society.

3- These rights and freedoms may in no case be exercised contrary to the purposes and principles of the United Nations.

Article 30

Nothing in this Declaration may be interpreted as implying for any State, group or person any right to engage in any activity or to perform any act aimed at the destruction of any of the rights and freedoms set forth herein.

Human Rights in Islam and the West:

A Comparative Encounter

We will now examine in detail the basic quintuple human rights through a comparative study of their related articles in the UN Declaration and the Universal Declaration of Human Rights in Islam.

The Sequence of the Discussion and Study

We will first make a study of the fundamental rights, such as the right to life. Then we will present the article concerning these basic rights, such as the right to life in Islam. Subsequently, we shall look into the corresponding rights as seen in the West.

The next step consists of a study of the points in common between these legal systems.

Eventually, the differences existing between them will be taken into consideration.

These basic rights, which are at same time the building blocks of human rights and freedoms in Islam, are as follows:

1. *The Right to Righteous Life*
2. *The Right to Dignity*
3. *The Right to Education*
4. *The Right to Committed Freedom*
5. *The Right to Equality*

A Basic Principle:

Righteous Life and
The Foundations of Basic Rights

"Life" in this context refers in fact to "righteous life," rather than life as such or absolute life, although associated with contempt, suffering, and torture.

The basic principle of life as understood by religion, science, philosophy and human good sense – which is usually manifested in spiritual literature of nations – is so evident and clear that it does not as such need to be further explained or articulated. There are several reasons for such sensitivity toward this phenomenon in human epistemic perspectives that we still mention hereunder:[117]

1- All men of ideas are unanimous in regarding the phenomenon of life in general and human life, in particular, the immensely significant and weighty issue in dealing with the world of existence. This unanimity is visible in all of the human quadruple epistemic perspectives – religion, science, philosophy and good sense.

2- Regardless of this unanimity, if we take the phenomenon of life in general and human life in particular into serious, having already put aside all pessimistic and prejudiced perspectives, we shall come across such wonderful forces and aptitudes as self-organization, knowledge, thinking, reasoning, conscience, will, knowledge by presence, perfectionism, positive love, discovery, imagination, constructive competition and hundreds of other capabilities that, if taken seriously, could demonstrate the essential value of our natural life. Alas, these marvelous possibilities of life and human characteristics have usually been underestimated due to their general accessibility and the contemporary research conducted upon them have only been done in a professional spirit rather than aiming to touch the realities and grasp their magnificence and value.

3- On the indispensability of human life, it will suffice to state that if this highly significant phenomenon is taken into earnest consideration of its capabilities and possibilities in knowing the reality – even a limited domain of it (i.e., nature) – such knowledge will be essentially flawed and devoid of any philosophical and scientific value, since every knowledge of the reality is achieved through human epistemic apparatus that is itself

---

117 - I discussed these issues in a lecture entitled "An Introduction to the Universal Declaration to Human Rights" delivered at the 6th Conference of Islamic Thoughts.

already irrigated by life.

4- To understand the reality of the world, we need to have sizable knowledge of the whole hierarchy of existence. It is needless to say that human life is the highest step in the hierarchy of existence since it is an only human life that has the capability to realize its axistential potentialities through an interactive relation with numerous kinds of beings in this world. The massive body of scientific, philosophical, literary and mystic literature on various aspects of human life shows the significance of this phenomenon in human episteme since time immemorial.

If we take "life," "dignity" and "freedom" as three entirely natural phenomena, their value curve shall remain at the level of naturality, and thus their related rights shall be decided according to the principles of naturalism. Thus conceived, these phenomena shall neither be of any value or have any significance to be demonstrated nor shall they be of rights to be observed.

It should be taken into prime consideration that if we regard life, dignity and freedom as three entirely natural phenomena that occur and disappear according to the laws of human nature in the spirit of positivists of the nineteenth century, we shall have no longer any occasion to demonstrate essential inherent rights for them beyond their natural values and bind people to commit themselves to them following their consciences although they would be against their social and individual benefits! It is needless to say that if we fail to demonstrate an inherent value for these phenomena, talking about the significance and magnificence of life shall be either a kind of ostentation or a means for deceiving shallow-minded people by the aggressive hunters of power and egotists.

It was indeed due to this very reason that such a magnificent phenomenon as life has continuously been abused by unfeeling despots during the long course of human history. Anastasia taxed people for the air they breathed![118] Nero wished people had one neck so he could chop it off and saw his name among the heroes! Tamerlane enjoyed spilling innocent blood! And Genghis Khan was so cursed and cruel that he would kill even the dogs and cats of his occupied cities.

This evil current originates from the ignorance of aggressive despisers of life toward its value and magnificence due to their being inebriated either by power or alcohol or pleasure or carnal desires. Even if we were to suppose that these egotists and assertive hunters of power were informed of the significance and magnificence of life, they would not still be able to grasp the true value of it due to their being inebriated by power and carnal desires. On the other hand, common people have, unfortunately, always preferred to be spectators of majesties and magnificent truths instead of being benefitted from them, for they constantly seek the knowledge of impressive realities

---

118 - Montesquieu, Charles Louis de Secondat, *De L' esprit de Lois.*

so as to gratify some of their carnal desires through them and not for their spiritual profits.

Life: Religion and Good Sense

Regarding the valuable works authored on various aspects of *menschenleben* along with the historical course of events and the ideas and behaviors of religious and moral people which originate in human good sense and pure conscience, life is a reality of wonderful potentialities that could be actualized and truly valued only through being oriented toward its right course.

Self-preservation in the sense of taking care of oneself against possible dangers is the most obvious reason of intrinsic value of life for those who are mentally intact. All human cultures bear witnesses to this inherent value. The following verses by Ferdowsi and Sa'adi, two renowned Iranian poets, are two distinguished instances of this human sensitivity toward the intrinsic value of life:

> *Do not annoy the ant carrying a grain,*
> *since it is a living being and life is sweet* [119]
>
> ***
>
> *I swear, O Sa'adi, on the lives of all the pure-hearted,*
> *that this worldly life does not worth your hurting others.* [120]

This spontaneous sensitivity has its origin in two basic factors:

1- Human intuitive knowledge of his life and its coordinates. Every mentally balanced human being understands the ultimate desirability of his life and the necessity of its continuation even in the face of unbearable bitters and hardships. This intuitive knowledge is not essentially didactic. It is needless to say, of course, that this basic knowledge is immune from ill-minded ideas, and it was for this very reason that some anthropologists have not declined to describe human life in the natural domain as "absolutely desirable." Furthermore, it has been due to this absolute desirability of life that no mentally balanced person has ever sacrificed his life for nothing but Supreme Being the Absolute.

Of course, we come across people in human history that have sacrificed their lives for reaching a secular goal. But if we take these self-sacrificing persons into serious consideration, we shall find that they have already absolutized their goals and then sacrificed their ultimately desirable lives for reaching them. For example, if we are to introduce philanthropy to someone as a matter of devotional significance, we shall need to promote it to the level of anthropolatry, since fondness toward something may not force someone to sacrifice his life for it unless he replaces this amiable

---

119 - Ferdowsi's *Shahnameh*.
120 - Sa'adi's *Gulistan*.

thing with the Lord, Who truly deserves life sacrifice, and wholeheartedly devote himself to this.

2- Beholding the intensive gravity of life, its positive features and the ultimate bitterness of the negative encounters along with it for other people. We are witnessing that people passionately defend their life against disturbing factors. These two features, the "intensive gravity of life" and "passionate defense of it," could demonstrate the absolute desirability of life in natural domains. Thus conceived, it could be said that the right to life is the first and most natural right that all living beings are entitled to, providing it does not disturb others' lives.

These two reasons regarding the fundamentality of right to life are both among the principles of common sense which is one of the primordial sources of Islamic articles of faith, obligations and rights; thus, we can reasonably conclude that the right to life, as decreed by common sense, is the first and most natural right in Islam.

The Right to Righteous Life in the Perspective of Islamic Rules and Texts

Although our previous debates on the reality of life demonstrate the value and natural quality of the right to life for all living beings and *homo sapiens* – except those living beings and humans that trespass up other creatures' rights – it shall nonetheless be very well-timed to point out some Islamic rules and texts in this regard:

1- We read in the Holy Quran that:

> *Look then at the signs of Allah's mercy, how he gives life to the earth after its death, most surely he will raise the dead to life; and he has power over all things.* (The Romans 30:50)

This verse describes vegetative life as Divine Mercy. Considering that vegetative life is a divine mercy, it can be concluded that animal life and consequently human life are certainly of a higher status. Therefore, all human beings are equally entitled to be benefitted from this divine mercy and nobody has the right to trample it. This could be deduced from the following verse:

> *And do not kill your people; surely Allah is merciful to you.* (The Women 4:29)

Thus, life is equivalent with Divine Mercy.

2- The Lord promises Hell to everyone who has been unjust toward their own soul through submitting to poor existential and social conditions:

> *Surely (as for) those whom the angels cause to die while they are unjust to their souls, they shall say: In what state were you? They shall say: We were weak in the earth. They shall say: Was not*

Allah's earth spacious, so that you should have migrated therein?
So these it is whose abode is Hell, and it is an evil resort.

(The Women 4:97)

3- When we ponder upon the rational basis of animal rights in Islamic jurisprudential resources, we will find that all of them are ultimately founded upon the inherent value of life and prohibition of killing a living being without reasonable grounds. Some great jurisprudents believe that all animal rights stipulated in Islamic texts are based on the intrinsic sanctity of soul. As an authentic *hadith* reads:

> *All [of these rights and regulations about animals] is due to the respect and reverence for the spirit.*

There is also another credible transmission that reads:

> *A woman who had tied a cat to a tree and caused the cat to die of thirst met divine punishment.*[121]

4- Gaming for revelry is prohibited in Islam and traveling for this purpose is a sin and quotidian prayers in such voyages must be performed as usual. There are several *hadith* on this matter upon which many fatwa have also been issued by jurisprudential authorities. We shall quote three of them hereunder:

* It has thus been quoted by Zorarah that, "One day I asked Imam Muhammad Al-Bagher (SWA):

> *If someone leaves his family to hunt and revels for two or three days, should he perform his daily prayers as usual or in a shortened form?" The Imam replied, "Since he left for revelry, he must perform them as usual."*[122]

* As Imam Sadegh (SWA) has been quoted, "If someone leaves his house for hunting as an attempt to provide foodstuffs for his family, he needs to perform daily prayers in a shortened form, but if he games for satisfying his lusts, he must say his prayers as usual and this act of him is not blessed.[123]

* Musa Marwzi has quoted Imam Musa Ibn Jafar (SWA) as saying that Holy Prophet Muhammad (peace be upon him) had stated that four things taint the heart and fill it with hypocrisy as water fills trees with life; examples are overindulgence in sensual pleasures, levity,

121 - Sheikh al-Horre al-Ameli, *Wasa'el al-Shi'ah*, On Blood-vengeance, Hadith 130, Vol. 19, p. 160. We have already driven and codified animal rights from an Islamic point of view in 32 articles based upon original Islamic resources in *A Translation and Interpretation of the Nahj ul-Balaghah*, Vol. 12, pp. 159-164. Also see M. T. Ja'fari, *Legal Inquiries* (2014). (Originally in Persian).
122 - Sheikh al-Horre al-Ameli, *Wasa'el al-Shi'ah*, On Blood-vengeance.
123 - Ibid.

subjecting oneself to royal service and gaming for revelry.[124]

5- Duck hunting at night is disapproved of. This judgment is documented to *hadith* that have been quoted on the issue, such as:

> ➤ Imam Al-Sadegh (SWA) quoted the Holy Prophet Muhammad (peace be upon him) as saying, "Do not hunt chicks in their nest and do not catch birds at night; wait until the break of dawn.[125]

> ➤ Imam Al-Sadegh (SWA) states that Holy Prophet has banished the believers from night hunt and stated that night is divine mercy on the birds so that they may be secure.[126]

As a result, hunting birds in their nests is forbidden according to these two *hadith*.

6- Abortion is prohibited in Islam upon strong jurisprudential reasons; everyone who commits it is regarded as a murderer and must pay the blood money of the fetus according to its embryonic age. Here we indicate some important reasons in this regard:

> ➤ Isaac Ibn Ammar was quoted as saying:

> *I said to Imam Musa Ibn Jafar (SAW) that a there was a woman who feared pregnancy and used medicine to abort what she had in her womb. The Imam replied, "No, (she should not abort it.)" I said, "But it is still just an embryo!" The Imam replied, "The embryo is the first stage of human creation."*[127]

> ➤ A hadith frequently quoted from Imam Al-Sadegh (SAW) and Imam Ali Ibn Al-Musa Al-Reza (SAW) reads:

> *The Prince of Believers, Imam Ali (SAW), ordained 100 dinars as the blood money of an abortive embryo; whereas a human zygote evolves through quintuple embryonic stages of zygote, clot, embryo, bone and flesh, the ordained blood money is paid according to these quintuple stages. But when the spirit is breathed into the embryo and changes it to a human being, the abortion shall be fined with the blood money off murder.*[128]

Regarding this Islamic jurisprudential judgment, it is clearly demonstrated that the right to life appears in this world from the very zygotic stage of embryonic evolution and anyone who trespasses this fundamental right shall be known as a murderer and will be punished according to Islamic provisions designated for suicide.

7- In Islamic jurisprudence, the human soul is seen as divinely sanctified;

---

124 - Ibid.
125 - Ibid.
126 - Ibid.
127 - Ibid.
128 - Ibid.

manslaughter is therefore prohibited, and those who commit homicide will face justice.

According to the following verse of the Holy Quran, all human souls are respected except those who ruin their lives by committing inhuman crimes:

> *Whoever slays a soul, unless it is for manslaughter or mischief in the land, it is as though he slew all men; and whoever keeps it alive, it is as though he kept alive all men; and certainly Our messengers came to them with clear arguments, but even after that many of them certainly act extravagantly in the land.*
> (The Dinner Table 5:32)

There are almost 14 instances of *hadith* in *Wasa'el Al-Shi'ah* (in the section titled "The Book of Blood Ransom") that clearly point out the prohibition of manslaughter. For example:

> *Once, Imam Al-Sadegh (SAW) was asked about those who committed homicide; the Imam stated that hell should be their punishment.*

Therefore, Islamic jurisprudence regards every human being – except those who have ruined their lives by manslaughter or mischief on earth – as entitled to the inalienable right to life; nobody is allowed to trespass or trample or abrogate this right, and it is incumbent upon all believers to protect innocent lives from harms and violations. Everyone who is capable enough of saving save a life and does not do so shall surely be considered as a partner in the murder. This judgment is documented to reasons stipulated in authentic Islamic sources, such as:

> *Muhammad Ibn Moslem has quoted Imam Muhammad Al-Bagher (SAW) as saying, "Verily, a man shall come on the Day of Judgment with a cup of blood in his hand. He will say, 'I swear to God I have not killed or participated in the act of killing anyone!' He shall be told, "You have reported on someone to a murderer and caused him to be killed; now you are the partner in a homicide.'"* [129]

There are also other *hadith* on the prohibition of participating in the killing of a believer, such as:

> *Everyone who participates in the killing of a believer shall enter the Day of Judgment with writing on his brow: "This is a disgrace and disappointment of divine mercy."*

It might be said that this quotation is merely about Muslims and does not apply to people of other faiths. This objection could be dealt with through a jurisprudential axiom that states when the absolute and the

129 - Sheikh al-Horre al-Ameli, *Wasa'el Al-Shi'ah*, Vol. 19, p. 8.

conditioned are both positive in their essence; they do not instantiate each other. For example, if a *hadith* orders us to respect the man of knowledge and another order us to respect the man of knowledge who is also just, the latter transmission (which is conditioned) does not instantiate the former. Therefore, the absolute reason, which is the quotation made by Muhammad Ibn Moslem does not restrict and instantiate those mentioned above one. Thus, the latter only further reiterates the prohibition by the condition of the believer.

8- One of the most significant reasons that demonstrate the intrinsic value and magnificence of human life in Islam is the prohibition of suicide. As God has stated in the Holy Quran:

> *Do not kill yourselves; surely Allah is merciful to you, and whoever does this aggressively and unjustly, we will soon cast him into the fire; and this is easy to Allah.*
> (The Women 4: 29-30)

Some exegeses of the Holy Quran have interpreted this verse as the prohibition of manslaughter and have translated the verse as "Do not kill each other; surely Allah is merciful to you." This line of interpretation is not correct for two reasons:

The First Reason: Regarding the generality of this verse that prohibits the very act of killing in general, suicide seems to be essentially in conflict with the above-mentioned jurisprudential axiom [that states when the absolute and the conditioned are both positive in their essence, they do not instantiate each other], particularly that human life on earth is a manifestation of omnipresent Divine Mercy. Thus, killing every human being regardless of their identity is strongly prohibited.

The Second Reason: Imam Al-Sadegh (SAW) has substantiated his view on the prohibition of suicide by quoting this verse:

> *Imam Al-Sadegh (SAW) stated, "Everyone who intentionally commits suicide shall be cast into the eternal fire of Hell. As God has stated, 'Do not kill yourselves'".*[130]

There are several quotations on the prohibition of suicide, among which the following has been ascribed to Imam Muhammad Al-Bagher (SAW):

> *The True Believer may be afflicted with every misfortune and die in every possible form, but he will never kill himself.*[131]

9- As the human zygote is entitled to the right to life in all its embryonic stages, it inherits like other human beings. Thus, if the father dies while

---

130 - Sheikh al-Horre al-Ameli, *Wasael al-Shi'ah*, On the Prohibition of Suicide, p. 13. (Originally in Arabic).
131 - Ibid.

the mother is still carrying a baby in her uterus, the inheritors have two ways before them:

a) They either should wait until the birth of the baby and to get their share of the inheritance after giving the newborn its share, or

b) They need to put aside two boys' shares and then enjoy their shares.

Thus, it is evident that Islam not only observes the human right to life in its weakest stages, but has also paid serious attention to the financial prerequisites of these weakest stages of right to survival.

10- The prohibition of sheltering the murderer. Several transmissions have been quoted on this issue in authentic Islamic resources, including 9 quotations cited in *Wasa'el Al-Shi'ah*.[132] The Holy Prophet Muhammad (peace be upon him) was quoted as saying:

> *"May the curse of God be on anyone who causes an accident or shelters the one who caused the accident!" The Prophet was then asked, "What do you mean by accident?" He replied, "Murder."*

11- As we have mentioned earlier, in Islamic jurisprudence, doing a slightest harm to human being causes punishment.

12- All religious injunctions and obligations in Islam are bounded to human physical and mental conditions, since all Muslim jurisprudents are unanimous in taking human capability as the basic rational prerequisite of all Shari'ah prescribed obligations; as a result, it is necessary to protect human beings from all physical and mental harms.[133] Generally speaking, life as understood by Islam is a lovely manifestation of Eternal Divinity that everyone is obliged to protect – whether their own life or other people's lives – against existed and possible harms as much as they *can*; otherwise, they shall be guilty and liable to be punished.

13- According to Islamic principles of jurisprudence, no one is allowed to sacrifice other lives for saving his own, since all lives are rays emitted from the same eternal source of light and no life is more valuable than other ones. An authentic narration reads:

> *Verily, dissimulation has been provisioned for safeguarding innocent bloods, and when the blood was doomed to be spilled, dissimulation is no longer prescribed.*

14- Everyone who is beholding the slaughter of a man while being able to save the innocent slain shall face the harshest punishment and his eyes shall be gouged out. Anyone who participates in killing a man shall be sentenced to life imprisonment. These judgments have been driven from concrete quotations that are unanimously agreed upon by

---

132 - Ibid, Vol. 19, p. 15-18.

133 - This is based upon the jurisprudential principle that reads, "There is no harmful thing in Islam".

jurisprudents, such as:

> *Imam Al-Sadegh (SAW) was quoted as saying, "Three men were summoned to Imam Ali (SAW); one had killed a man while the other kept the victim, and the third was watching. The Imam sentenced the eyes of the beholder to be gouged out, sentenced the keeper to life imprisonment and the murderer was sentenced to execution."*[134]

The beholder's sentence, according to rational and transmitted reasons, is conditioned upon his ability to save the slain indeed. It might be said that the sentences issued in this transmission are tough and thus could have been reduced to short-term imprisonments and lashing.

This objection bespeaks on behalf of critiques of the Islamic law of retaliation, mostly uninformed people and some thinkers of legal matters who have insufficient knowledge of the philosophy of the law of retaliation in Islam, the philosophy of which we are going to explicate hereunder.

The Law of Retaliation: Why?

The objections to the Islamic law of retaliation all have their origins in the ignorance of the objectors to the grand philosophy of retaliation in Islam, which is informed by the inherent value and magnificence of human life. These objections could be tackled by following considerations:

a) It is not so that every murderer shall be sentenced to retaliation; this sentence is restricted to voluntary homicide and its execution depends upon the avenger of blood's opinion unless it is demonstrated to judicial authorities that the convict is a murderer by nature. Thus, it is only in such cases that the sentence of retaliation is exercised.

This demonstrates that retaliation is not the only sentence for the one who has committed homicide. This also shows how serious Islam is in protecting human lives and innocent bloods. Could there be any provision more logical and acting as a stronger guarantee for safeguarding the magnificent and invaluable human life, which is a manifestation of the Divine Majesty? On the other hand, it is the murderer himself that has devalued his life by committing voluntary homicide.

Retaliation, as one of triple sentences of homicide, bears a grand philosophy thin not always taken into account by egotist legal experts. Retaliation extinguishes the inner fire of avengers of blood and tackles the possible mental disorders.

b) The possibility of mental instability in the murderer, even when the crime is being committed, nullifies the sentence of retaliation according to the jurisprudential principle of *"even the slightest uncertainty nullifies the sentence"*.

c) As we have mentioned earlier, objections to the Islamic Law of Retaliation basically originate from general ignorance to the truth and the intrinsic value and magnificence of human life. Those shallow-minded defenders of the murderer's right to life do not know that their baseless sentiments expose all human lives to danger since one could voluntarily commit homicide without facing justice. Consequently, these shallow sentiments could undermine the inherent value and magnificence of human life. As a result, the law of retaliation could reduce the rate of homicide and reveal the true significance of human life.

It might be said that Islamic law allows the murderer to be released by paying the blood money with the Avengers' consent.

This objection could be tackled with reference to the previously mentioned Grand philosophy of retaliation; as we have already mentioned, this harsh statement is supposed to fill the murderer with terror. It is also retaliation that reveals the true essence of Islamic remission. All of these issues debated here on the significance and inherent value and magnificence are documented to the following divine verse of the Holy Quran:

> **And there is life for you in (the law of) retaliation, o men of understanding, that you may guard yourselves.**
>
> (The Cow 2:179)

Obviously, this is not to say that retaliation resurrects the slain or creates a new man; rather, it signifies that retaliation is the best instrument to fill the aggressive criminals with terror so not to think even about victimizing other peoples for reaching their evil purposes.

15- Negligence in the case of innocent blood shed is a mortal sin and surely makes one the participant to the crime. As Imam Muhammad Al-Bagher (SAW) has been quoted as saying:

> *Some people came to Prophet Muhammad (peace be upon him) and said, "O' Messenger of Allah! Someone has been murdered in Johaynah." The Prophet immediately left his home for their mosque. Having heard about Prophet's arrival, the people gathered in the mosque. "Who has murdered this man?" the Prophet asked. They answered, "We do not know." "How surprising!" the Prophet stated. "A Muslim has been slaughtered in a Muslim community and nobody knows who his murderer is?! I swear to God Who has commissioned me as His prophet by truth, even if all the people on earth and heavens by their common consent participate in*

murdering a Muslim, they all shall be thrown into fire by their faces."[135]

This prophetic transmission reveals the true magnificence of human life indeed. Let us now pay more attention to this brilliant quotation from the Holy Prophet (PBUH) that reads, "If all people on earth and heavens (even being billions in number) by their common consent participate in murdering a Muslim, they all shall be sent to Hell." Thus conceived, the right to life is not merely a right in the current meaning of the term but an *"Ordinance"*.

What should be taken into prime consideration here is that right in this context has an imperative resonance; that is to say, the right to life is not merely a right in a purely natural sense, but it is essentially a normative concept belonging to the realm of *oughtness*. To this very reason, such basic concepts as life, dignity and freedom should be understood as divine ordinances rather than as rights that could be abrogated, curtailed or trespassed.

Human life as understood by Islam is a two-fold phenomenon that can once be conceived in relation to:

a) humanity and, from a different point of view,

b) it can be understood in relation to Divinity as well.

Life in Relation to Humanity

Life in relation to humanity is man's absolute desideratum in natural domains that he, like other animals, seeks to preserve it through his spontaneous forces and the free-will that distinguishes him from other creatures. Thus, every intelligent man surely deprives himself of one thing only for the sake of a higher profit – although this may be a spiritual ideal – or not to sustain a bigger loss. When we suppose that there is nothing called life, neither profit nor loss shall be at stake, since all profits and losses are bounded to life. What difference does it make for a dead fish on the shore whether you spray water onto it or not?! Therefore, life is neither conveyable nor eliminable. As we have mentioned earlier, life could only be exchanged by another eternal life through self-sacrificing for the Lord.

Life in Relation to Divinity

No mentally balanced, enlightened human being would doubt that God is the Absolute Owner of life and death.

> *I did not came here by myself so to leave it all alone*
> *Whoever brought me here shall lead me back to my home*

This is a self-evident truth that does not need to be demonstrated. However,

---

135 - Sheikh al-Horre al-Ameli, *Wasael al-Shi'ah*, Vol. 19, p. 9.

there are several thoughtful verses in the Holy Quran that remind the believers that the Lord is the one who gives life and takes it back; we shall now indicate hereunder some examples of them:

> *So when I have made him complete and breathed into him of my spirit, fall down making obeisance to him.*
> (The Rocky Tract 15:29)

This very theme has been presented on more than one occasion in the Holy Quran (i.e., The Prostration 32:9). Such verses are stating that human life has emanated from a divine source of being without being caused or mediated by any natural means.

By the same token, death – which signifies the separation of the soul from the body – is directly related with Divine Providence, although life and death appear to be two consecutive natural phenomena closely bounded to the eternal laws of nature. There are other verses in the Holy Quran that simultaneously ascribe life and death both to Divine Will, such as:

> *And He it is who has brought you to life, then He will cause you to die, then bring you to life (again); most surely man is ungrateful.*
> (The Pilgrimage 22:66)

> *And most surely we bring to life and cause to die.*
> (The Rocky Tract 15:23)

> *Allah takes the souls at the time of their death.*
> (Crowds 39:42)

Moreover, in some verses the angels are introduced as the agents of death, such as the following verse of the Holy Quran that reads:

> *Say: the angel of death who is given charge of you shall cause you to die ...*
> (The Prostration 32:11)

They are not surely in conflict with Divine Sovereignty as the Grim Reaper is merely a divinely commissioned agent to collect the souls when the people die, as some angels exercise Divine Will in the creation of human bodies and truly God is the Absolute Creator and other beings are merely mediators. Indeed, as the Holy Quran has stated:

> *He is Allah the creator, the maker, the fashioner; his are the most excellent names; whatever is in the heavens and the earth declares his glory; and he is the mighty, the wise.*
> (The Mustering 59:24)

The mediation of angels in human creation and death shows the value and magnificence of human life since they have no hand in the creation of *res congelatate* and *res vegetabilitas*.

Human Rights in Islam and the West in a Comparative Encounter 136

1 The Right to Righteous Life

Universal Human Rights in Islam

Article 1:

I)   Life is a God-given gift, and the right to life is guaranteed to every human being. It is the duty of individuals, societies, and states to protect this right from any violation, and it is prohibited to take away life except for a Shari'ah-prescribed reason.

II) It is forbidden to resort to such means that may result in the genocidal annihilation of humanity.

III) The preservation of human life throughout the term of time willed by God is a duty prescribed by Shari'ah.

IV) Those oppressed people whose life and dignity have been threatened by natural forces or by the oppressors shall be obligated to protect their life and dignity against the threats by any legal means possible. Anyone who does not stand up for the fulfillment of this obligation would have indeed helped natural forces and oppressors in weakening themselves and shall be among those whom, as the Holy Quran has stated:

---

136 - In this comparative study, the articles recommended and ratified in the Universal Declaration of Human Rights in Islam, issued by the Islamic Conference Organization in 1990 have been compared with the articles included in the Universal Declaration of Human Rights approved by the United Nations. The right concerned will first be studied as a whole. Then, the corresponding articles in the Islamic and Western declarations will be included and the common points existing between them will be discussed. Finally, the differences between the Universal Declaration of Human Rights in Islam and the West will be pointed out. The titles which constitute the basic rights in Islam, which also form human rights as seen in Islam, and the sequence for the discussions in this research is: a) the right to righteous life, b) the right to dignity, c) the right to education, d) the right to responsible freedom, and e) the right to equality in regard to laws.

> *The angels cause to die while they are unjust to their souls, they shall say: In what state were you? They shall say: We were weak in the earth. They shall say: Was not Allah's earth spacious so that you should have migrated therein? So these it is whose abode is Hell, and it is an evil resort.* (The Women 4:97)

Needless to say, migration is merely one of the means to drive away threats.

V) Abortion is forbidden except for a Shari'ah-prescribed reason. [137]

The UN Declaration

Article 3
Everyone has the right to life, liberty, and security of person.

Article 5
No one shall be subjected to torture or cruel, inhuman or degrading treatment or punishment.

Note: Whereas the articles of the Universal Declaration of Human Rights in Islam have been arranged in this book on the basis of the quintuple basic rights, and since no such arrangement has been made in the UN Declaration, we have to discuss the articles where we need to do so as the articles do not address the quintuple basic rights independently, like Article 3, which includes three basic rights of life, freedom and security of person. In such cases, we shall discuss the right that is at issue and the other rights stipulated in the article shall be relegated to their occasion.[138]

Shared Characteristics

1. Right to righteous life
2. Rights to freedom
3. Right to security

---

137 - The explanations and reasons underlying each of the articles and basic principles of these rights (the right to life, the right to education, the right to dignity, the right to committed freedom and the right to equality) have been fully dealt with in their corresponding sections. Therefore, we will not repeat them in our comparative studies here.

138 - The articles dealing with man's rights and freedoms in both legal systems – the Islamic point of view compiled at the Islamic Conference and that of the West – are, in regard to the basic principles of rights (the right to life, the ⇨ right to education, the right to dignity, the right to committed freedom and the right to equality) not so defined and clear-cut to be able to assign each article to a basic principle. Thus, in each case, we have analyzed each article considering the five principles mentioned above.

4. The prohibition of torture

5. The prohibition of cruel treatment or punishment

6. The prohibition of inhuman conducts (contempt)

All of these rights are agreed upon by both two Islamic and Western legal systems as basic natural rights of humanity.

Differences

1- The Islamic Declaration's Article 1, Clause I, declares life as a "God-given gift," while there is no such phrase in the UN Declaration. This silence about the origin of human life devalues the proclaimed rights for man or at least obscures them as the reader does not know who this man is. Needless to say, this obscurity certainly dismantles the stipulated rights in the Declaration or at least makes them impossible to be implemented.

    Although the first article in the UN Declaration reads, "All human beings are equally endowed with reason and conscience," and this may be somehow an indication to transcendental aspect of human nature and man's dependence on Divine God, this mere indication nonetheless could not demonstrate any value for humanity.

2- Although the Preamble to the UN Declaration has implicitly obligated the member states to observe and exercise the rights related to the basic right to life, whereas the member states have failed to reach common grounds in the management of their political, economical, religious, moral and cultural affairs, it thus seems almost impossible for these rights to someday find the true occasion to be observed and implemented. Consequently, it should be said that these rights will be implemented by the dominance of dominant powers for securing their interests.

3- In the second clause of Article 1 of the Islamic Declaration, it has been stipulated that "It is forbidden to resort to such means as may result in the genocidal annihilation of mankind" while there is no trace of such prohibition in the UN Declaration. It might be said that in the third article of the UN Declaration, it has been clearly stipulated that all human beings are equally entitled to have the right to life, and this is sufficient for the purpose mentioned above. To state the matter otherwise, when the article clearly stipulates the eligibility of all human beings to the right to life, it implicitly proclaims the prohibition of abrogation of this basic right. This is totally right, but *clarity* is essential in legal documents, and legal articles must be clearly stipulated so as to be safeguarded from misinterpretations and possible misuses.

4- In the third clause of Article 1, there is a remarkable issue: "The preservation of human life throughout time willed by God is a duty prescribed by Shari'ah". This duty does not mean that we need to know firstly the term time willed by God and then try to preserve human life; rather it means that not only is no one allowed to violate this divine right, but it is also the duty of all humans to preserve and safeguard it against possible harms.

This clause has stipulated obligations that reveal the immense significance of the right to life for all human beings. This can be explicated as follows:

a) Everyone is obliged to protect his life and no one is allowed to say, "This is my own life and I want to annihilate it!" Moreover, no one can decide to transfer it to others, sell it, or commit other misappropriations.

b) It is incumbent upon everyone whose life and dignity have fainted either by natural causes or by aggressive hunters of power to rise and re-colorize them with every legitimate means accessible. Anyone who does not perform this duty shall be regarded as an accomplice to the crime. Such a person will have thus committed a mortal sin, according to the verses of the Holy Quran. As we have seen earlier, these duties have not been stipulated in the UN Declaration.

5- The fifth clause reads, "Abortion is forbidden except for a Shari'ah-prescribed reason." This is among the clearest reasons of human inherent dignity, value and magnificence. This clause clearly shows Islam's sensitivity toward human rights in every stage of man's life. This basic and immensely significant right is absent in the UN Declaration.

The Islamic Declaration

Article 2 [139]

I)   Everyone shall have the right to live in a clean environment, away from vice and moral corruption, an environment that would foster his self-development and it is incumbent upon the State and society in general to afford that right.[140] Everyone shall have the right to medical and social care, and to all public amenities provided by society and the State within the limits of their available resources.

II) The State shall ensure the right of the individual to a decent living which will enable him to meet all is requirements and those of his dependents, including food, clothing, housing, education, medical care, and all other basic needs. [141]

---

139 - In the Cairo Conference, a clause was added to Article 2, stating that, "The health and soundness of the human body is a right that is non-violable; manipulating or distorting physical health is not advisable except for Shari'ah-prescribed cases. It had been said that this clause did not exist in the statement issued by the Tehran Conference, whereas it in fact did exist in Clause II of Article 2 as well as Article 4.

140 - We have brought this again as Clause IV of Article 6 in the Right to Dignity, since this clause is related with the basic right to dignity.

141 - This clause is analyzable as follows:

   I) The Right to Dignity (The state shall ensure the right of the individual to a decent

Note: Such social services and a decent life exclusively belong to those who that have not divested themselves of them by their free wills.

The UN Declaration

Article 25

Everyone has the right to a standard of living adequate for the health and well-being of himself and of his family, including food, clothing, housing and medical care and necessary social services, and the right to security in the event of unemployment, sickness, disability, widowhood, old age or other lack of livelihood in circumstances beyond his control.[142]

Shared Characteristics

 a) The right to health and clean environment
 b) The right to medical and social care
 c) The right to well-being and social services including food, clothing, housing and other necessary needs

Differences

1- In the Islamic Declaration, the state is obliged to afford these rights within the limits of its available resources. This applies to all human conditions such as unemployment, sickness, disability, widowhood, old age, and all other necessary requirements; while this generalization has been done in the UN Declaration in a very elaborate fashion. As a result, there is no major difference between the two Declarations on the rights at issue.[143]

2- The Islamic Declaration defines the ideal life regarding human dignity, which is a more general and universal concept than "well-being" that seems not to be achievable for all human societies. There are almost eight verses in the Holy Quran within which this concept has been reproved. However, we could say that "well-being" in this context means something

living which will enable him to meet all is requirements and those of his dependents).

 II) The Right to Life (food, clothing, housing, education, medical care).

 III) Other Rights (other basic needs).

142 - The second clause of this article shall be debated in Article 11.

143 - We suffice here to an example in order to demonstrate the universality of this right. In *Wasa'el al-Shi'ah* authored by Sheikh al-Horre al-Ameli, Book of Al-Jihad, Vol. 11, p. 49, it has been quoted from Tusi's *Al-Tahdhib*, that once a blind old man was begging. Imam Ali (PBUH) saw him and addressed the people around: "What is this?! Why is there begging in the Islamic community?" The people answered, "He is a Christian." The Imam stated, "You have been benefited from this man in his springtime, and now that he has become old, you have deprived him of his rights?! Pay him a pension from public treasury of Muslims."

like "comfort," that could be equivalent with dignity.

The Islamic Declaration

Article 3

In the eruption of war and case of armed conflict, it is not permissible to kill non-belligerents such as senior man, women, and children. The wounded and the sick shall have the right to medical treatment; moreover, prisoners of war shall have the right to be fed, sheltered and clothed. It is prohibited to mutilate dead bodies. It is prescribed to exchange prisoners of war and to arrange visits or reunions of the families separated by the circumstances of war.[144]

Critical Assessment

This article does not exist in the UN Declaration. As a result, it needs to be debated by Western scholars why this crucial article has sorely been neglected in the UN Declaration. It might be said that this article and other similar articles do belong to international conventions on war and peace. This answer does not seem to be right, since if such highly respected human rights, such as this one, are to be taken into earnest consideration in a document of such importance as the Declaration of Human Rights and to be demonstrated with logical reasons for nations and states, it could prevent possible violations to life and its dimensions; although these rights could also be debated in other legal conventions, they nonetheless need to be stipulated in the Universal Declaration of Human Rights, as they are closely related to human life.

---

144 - This clause as well as the second clause can be analyzed to:

I) - The Right to Life: (In the eruption of war and in case of armed conflict, it is not permissible to kill non-belligerents….)

II) - The right to Freedom: (It is a duty to exchange prisoners of war and to arrange visits or reunions of the families separated by the circumstances of war.)

III) The right to Life and its Derivatives: (It is prohibited to fell trees, to damage crops or livestock, and to destroy the enemy's civilian buildings and installations by shelling, blasting or any other means).

In the Cairo Declaration, "eruption of war" has been replaced by "the use of force". This replacement does not seem to be correct, since the use of force is conceptually more extensive than war and may not include the corresponding collateral damages.

The Cairo Declaration does also proclaim it a duty to exchange prisoners of war and to arrange visits or reunions of the families separated by the circumstances of war while the Tehran Charter had declared it a prescribed task. Since circumstances of war vary in prescriptive language, in this case it seems to be more intelligible than the imperative one. Prescription in this context is more consistent with the essentially context-bounded provisions of Islamic jurisprudence indeed.

The Islamic Declaration

Article 4:

It is not permitted without a legitimate reason to arrest an individual, or restrict his freedom, to exile or to punish him. It is not permitted to subject him to physical or psychological torture or any form of humiliation, cruelty or indignity. Nor is it permitted to subject an individual to medical or scientific experimentation without his consent or at the risk of his health or of his life[145]. Moreover, it is not permitted to promulgate emergency laws that would provide executive authority for such actions.

Note: This article is one of the highly respected human principles that originate in Islam. It can be analyzed as follows:

1- The Right to Freedom: (It is not permitted without a legitimate reason to arrest an individual, or restrict his freedom, to exile or to punish him). As we shall point out in our coming debates on the general principle of freedom, this general principle – regarding the intelligible interpretation that we shall provide for it – is indeed the primary and necessary prerequisite of an ideal life. Moreover, the prohibition of subjecting an individual to medical or scientific experimentation without his consent is closely related to the right to freedom. Of course, when these medical experimentations are being done for humane purposes with the consent of the individual, there is no objection, but if these experimentations are harmful to human beings, no one is allowed to endanger their life by such undertakings due to their right to freedom.

2- The Right to Life (It is not permitted to subject a man to physical or psychological torture). Although the right to physical and mental immunity from torture is not among direct prerequisites of the right to life, life nonetheless becomes painful and even unbearable with the absence of health, and then torture could be prohibited as something harmful to life.

3- The Right to Dignity (It is not permitted to subject a man to any form of humiliation, cruelty or indignity). As we shall say in our coming debates on the general principle of inherent dignity, the history of humanity has simultaneously been witnessing numerous bloody massacres and also millions of martyrs that sacrificed their lives in protection of human dignity.

---

145 - As stated in the Holy Quran, "And make not your own hands contribute to [your] destruction."(The Cow 2:195)

The UN Declaration

Article 5

No one shall be subjected to torture or cruel, inhuman or degrading treatment or punishment.

Article 9

No one shall be subjected to arbitrary arrest, detention or exile.

Article 11

(2) No one shall be held guilty of any penal offense on account of any act or omission which did not constitute a penal offense, under the national or international law, at the time when it was committed. Nor shall a heavier penalty be imposed than the one that was applicable at the time the penal offense was committed.

Article 14

Everyone has the right to seek and to enjoy in other countries asylum from persecution.

Shared Characteristics

1. The prohibition of arbitrary arrest
2. The prohibition of restricting one's "committed" freedom
3. The prohibition of exile
4. The prohibition of punishing someone without legitimate reasons and imposing heavier penalty than what was applicable at the time the penal offense was committed
5. The prohibition of physical and psychical torture
6. The prohibition of any form of humiliation, cruelty or indignity.

Differences

1- The fourth article of the Islamic Declaration clearly stipulates that "it is not permitted without a *legitimate reason* to arrest an individual, or restrict his freedom, to exile or to punish him;" there is no such stipulation in the UN Declaration, however. Nevertheless, since the articles stipulated in the UN Declaration are all subjected to the condition of consistency with the constitutions of member states, it could be seen as an implicit stipulation of the indispensability of legitimacy in such cases.

2- The articles in the UN Declaration that address the issue of freedom do not clearly stipulate its essential relation with *commitment* unless in cases in which other peoples' rights are at stake. In the Islamic Declaration, wherever human freedom is at issue as a right, it is always stipulated that it should not violate other people's rights and destroy the "intelligible life" that Islam has risen to make a reality. Thus, as it shall be articulated in coming debates on freedom, *freedom does always involve commitment.*

3- The UN Declaration has not addressed the highly significant issue of subjecting human individuals to medical experimentations; in the Islamic Declaration, on the other hand, since all human beings are thought to be in charge of their body and soul, such medical experimentations are forbidden unless they are

a) being done with the consent of the individual himself, and

b) without jeopardizing his life.

4- It has also been stipulated in defense of this fundamental right in the Islamic Declaration that, "Nor is it permitted to promulgate emergency laws that would provide executive authority for such actions." There is no such stipulation in the UN Declaration, which seems to be a fatal negligence.

It needs to be clarified that the prohibition of the promulgation of emergency laws that would provide executive authority for such actions is not an extension of secondary rules that are context-bounded and supposed to answer the social needs. However, the secondary rules are ultimately reducible to primary prescripts.

The Islamic Declaration

Article 5

Everyone shall have the right to live in a clean environment, whether in urban or rural districts, an environment that would foster his self-development and it is incumbent upon the State and society, in general, to afford that right.

Critical Assessment

It is most surprising that the UN Declaration lacks this crucial article that seems to be one of the most necessary dimensions of natural life. This terrible negligence appears to have originated out of the Western forgetfulness of the rights of the natural environment that has given rise to contemporary environmental crises that engulfed all human societies. This is the gravest shortcoming in the UN Declaration that needs to be addressed by the scholars the soonest.

2
The Principle of Human Dignity

The sun, the moon, the brilliant stars, with the same eyes they have seen millions of human beings die as victims of defending the human right to life, have also witnessed the broken cages of the bodies of millions of people martyred in defense of the human right to dignity.

The inherent human dignity is a divine bounty like "reason" and "conscience," which have been conferred upon humanity by God the Almighty. These divine bounties have such wonderful potentialities that could be actualized by the assistance of "free will" through evolutionary activities of the human self in the course of "intelligible life."

The Right to Human Dignity

To understand the right to human dignity, we will first need to outline – although in a nutshell – the terminological meaning of dignity. Regarding all of the different usages of the term, we could say that dignity in this context implies the quality of being cleaned out of all impurities and the peculiar honor and perfection that belongs to the one to whom the dignity is ascribed. Islam has proven two kinds of dignity for humanity as they are explained hereunder:

1- Inherent dignity as a natural mode that all people enjoy as long as they have not divested themselves of it by betraying or committing a crime against themselves or others.

2- Acquired dignity that is developed by putting the positive potentialities and forces of human nature into operation and competing in the course of growth, perfection, and pious deeds. This dignity is based on human free will and makes up the ultimate value of humanity indeed.

Inherent Dignity[146]

We shall begin with the inherent and spontaneous dignity that has been conferred upon humanity by God. There are several verses in the Holy Quran and prophetic transmissions that indicate this dignity. We shall now point out here a few *hadith* and verses of the Holy Quran that have been used by many scholars to demonstrate inherent human dignity:

---

146 - I have presented these debates in the form of a lecture at the international Conference on Human Rights held in the Tehran School of Law in 1980.

And surely we have honored the children of Adam, and we carry them in the land and the sea, and we have given them of the good things, and we have made them excel by an appropriate excellence over most of those whom we have created.

(The Night Journey 17:70)

This holy verse clearly demonstrates the inherent dignity that has been conferred by God upon human beings, the children of Adam, through which they are being distinguished from other creatures.

Accordingly, all human individuals are obliged to recognize and observe this primordial right of dignity. This inherent dignity and honor have its origin in the essential relation that man has with his Creator, as has been articulated in the following verse:

So when I have made him complete and breathed into him of my spirit, fall making obeisance to him.

(The Rocky Tract 15:29)

This verse reveals that human individuals, besides their right to life – which has to be observed – also have the right to inherent dignity, which could be enjoyed as long as they have not divested themselves of it by betraying or committing a crime against themselves or others.

All revealed religions and moral and legal schools unanimously take this inherent dignity as an inalienable right of humanity that must be observed by society and the state. Sadly, however, many contemporary legal systems – including the occidentally-motivated UN Declaration – have solely confined human dignity in his inherent dignity and do not speak of a higher dignity – that we call *acquired dignity*. As a result, they impede human movement in the course of intelligible life.

The idea that legal issues are totally unconnected with the realm of values is the very confusion that has given rise to the contemporary intellectual deadlock that is gradually uprooting human life from the earth. As stated by those vigilant scientists who have not been sedated by money, power or fame, "The have changed the Earth from an extremely beautiful planet in which human beings lived with desirable liveliness into a burning motor which is speeding toward the annihilation of human life at an amazingly immense rate."[147]

Acquired Dignity

There is a higher dignity in human beings besides their inherent dignity that is *achieved* based on an individual human commitment to divine ordinances. The following verse of the Holy Quran is among those verses that elaborate on the prerequisites of this very dignity:

---

147 - See *"The Declaration of the Conference on Survival in the 21st Century, Vancouver"* in this book.

> *O you men! Surely we have created you of a male and a female,*
> *and made you tribes and families that you may know each other;*
> *surely the most honorable of you with Allah is the one among you*
> *most careful (of his duty); surely Allah is knowing, aware.*

(The Chambers 49:13)

Thus, it is not so that human beings are eternally honorable creatures; however, this honor is something that could solely be achieved through the actualization of the positive potentialities and aptitudes inherent in human nature. As a result, those aggressive hunters of power that make everything a victim of their evil and egotistic purposes not only are not entitled to be benefited from the right to dignity and respect, but they must also be punished for violating other peoples' rights and ruining their lives.

It shall be of avail here to discuss a few quotations on the matter:

1- Muhammad Ibn Jafar Al-Oghba quotes Imam Ali (SAW) as saying in one of his sermons:

> *O' People! Verily Adam has not fathered you as bondmen and bondwomen. All people are free indeed, but God has assigned the affairs of some of you to be managed by others among you.*[148]

Not only has the quotation mentioned above clearly proclaimed the prohibition of slavery in Islam, but it has also demonstrated inherent human dignity by saying that all human beings are born free. Moreover, the Holy Quran reads:

> *Allah does not forbid you from respecting those who have not made war against you on account of your religion, and have not driven you forth from your homes, that you show them kindness and deal with them justly; surely Allah loves the doers of justice.*

(That to Be Examined 60:8)

2- Addressing Malek as the governor of Egypt, Imam Ali (SAW) writes in a state correspondence:

> *Inform your heart with the love, benevolence, and mercy to your people, and don't behave with them like a bloodsucking predator lying in ambush to hunt them, since they are from two groups: they are either your religious brothers or your fellow in kind.*[149]

It is obvious that no mercy and benevolence for people is higher than helping them reach their primordial and natural rights. Although some of them are incapable of putting their positive potentialities and aptitudes into operation, they are still human beings and need to be respected.

---

148 - Fayz Kashani, Mullah Mohsen, *Al-Wafy*, Vol. 14, p. 20.
149 - *Nahj ul-Balagha*, Letter 53.

3- Mohadeth Qomi quotes a transmission as follows:

> ***Hussein Ibn Khalid says, "I asked Imam Reza (SAW) one day, 'People quote the Holy Prophet Muhammad (peace be upon him) as saying that God has created man in His form. Is that correct?' Imam Reza (SAW) replied, 'Curse on them! They have deleted the opening words of transmission; [it is, in fact, as this:] The Holy Prophet was passing by when he saw two men cursing at each other. One of them told the other, 'May God make you ugly with all those who are in your form!' The Holy Prophet then said, 'Do not say that, for God has created all people in his form.'"***[150]

4- Imam Ali (SAW) wills to his sons not to mutilate Ibn Moljam and states:

> ***Never mutilate the murderer's body, since I heard from the Prophet Muhammad (SAW) that, "Beware not to mutilate, even may it be a rabid dog or a madman."***[151]

Mutilation means the amputation of parts of the human body before or after his death for disgracing him. This quotation from the Holy Prophet (PBUH) clearly shows the necessity of observance of human dignity both during man's lifetime and after his death.

5- Mosad Ibn Sedghah has quoted Imam Al-Sadegh (SAW) as saying:

> *Imam Ali (SAW) sent 900 kilos of palm dates to a man who was benevolent and never would ask anyone for help. Some told the Imam, "For God's sake! He did not ask you for anything, and you gave him 900 kilos of palm dates while 180 kilos would be enough for him!" The Imam stated, "May God never allow people like you to increase in number. I bestow, and you begrudge! I swear to God if I do not give him what he expects from me unless he asks me, for sure I have not given him anything without having already taken its price from him. That is to say; I have compelled him to sweat for it on his face that he puts it on the soil in his prayers for God."*[152]

Could one bring something clearer than this for demonstrating human dignity and honor?

Here we need to remind the reader that if we regard life as a merely natural, spontaneous phenomenon without a transcendental meaning, we shall achieve no success in demonstrating any right for life – let alone an inherent dignity that must be observed by all individuals.

Dignity: A Right Which Must Mutually Be Observed

It might be objected that the impossibility of this issue is so clear that it does

---

150 - Sheikh Abbas Qomi, *Safinat Al-Bihar*, Vol 2, p. 54-55.

151 - *Nahj ul-Balaghah*, Letter 47.

152 - Sheikh al-Horre al-Ameli, *Wasa'el Al-Shi'ah*, Vol 2, p. 118.

not need even to be addressed any more. As we have mentioned earlier, we need to take it into earnest account that this issue is not a simple question to be answered by a "yes" or a "no"; in fact, it has numerous dimensions that must be addressed independently. Although this question has been answered concisely in the course of our previous debates, it seems that we nevertheless need to readdress it here with all its specifics.

The in observance of other peoples' right to inherent dignity and honor is not the effect of a determinate cause; as a result, we need here to ask about the causes of humiliating and despising others:

1- If carelessness and indifference toward other peoples' right to dignity originate in egotism, selfishness, and indecency, these are indeed the qualities that make their owners even worse than quadrupeds; in fact, this has also been eloquently revealed through the glorious words of the Holy Quran:

> *And certainly we have created for Hell many of the jinn and the men; they have hearts with which they do not understand, and they have eyes with which they do not see, and they have ears with which they do not hear; they are as cattle, nay, they are in worse errors; these are the heedless ones.* (The Heights 7: 179)

2- If the in observance of other people's rights to dignity happens as an effect of simple ignorance toward the meaning of humanity and the existential dimensions and values which are the sources of human primordial dignity and honor (in the sense that he knows that he is ignorant of these fundamental dimensions of humanity), the agent is no longer obliged to commit himself to this duty, as knowledge is a necessary prerequisite of any obligation. Such ignorance seems, however, to be inconceivable in a cultured society with conscientious and intelligent citizens, since every conscientious and intelligent human being is well aware of the bitterness of humiliation. Nevertheless, such an ignorance of inherent human dignity does not divest the ignorant of their right to human dignity, unless they abuse this observance.

3- If this heedlessness toward human primordial right to dignity and honor has its origin in a *double* ignorance, then it would mean that one has lost one's way in knowing and evaluating human dignity and honor while having the belief that man is an egotist animal who utilizes his forces and natural dispositions only to satisfy his selfish desires, like Hobbes and Machiavelli!! Although double ignorance in this sense could also have been an effect of negligence like simple ignorance, such negligence is nonetheless only conceivable for shallow-minded people rather than for well-practiced intellectuals. It is, in fact, excessive egotism that gradually blinds the vision of these scholars. Having misinterpreted and undermined their dignity, honor and existential value, these thinkers proceed to generalize their blind misinterpretations of other people's.

Should we unjustly align these thinkers, who have led humanity to the swamp of self-alienation, with the shallow-minded simple?!

4- Mammonism in the sense of the greedy chase of wealth, office and fame seem to be the most pervasive cause of trampling peoples' dignity. In those societies, in which the upper hand has been given to technology, the workers and employees' rights to dignity are trespassed in broad daylight, and they are treated by their employers like a bright gorilla!! The employee's wage is usually settled to his satisfaction rather than according to the true value of his services, and this is an issue that has not seriously been addressed by any school of thought yet!

Today human lives do not listen to any principle or law insofar as the scholars of humanities within academia are dictated to write:

> *The most basic human derive in all dimensions of life is the libido (sexual instinct)!! And although its gratification in animals is conditioned upon a law, in human beings it should not be restricted by any conditions or law!! Also, everyone who challenges this theory is an anti-scientist!! Conscience does not have authenticity and is nothing but the commands and injunctions that are prescribed to man in his childhood and youth!! And everyone who challenges this theory is an anti-scientist!! All human ideas, discoveries, aesthetic, scientific, philosophical, political and literary sentiments along with all human mental projections, wills and imaginations are functions of conditioned mental processes!! And everyone who challenges this theory is an anti-scientist!! The world in its current state is the result of natural selection and survival of the fittest!! And everyone who challenges this theory is an anti-scientist!! All human intellectual and physical actions are based on utilitarianism!! And everyone who challenges this theory is an anti-scientist!! We need to resort to war or any unethical means to stave off the explosion of population as Malthus has suggested!! And everyone who challenges this theory is an anti-scientist!! Machiavellianism is the best political idea of all times!! And everyone who challenges this theory is an anti-scientist!!*

We know how many epics have been composed and how many bombastic and baseless claims have been made to justify the hegemony of these evil ideas within human academic sciences while the Universal Declaration of Human Rights is grounded upon human inherent dignity and honor!! Do contemporary thinkers not see this *paradox*? Or do they, in fact, see it, but since they are overwhelmed with the prevailing atmosphere, they pretend not to?!

The Hierarchy of Dignity

It would be nonsense to claim that all human beings are equally entitled to have the right to dignity. Is it intelligible indeed to think that Imam Ali (SAW) has an equal right to dignity to Ibn Moljam, the man who killed him? Which school of thought regards Moses, Jesus and Muhammad (peace be upon them) equally eligible regarding the right to dignity to Pharaohs, pagans and aggressive hunters of power?

It seems that every legal, cultural, political and moral thought that tries to align the enemies of truth and humanity with enlightened souls and minds by seeing them equally entitled to the right to dignity and honor shall dig under the foundations of human dignity and honor. The Holy Quran has strongly renounced such equality:

> *"Surely the most honorable of you with Allah is the one among you most careful (of his duty)."*

(The Chambers 49:13)

As we have mentioned earlier, according to reason, conscience, and authentic Islamic texts, human dignity is divided into two kinds: natural dignity and divine dignity.

1- The Natural or Primordial Dignity of Humanity: This kind of dignity is the divine bounty that has been conferred upon every human individual by God the Almighty. As we have mentioned previously, this is the very truth that has been revealed in the following verse of the Holy Quran:

> *And surely we have honored the children of Adam, and we carry them in the land and the sea, and we have given them of the good things, and we have made them excel by an appropriate excellence over most of those whom we have created.*

(The Night Journey 17: 70)

2- The Divine Dignity of Humanity: This kind of dignity is developed by putting the positive potentialities and forces of human nature into operation and competing in the course of growth, perfection, and pious deeds. This dignity is based on human free will and makes up the ultimate value of humanity indeed. This is the very *dignity* that the Lord has spoken of in the Holy Quran (The Dwellings 49:3).

It is needless to say that both of these dignities are hierarchical in their essence in the sense that human individuals enjoy different levels of dignity by their knowledge of the essential value and magnificence of humanity that plays an indispensable managerial role in human life in a meaningful world.

We shall now readdress here the previously discussed six groups of human beings[153] in the light of the twofold dignities:

I) Those human beings who have not been evolved on their characters and have no epistemic and moral qualities – but for what is necessary for living a merely natural life. This bunch of people could be appropriately classified as "Primitives."

---

153 - See the chapter entitled *"Divisions of Human Characters in The Universal Islamic Declaration of Human Rights"*, in this book.

The dignity of this group is demonstrated upon two frequently cited verses of the Holy Quran, i.e. "*And surely we have honored the children of Adam*" (The Night Journey 17:70) and "*Allah does not forbid you respecting those who have not made war against you*" (That to Be Examined 60:8), and also in Imam Ali's letter assigning Malek to govern Egypt, where he writes:

> *Inform your heart with the love, benevolence, and mercy to your people, and don't behave them like a bloodsucking predator lying in the ambush to hunt them, since they are from two groups: either your religious brother or your fellow in kind.*[154]

Moreover, another renowned quotation from the Holy Prophet Muhammad (PBUH) reads:

> *All people are members of Allah's family, and their most blessed one with the Lord is the one who is most beneficial for the members of Allah's family.*[155]

It is this very natural dignity according to which all people are equally entitled to be members of Divine Family.

II) Those human beings who have embarked upon the path of epistemic and moral evolution and achieved the needed qualities for entering the realm of social life and peaceful coexistence. These two groups enjoy natural dignity alike, although the second group, due to its partial readiness for peaceful coexistence, is more honorable. The reason for this existential excellence could be sought for in the following sentence from Imam Hussein's Ashura speech which reads:

> *If you are not religious and do not fear from the Day of Judgment, at least you can be liberal-minded [faithful to primordial features of humanity and principles of conscience].*[156]

Having said this, the Imam intends to remind the blind-hearted enemy about the necessity of the observance of commonly approved social conventions of time, one of which states that, "*In the event of the use of force and in case of armed conflict, it is not permissible to kill non-belligerents such as old men, women, and children*". Thus, Imam Hussein (PBUH) terms the observance of commonly approved social conventions of time as liberal-mindedness (*Al-hurriyyah*). It is needless to say that this grade of sociability is not achievable unless the man abandons his animal sensual desires. The more places man takes in the course of intellectual evolution, the more dignity man shall enjoy.

---

154 - *Nahj ul-Balagha*, Letter 53.
155 - Sheikh al-Horre al-Ameli, *Wasa'el Al-Shi'ah*, Vol. 6, p. 510.
156 - Abu Muhammad al-Hassan bin Ali bin al-Hussein bin Shu'ba al-Harrani, *Tohaf Al-Ughul ("The Masterpieces of the Mind")*, p. 114. (Originally in Arabic).

III) Those human beings who have gone ahead of the second group and recognized that this life and world could not be interpreted and justified without recourse to the world beyond it, while their mind and conscience order them to provide an intelligible interpretation and justification for this life and this world. To this very reason, they commit themselves to some duties to be able to be connected with the transcendent origin of existence. Despite their being unaware of prophetic teachings, these people excel over the two previously discussed groups as they have truly recognized that life and the human self-need to be interpreted and justified. This recognition, in turn, needs dispensing with sensual desires and carnal pleasures.

IV) Those human beings who, besides being intellectually committed persons in a sense mentioned above, also believe in one of the Abrahamic Religions such as Judaism, Christianity, Islam and Zoroastrianism[157], and are committed to their *Shari'ah*.

Needless to say, if this group were true disciples of their claimed faiths, they could enjoy more dignity than those of the three previous groups, since due to their allegiance to a school that is documented to divine revelation they are more ready to leap into the evolutionary course of perfection.

V) While believing in all previous Abrahamic Religions, Muslims have committed themselves to the religion that has been revealed to Muhammad, the son of Abdullah (PBUH). This religion, according to verses of the Holy Quran, is called Islam and is an expression of Abraham's Religion, which is the whole of Revealed Religions. Such a human being is in fact engaged in the belief of all prophets appointed by God and in the religion propagated by Noah, Abraham, Moses, Jesus and Muhammad ibn Abdullah (PBUH). As eloquently stated by the Holy Quran:

> *He has made plain to you of the religion what he enjoined upon Noah and that which we have revealed to you and that which we enjoined upon Ibrahim and Moses and Jesus that keep to obedience and be not divided therein; hard to the unbelievers is that which you call them to; Allah chooses for himself whom he pleases, and guides to Himself him who turns (to him), frequently.*
> (Consultation 42:13)

As everyone who truly believes either in Abraham, Moses or Jesus shall surely believe in Muhammad Ibn Abdullah (PBUH) and the fact that the Muslims' excellence in dignity and honor is the direct effect of his vigilance in resorting to reason, conscience, primordial nature and transcendent sensations to choose the soundest and the best values and ordinances. On human dignity, Imam Al-Sadegh (SAW) has been

---

157 - Providing this religion sees itself as an Abrahamic Religion.

quoted by Isaac Ibn Ammar as saying:

> *"O' Isaac! How do you pay your charity tax*[158]*?" "They [indigents] come to my house, and there I pay them my charity tax," I said. "O' Isaac! You have humiliated them by your task," the Imam stated. "Beware that verily God the Almighty says, 'Everyone who humiliates one of my friends has indeed declared war on me. '"* [159]

As we can see, acquired dignity is so magnificent that treating such a dignity with insolence is taken to be tantamount to declaring war upon God the Almighty.

VI) Those enlightened souls and minds that have to be conferred with eternal quality of *Taghva* (Piety)[160] which is insisted on in the following verse of the Holy Quran: *"Surely the most honorable of you with Allah is the one among you most careful (of his duty)"* (The Chambers 49:13). The highest degree of dignity belongs to this group of human beings.

The Pious

The pious are those who preserve their *essences* (self, ego, and character) from impurities and ruining factors and give the helm of their beings to the divine substance lied in their essences and made serious efforts to actualize their *selfhood*. Thus conceived, piety could be defined as *"self-preservation in the light of divine perfection."* Piety, as understood in this way, is achievable in all of the sextuple groups minus the first one in various degrees. That is to say, every human being in these five groups can enjoy piety through obtaining self-consciousness and harnessing their carnal desires. As a result, these five groups can enjoy divine dignity in various degrees.

The right to dignity, like other basic rights, is an "ordinance," not merely a right in its legal sense. As we have mentioned earlier in our debates on the right to life that this right is not a concession that could be conveyed or annulled, it is also the case with the right to dignity and other fundamental rights to education, freedom, and equality.

According to Islam, nobody is allowed to convey or annul what has been conferred upon him as a divine dignity by God the Almighty. For example, nobody could say that "I have conveyed my right to self-respect to such and such a person for such amount of money, or have annulled it, so now I do not have now any dignity, and everyone is allowed to humiliate me." As the defense of human dignity and honor is an obligation in Islam, in the same

---

158 - In Arabic, "Zakat" originally means the amount payable by a Muslim as part of his religious obligation (Translator).

159 - Majlesi, Muhammad Baqir, *Bihar Al-Anwar*, Vol. 20, p. 21.

160 - The spiritual quality which helps the believer to be spiritually and physically committed to his duties.

way, the guidance of someone who has supposedly turned his back to his primordial right to dignity is also prescribed.

> *"Nobody would treat with insolence toward other peoples' dignity unless having already lost their dignity."*

We need to pay serious attention to the point that a life without human dignity and honor not only is not a human life, but it is even lower than animal life, since it is obvious that a human being without dignity and honor could brutally violate and trample other peoples' dignities and honors for the gratification of his selfishness and carnal desires. On the other hand, the most predacious of beasts do not have the ability to harm human dignity; in the most, they may only cause damages to the human body when they are hungry or due to their brutal nature not in a hostile manner. In short, if one is well aware of the significance of human dignity and honor and enjoys this magnificent capital, one would never humiliate other people or treat them with insolence regarding their dignities and honors.

A Paradox Encountered

Every legal system that is to defend the freedom of expression and opinion needs to take this important point into serious consideration that absolute and unrestricted freedom of expression could lead to abuses of human dignities and other accepted and intelligible social premises. Since we do regard the freedom of expression, like other freedoms, only as highly relevant means for achieving the loftiest human ideals, freedom of expression – despite its vital significance for us – is therefore in our view conditioned upon it's not harmful to human dignity and honor. This is the view that Islam holds on freedom, i.e. the most significant divine bounty by which human being can reach perfections. Unfortunately, this is the very point on freedom of expression and opinion that has been sorely neglected in the UN Declaration on Human Rights. This legal system, that is in its compilers and writers' view the excellent product of ancient cultures and legal and political systems of the past, leads to a paradox which is indeed the result of binding all human beings to observe human inherent dignity on one hand, and insistence on the absolute freedom of expression and opinion on the other.

I have discussed this issue with many legal scholars – particularly with dozens of experts who were attending a conference on human rights held in the Philippines, including Paul Marx, a member of the UN Commission on Human Rights – but each time I heard the same stereotype answer, i.e. "human dignity must be observed." I hope the legal experts both in the East and the West will take this issue seriously and try to find a real solution for it. This paradox could be outlined as follows:

The UN Declaration has insisted, on several occasions, on the necessity of observance of human dignity:

1- The first paragraph of the Preamble, which elaborates on the motives of the codification of the Universal Human Rights, reads, "Whereas recognition of the inherent dignity and the equal and inalienable rights of all members of the human family is the foundation of freedom, justice, and peace in the world."

2- Article 1 reads, "All human beings are born free and equal in dignity and rights. They are endowed with reason and conscience and should act towards one another in a spirit of brotherhood."

3- Article 5 states that "No one shall be subjected to torture or cruel, inhuman or degrading treatment or punishment."

4- According to Article 12, "No one shall be subjected to arbitrary interference with his privacy, family, home or correspondence, nor to attacks upon his honor and reputation. Everyone has the right to the protection of the law against such interference or attacks."

5- Article 26, Clause 2 states that "Education shall be directed to the full development of the human personality and the strengthening of respect for human rights and fundamental freedoms. It shall promote understanding, tolerance, and friendship among all nations, racial or religious groups, and shall further the activities of the United Nations for the maintenance of peace."

These articles, along with the paragraphs of the Preamble, eloquently show that inherent human dignity is among the most basic of human rights stipulated in different ways and on several occasions due to its extreme significance. We shall now review the occasions in the UN Declaration wherein the freedom of expression and opinion have been declared as an extension of unalienable human rights in an absolute and unrestricted fashion.

Article 19 of the UN Declaration reads, *"Everyone has the right to freedom of opinion and expression; this right includes freedom to hold opinions without interference and to seek, receive and impart information and ideas through any media and regardless of frontiers."*

Now the question is that if the UN Declaration on Human Rights has declared human dignity as a basic right that must be observed by all human individuals, how can it regard unrestricted freedom of expression and opinion as a legitimate right that could be abused as an excuse to trespass other peoples' dignity and honor?! We need to ask where should those whose dignity and honor have been violated in the name of absolute freedom of expression and opinion seek justice?!

The impartial scientific and philosophical discussions of ideas are, of course, other issues and I do not think we could find someone who would declare them as an "insult."

The Islamic Declaration

Article 6

I) All human beings form one family whose members are united by submission to God and descent from Adam. All men are equal regarding basic human dignity and basic obligations and responsibilities, without any discrimination on the grounds of race, color, region, language, sex, religious belief, political affiliation, social status or other considerations. True faith is the guarantee for enhancing such dignity along the path to human perfection. No one shall be allowed to abrogate this inherent dignity from a human individual except due to a felony, treason, corruption or polytheism, since the one who associates aught with the Supreme Being – the source of all human values, goodness, and perfection – or deny his omnipresent existence, betrays himself. Moreover, if he is a socially influential figure, he would be betraying his society, and one who is disloyal to his society has surely abrogated his inherent dignity unless he is intellectually and conscientiously weakened.[161] Moreover, all human individuals are equally eligible to the primordial right of inherent dignity regardless of their political ties and social class.

II) The abrogation of one's right to inherent dignity due to the above-mentioned reasons shall not also abrogate his right to life until man has not faced his verdict issued by Islamic Shari'ah authorities; for instance, when someone commits murder, although he has himself abrogated his right to dignity by homicide – since by killing of a human being he has deprived someone of his basic right to life. However, the murderer's right to life is preserved before the execution of his verdict, and no one shall deprive him of food, housing, clothing, and medical treatment.

III) All human individuals are the members of Allah's family and their most blessed one with the Lord is the one who is most beneficial for the members of Allah's family. Verily, no one is superior to the other, unless upon *Divine Awe* (acquired existential nobility by being more committed to divine obligations) which all ideal human values are related to. Moreover, good opinions and acts in the quadruple relations (human relations with oneself, human relations with God, human relations with the world, and human relations with his fellow human beings) are guarantees for this existential nobility in the path of Intelligible Life.

---

161 - The intellectual and conscientious weakness of an average mind in understanding divine unity appears to be impossible, since human primordial nature is indeed in charge of understanding the divine unity of the Lord and it would hardly be contaminated to the degree that it might fail to touch this basic reality. Moreover, the essential baseness of felony and corruption in the human society is intuitively understood by enlightened conscience and common sense.

IV) Every human being has the right to live in a morally clean environment that would foster his self-development and it is incumbent upon the State and society, in general, to afford that right.

The UN Declaration

Preamble: Whereas recognition of the inherent dignity and the equal and inalienable rights of all members of the human family is the foundation of freedom, justice, and peace in the world,

Whereas disregard and contempt for human rights have resulted in barbarous acts which have outraged the conscience of humanity, and the advent of the world in which human beings shall enjoy freedom of speech and belief and freedom from fear and want has been proclaimed as the highest aspiration of the common people,

Whereas the peoples of the United Nations have in the Charter reaffirmed their faith in fundamental human rights in the dignity and worth of the human person and the equal rights of men and women, they have also determined to promote social progress and better standards of life in larger freedom.

Article 1

All human beings are born free and equal in dignity and rights. They are endowed with reason and conscience and should act towards one another in a spirit of brotherhood.

Article 5

No one shall be subjected to torture or cruel, inhuman or degrading treatment or punishment.

Article 12

No one shall be subjected to arbitrary interference with his privacy, family, home or correspondence, nor to attacks upon his honor and reputation. Everyone has the right to the protection of the law against such interference or attacks.

Article 25

Everyone has the right to a standard of living adequate for the health and well-being of himself and of his family, including food, clothing, housing and medical care and necessary social services, and the right to security in the event of unemployment, sickness, disability, widowhood, old age or other lack of livelihood in circumstances beyond his control.

Shared Characteristics

1- Safeguarding inherent dignity for all human individuals.
2- No human being shall be humiliated without reason.

3- inherent Human dignity has brought about particular rights and duties for human individuals.

4- All men are equal regarding basic human dignity and basic obligations and responsibilities, without any discrimination on the grounds of political affiliation and social status as long as they are not ruining inherent human dignity.

5- No one shall be subjected to torture or cruel, inhuman or degrading treatment or punishment.

6- No one shall be subjected to attacks upon his honor and reputation.

7- Everyone has the right to a standard of living adequate for the health and well-being of himself and of his family, including food, clothing, housing and medical care and necessary social services, and the right to security in the event of unemployment, sickness, disability, widowhood, old age or other lack of livelihood in circumstances beyond his control.

Differences

1- One of the most fundamental differences between the Islamic and the UN Declarations on Human dignity is their divide on making a distinction between inherent dignity and acquired dignity.

Note: In other words, the occidentally-oriented UN Declaration addresses issues such as dignity, honor, name and reputation in its preamble and articles without distinguishing the two kinds of dignity (primordial and divine).

It seems that this inattention to acquired dignity as such could be one of the highly significant reasons for the mental stagnation of human beings and their deprivation from intellectual and spiritual evolution. Acquired dignity, also termed as dignity based on divine values, consists of an excellent human quality that is *achieved* through the observance of one's own rights along with those of others and fulfillment of obligations and duties – not by virtue of individual material goals – but in the wake of a deep sensation rooted in human conscience that has been conferred upon human beings by God the Almighty as the primordial source of spiritual and intellectual evolution.

As we have mentioned earlier in our general discussions on "right to dignity," both kinds of dignity have been clearly elaborated in several verses of the Holy Quran. Inherent dignity has been eloquently articulated in the Holy Quran as, "*And surely we have honored the children of Adam*" (The Night Journey 17:70). This verse reveals that all human beings are entitled by their nature to be honored, and it is needless to say that this inherent dignity – despite its being the source of particular rights and obligations for human beings, however, according to particular moral and scientific reasons and revealed religions – could not be the source of human excellence and perfection alone, and requires continuous efforts to be made for self-purification and fulfilling social and individual obligations.[162]

2- Having taken the lead within academia, leviathanism has brought grievous havocs upon the pantheon of human sciences and made the understanding of inherent human dignity in academic terms impossible[163], while Islam views this inherent dignity as a divine bounty that has been conferred upon humanity by God the Almighty.

3- The right to inherent dignity is abrogated in such cases as homicide and treason, but this abrogation does not have any impact on the basic right to life.

4- The UN Declaration lacks a convincing reason to rationally demonstrate that all human individuals are the members of the same family. Islamic sources, on the other hand, resorting to the principles of primordialism and introduce human beings the members of a Divine Family:

All people are members of Allah's family, and their most blessed one with the Lord is the one who is most beneficial for the members of Allah's family.[164]

5- The Islamic Declaration clearly stipulates that "every human being has the right to live in a morally clean environment would foster his self-development and it is incumbent upon the State and society, in general, to afford that right;" on the other hand, there is no such moral concern in the UN Declaration. However, there are two cases in this declaration that are seemingly alluding to the so-called right to "moral becoming":

I) The second clause of Article 26 reads, "Education shall be directed to the full development of the human personality and the strengthening of respect for human rights and fundamental freedoms. It shall promote understanding, tolerance, and friendship among all nations, racial or religious groups, and shall further the activities of the United Nations for the maintenance of peace."

II) Article 29 reads, "In the exercise of his rights and freedoms, everyone shall be subject only to such limitations as are determined by law solely for the purpose of securing due recognition and respect for the rights and freedoms of others and of meeting the just requirements of morality, public order and the general welfare in a democratic society." Moreover, as previously mentioned, the second clause of Article 26 states that "Education shall be directed to the full development of the human personality."

---

162 - See the previous discussion on dignity.
163 - In other words, from an academic point of view, the capability to prove dignity for all human beings still does not exist, and Thomas Hobbes's leviathanism is still regarded as the base for the knowledge and the assessment of human beings in academic circles and universities all over the world.
164 - Muhammad Ibn Yaqoub Kulayni, *Usul al-Kafi*, Vol 2, pp. 6-7.

Regarding the contemporary situation of human sciences within academia – as we have elaborated on earlier – "the full development" in this context could not be understood as signifying moral development, since when we turn to academic textbooks on ethics, we see that they usually define morality as a set of rules of conduct that have been settled by the society and do not maintain any authenticity for it as it is not demonstrable upon the principles and foundations of *die Geisteswissenschaften der Gegenwart*. Moreover, regarding the culture of excessive hedonism and utilitarianism that is dominant today in the most Western and West officiated countries, "the full development" here could not have any meaning but the realization of all potentialities and conditions of merely natural life and not the intelligible life that has always been the ideal of all holy prophets, theosophers, moralists and true mystics.

In regard to the second clause of Article 29, on the other hand, we have to say that if the condition of "in a democratic society" had not been stipulated, it could be said that "meeting the just requirements of morality" in this context is a universal invitation toward highly respected principles of morality. But as we know, the just requirements of morality in Western countries today are the principles that secure individual freedoms and privacies from possible violations.

The Islamic Declaration

Article 7

I) The woman is equal to the man in human dignity, and has rights to enjoy as well as duties to perform; she has her civil entity and financial independence, and the right to retain her name and lineage.

II) The husband is responsible for the support and welfare of the family.

Article 10

I) The family is the foundation of society, and marriage is the basis of its formation. Men and women have the right to marriage, and no restrictions stemming from race, color or nationality shall prevent them from enjoying this right.

II) Society and the State shall remove all obstacles inhibiting marriage and shall facilitate the marital procedure. They shall ensure family protection and welfare.[165]

---

165 - Although this article shall be presented and discussed in its own appropriate place and in line with the sequence, it has also been included here due to its total relevance with Article 7.

The UN Declaration

Article 16

1- Men and women of full age, without any limitation due to race, nationality or religion, have the right to marry and to found a family. They are entitled to equal rights as to marriage, during the marriage and at its dissolution.

2- Marriage shall be entered into only with the free and full consent of the intending spouses.

3- The family is the natural and fundamental group unit of society and is entitled to protection by society and the State.

Two Significant Issues

We need to address here two highly significant issues before proceeding to our comparative remarks on these articles:

I) The statement that "the family is the natural and fundamental group unit of the society" is an undoubted fact as seen by fields such as ethnic-sociology, religion, psychology and other branches of human sciences. But if this fundamental fact of the family is documented to human whims and baseless ideas like other human affairs, it shall undergo serious changes in varying the situations of human life. As a matter of fact, nowadays we see that humanity has been reduced to animal lusts and carnal desires due to unrestricted freedoms propagated under the impulse of excessive utilitarianism and overindulgence in sexual desires by some uncommitted thinkers who are breaking the primordial principles of morality in the name of liberalism so as to prove themselves competent enough to be awarded prizes.

It was this very deviation from Divine Law that has finally dug up the foundations of the family in the contemporary age. These so-called proponents of liberalism are propagating with utmost impudence in such sexual deviations as individual freedoms that one would be ashamed of even mentioning their names.

The hegemony of these devilish views in the West is so clear that it does not seem to need to be demonstrated by extra reasons. What we are going to mention here is that an occidentally-motivated declaration on human rights cannot speak of the family as a fundamental group unit in society as almost all prevailed cultural symbols in Western countries, and sadly, even the semi-scientific works published in those countries, are undermining the building blocks of family.

II) The rights that have been stipulated in UN Declaration about family and woman are based on such freedoms that are neither natural nor logical, since firstly, if they were logical, the family in Western countries and those Eastern countries intoxicated by the West should not have been so disordered in this regrettable form that so many physical and mental disorders have been brought about – most grievous of all is the self-alienation that has engulfed all these countries. Secondly, the occidentally-oriented UN Declaration has not unfortunately distinguished between equity and justice in a clear fashion.

It is not logical indeed to divide humanity in two poles of male and female in the name of equality and reduce the woman down to a uterus and menstruation!! If Western culture, which is the main source of inspiration for the UN Declaration, does not accept the truth that "justice based on the rule of law and reality is better than baseless equality" and try to redress the mistakes made in the past, it shall not succeed in providing a defendable logic for justifying its statements on male and female freedoms.[166]

Shared Characteristics

1- The woman is equal to the man in human dignity, and has rights to enjoy as well as duties to perform.

---

166 - For more details on our views on these issues, see the eleventh volume 11 of M. T. Ja'fari, *A Translation and Interpretation of Nahj ul-Balaghah.* (Originally in Persian). We shall provide hereunder an outline of the topics discussed there that may assist the reader to easily find her/his needed materials:

- Male/female divide dilemma/ 240.

- Is there any remedy for the dilemma? / 248.

- Is woman dependent on man? / 252.

- Are women more persistent on their mistakes than men? / 255.

- The common views on the peculiarities of two sexes/ 259.

- Man and Woman: Two Perspectives on Life/ 262.

- The human identity of man and woman in Islam/ 265.

- The second dimension: man and woman as two pillars of family/ 267.

- The analysis and explication of: *"men are the protectors of women"* (4: 34)/ 270.

- The man led family and its relation with society/ 273.

- Three solutions for woman's violation from conjugal rights/ 277.

- Man's violation from conjugal rights/ 280.

- Should women call off their rights when the man violates conjugal rights? / 283.

- Is woman a farmland for man? / 284.

- The differences between men and women in three issues/ 286.

- Ado on Male and Female reasons/ 291.

- Male/female equality in practical reason/ 298.

- Evil/good woman dilemma/ 307.

2- Women have a civil entity as much as men do, and are equally entitled to enjoy all of the necessities of a decent life.

3- The woman is independent of her financial obligations, like the man.

Also, while this has not been stipulated in the UN Declaration, it is wholly by all Western legal trends.

4- Marriage shall be entered into only with the free and full consent of the intending spouses.

5- The family is the natural and fundamental group unit of society and is entitled to protection by society and the State.

Differences

1- In Islam, the man and the woman are both equally obliged to observe the condition of religion in their marriage in the sense that they are not allowed to marry non-Muslim women or men. The reason for this injunction is very clear since Islam is a primordial religion and everyone who has chosen it as their belief have in fact decided to allow their primordial nature to flourish and such a person cannot share his love with someone who does not believe in Islam.

On the other hand, since Islam regards religious life as the only *lebenform* that could be meaningfully interpreted, irreligious life in its view is thus not logical at all. Children are an indispensable part of marriage. There is no doubt that Islam, which sees this world as the passageway that brings us to the eternal life as the locus of perfection and peace, shall not allow its believers to live an animal-like, unrestricted and purposeless life and after a while to disappear into nothingness; consequently, it strongly orders believers to rear their children according to an orthodox set of beliefs for a human and divine life. Now, if one of the parents is not a Muslim, it shall result in many insoluble difficulties in child-rearing. This kind of marriages usually causes the children to live without religion – and, as we know, an irreligious life has no identity. Moreover, since parents are not able to reach a viable consensus on this matter, they always prefer pass by this vital issue in silence.

2- Whereas "men and women are entitled to equal rights as to marriage, during marriage and at its dissolution," the man is thus not obliged to pay alimony or dower to his wife, according to the UN Declaration, while Islam has assigned it to the woman – of course, not compulsorily – to manage the internal affairs of family by her treasury of purely human affections. It is for this very reason that Islam has obliged the man to pay his wife alimony and an intelligible amount of dower.

3- Whereas the UN Declaration has stipulated that "men and women are entitled to equal rights during marriage and at its dissolution," it becomes clear that it takes man and woman as equally entitled to the right to divorce.

Islam does not approach this issue with such simple-mindedness that the occidentally-oriented UN Declaration has shown in dealing with it since women are more sensitive toward marital problems due to their emotional nature and often apply for divorce without strong reasons. We will suffice here to a statistic printed in one of Iran's daily newspapers that read:

> About 90% of petitions for divorce in France in the year 1890 have been filed by women.[167]

Furthermore, children need to be reared right from their suckling period under their mothers, for hiring a babysitter or sending them to baby farms or nurseries could deprive them of human emotions and affections and cause them to be involved in nihilism and nothingness in their youth; as it has been claimed by some thinkers in the West, "These youths are only good for the army, not for human purposes".

Precisely speaking, this is the very point that has already been stipulated in the second clause of Article 25 of the UN Declaration, which reads "motherhood and childhood are entitled to special care and assistance." Islam assigns it firstly to the man to provide the needs and take care of the mother and her baby, and it is only when the father is disabled or the mother and baby are deprived of family care for any reason whatsoever that the society and the state are obliged to perform their duties. Therefore, the occidentally-motivated UN Declaration has to accept that beside their social and individual rights; human beings need to be protected in some ways.

4- There is an extremely significant issue that is always neglected by the West in cultural and legal debates, and that is the fact that young people, regardless of their higher education, are still unable to understand many of the colossal truths of life and distinguish between committed and uncommitted lives. The dominance of sexual desires in this season of human life even worsens the situation.

To state the matter differently, young people who decide to marry are naturally overwhelmed with their sexual instinct, and this overshadows other issues of life, and as the time goes by, the sexual desires leave the scene, and the overshadowed issues show themselves up. It is due to this very reason that Islam insists on the permission of parents of the maiden as the precondition for the marriage, since girls are not conscious of life affairs as much as boys, due to their sexual differences and religious considerations and thus are vulnerable and need to consult with their parents (or everyone who is her guardian) on the biggest decision of their lives. Nevertheless, the guardian must be a competent person; otherwise, it is incumbent upon the society and the state to decide on this immensely significant issue.[168]

---

167 - *Keyhan Newspaper*, No. 6627, September 7, 1965. (Originally in Persion).

168 - We know that issues such as the necessity of the guardian's permission for the

Explication: Many irrational attacks have been conducted against Islamic jurisprudence by uninformed persons under the plea stating why Islam has not declared these creatures as equal. As a general answer to this objection, we need to mention that the legal differences between the man and woman originate in their physical and psychological differences between the two sexes. According to the findings of scientific research done by distinguished researchers such as Professor Rigue on the physical and psychological differences existing between these two sexes, the belief in equality of man and woman is either for the chase of fame or because of ignorance to existential coordinates of these creatures. These physical and psychological differences between these two sexes occur on more than one hundred occasions.[169]

We need here to address an extremely significant issue that could serve as the thread of Ariadne in solving other intricate issues around the male/ female dilemma. It is this very issue that shows itself up in the law of retaliation, stating that if the murderer is a woman who has killed a man, she shall be retaliated on the condition that the avenger of blood not to accept the blood money and does not forgive the murderer. But if a man has murdered a woman, his retaliation shall be conditioned upon paying half

---

marriage of a maiden are not understandable for most Westerners as many social and cultural phenomena that are seen as regular by them are not fathomable for us as Muslims, such as:

I)   The relationship between a man and woman, one of the most sensitive and significant of human relationships, has to be within a legal framework; it is not at all like animals whose relations are only conditioned upon blind desires.

II)   In Islam, the human self has a divine aspect which is counted as the source of human inherent dignity. Therefore, for evolving this divine aspect, we ⇨ humans need not to overindulge with sexual desires in an unrestricted fashion.

III) Islam does not see the woman as the means of pleasure for man – although pleasure is naturally a necessary item in a successful sexual relationship – since in Islam man and woman are equally entitled to the right to inherent dignity, and no one is thus allowed to trespass this divine ordinance and describe a woman as a means of pleasure for man.

IV) Islam does not take it necessary to arouse sexual consciousness in the society by means of explicit materials and pornographies as it is done now in the West; however, it proclaims that we need to cultivate the spirits of human individuals and make them ready for an intelligible and meaningful life. The aggressive hunters of power do not want to confess that many brilliant minds, like Avicenna, Averroes, Razi, Al-Biruni, Rumi and Mulla Sadra, have been cultured in the past without sexual teachings. These aggressive hunters of power seem to claim that, "We have solved all problems and there is no pain needs to be redressed; we humans have studied learned our lessons of the book of existence!!" The reason for such claims could be sought for in such books as Alexis Carrel's *Man the Unknown* (1935).

169 - See, for instance, Motahhari, Morteza, *Women's Rights in Islam*, pp. 167-178.

of the murderer's blood money by the avengers of blood. It has been said that this is an explicitly unjust discrimination between the two sexes. This objection has a clear answer, as the necessity of paying half of the murderer's blood money is essentially an economic issue and does not have anything to do with the inherent dignity and sexual discrimination.

It is needless to say that the major burden of earning a living for the family is on the shoulders of man; thus, the absence of a man in a family could expose it to the bitterness of poverty. The absence of a woman in the family, on the other hand, although a dear emotional loss, will not have such grievous economic echoes. This is to say; this jurisprudential judgment is not an insult or discrimination about women's inherent dignity as a human being, but it shows that justice is the building block of Islamic jurisprudence.

The objection that "today women are participating in major economic activities shoulder to shoulder with men" and this jurisprudential judgment does not have occasion anymore, although seemingly attractive, it is not logical concerning the grievous havocs that have been brought upon families due to the participation of women in economic activities. Generally speaking, we need to either leave off the idea of fundamentality of the family in the human society – believing that man must gratify his sexual instinct at any price – or accept this as an indispensable reality that women should return to their homes and revive the lost warmth of their family.

Needless to say, this shall cause man and woman to have different rights and obligations without losing their inherent dignities since primordial human dignity is one thing and the principles governing the natural course of life is another.

The Islamic Declaration

Article 8

Just as in life, so also after death, the sanctity of a person's body shall be inviolable. It is the obligation of believers to see that a deceased person's body is handled with due solemnity.

The UN Declaration

Article 25

Everyone has the right to a standard of living adequate for the health and well-being of himself and of his family, including food, clothing, housing and medical care and necessary social services, and the right to security in the event of unemployment, sickness, disability, widowhood, old age or other lack of livelihood in circumstances beyond his control.

Shared Characteristics

Both declarations insist on the necessity of the observance of individual respect and honor.

Differences

The UN Declaration does not give any indication of the human right to dignity and honor after one's death, while the fortification of human dignity needs this inalienable right to be stipulated. Regarding this right along with the prohibition of abortion, we can demonstrate that Islam regards human beings entitled to the right to inherent dignity *from the cradle to the grave.*[170]

The Islamic Declaration

Article 9

I)   Everyone shall have the right to live in security for himself, his religion, his dependents, his honor and his property.

II) All monotheistic beliefs including Judaism, Christianity, Islam, Zoroastrianism and Sabaism shall be protected by the rule of law. Non-revealed beliefs[171] are, on the other hand, not eligible for this right.

III) Everyone shall have the right to privacy in the conduct of his private affairs, in his home, among his family, concerning his property and his relationships. It is not permitted to spy on him, to place him under surveillance or to besmirch his good name. The State shall protect him from arbitrary interference.

IV) A private residence is inviolable in all cases. It will not be entered without permission from its inhabitants or in any unlawful manner, nor shall it be demolished or confiscated and its dwellers evicted except upon Shari'ah-prescribed reasons.

Note: Whereas the exercise of the latter clause has been assigned to Shari'ah authorities, it is incumbent upon the Muslim Judge to decide with ultimate caution.

The UN Declaration

Article 3

Everyone has the right to life, liberty, and security of person.

---

170 - For a more detailed discussion on this issue, see the chapter entitled "*Righteous Life and the Foundations of Basic Rights*", in this book.

171 - Article 19 describes the non-revealed beliefs' position in the Muslim society.

Article 12

No one shall be subjected to arbitrary interference with his privacy, family, home or correspondence, nor to attacks upon his honor and reputation. Everyone has the right to the protection of the law against such interference or attacks.

Article 22

Everyone, as a member of society, has the right to social security and is entitled to realization, through national effort and international cooperation and by the organization and resources of each State, of the economic, social and cultural rights indispensable for his dignity and the free development of his personality.

Shared Characteristics

1- The right to security of person, honor, family and finance in national and international scales.

2- Everyone has the right to privacy in the conduct of his private affairs, in his home, among his family, concerning his property and his relationships.

3- No one is allowed to attack people's reputation and honor.

4- It is incumbent upon the society and state to protect individual privacies against possible transgressions.

5- A private residence is inviolable in all cases. It will not be entered without permission from its inhabitants or in any unlawful manner, nor shall it be demolished or confiscated and its dwellers evicted except upon Shari'ah-prescribed reasons.

Differences

1- The second clause of Article 9 of the Islamic Declaration restricts religious security to monotheistic beliefs that are documented in a revealed book. Regarding the sore fact that human history has witnessed numerous evil minds that have led humanity to the verge of destruction by way of religion – which is one of the extremely significant *existential* dimensions of humanity – this restriction seems to be wholly intelligible. Whereas Islam is a religion for all seasons of human life and has proposed a comprehensive program for all aspects and dimensions of *menschenleben*, it cannot reduce religion into a merely individual phenomenon that secures personal solace. It is due to this very reason that Islam does not accept religion as a truly revealed belief, but rather, according to reliable records of divine words substantiating the authenticity of that belief.

I wonder why Western thinkers, although having observed the objective consequences of the bitter absence of religion in social and individual lives, still do not want to take religion seriously as an identity-giving phenomenon and reveal its positive and effective sides to human societies. There is no reason for this inattention and hostility toward the deepest factor of self-growth but excessive utilitarianism and hedonism, and in general, the egotists that would not be tolerated by any divine religion. This is the very reason that not only has hindered the true recognition of divine religions, but has also succeeded in digging up the foundations of morality in human societies, and in doing so, has reduced the man to an unconscious machine, a plaything for the aggressive hunters of power.

2- The inviolability of private residences has been stipulated in the UN Declaration in an unconditional manner, while in the Islamic Declaration, this right is conditioned upon provisions of Shari'ah Law. The reason for this conditionality is clear, as a private residence could be used for socially and individually ruining inhuman and immoral purposes.

Generally speaking, since Islam simultaneously lays serious emphasis on both individual and social aspects of human existence, individual freedoms thus naturally need to be in line with the social value system.

3
The Principle of Education [172]

One of the most wonderful features of education is that not only does it have the ability to adjust and justify the inherited, natural, environmental, cultural and social factors for achieving the ideals of individual and social life, but also with enough consciousness, proficiency, and sincerity on behalf of the teacher and educator as well as the receptive character of the trainee, it could change a blood-sucker to a just and fair person within one day; on the contrary, under the same circumstances it is nonetheless also able to metamorphose a just person into a blood-sucker.

Introduction

Here we need to sketch a short introduction on the vital significance of education before turning to our comparative studies on the basic right of education:

There is no doubt that correct education is the most fundamental factor in legal reformation – even in the smallest of human communities – let alone in the legal reformation of all human societies, which is the aspiration of universal legal systems.

Precisely speaking, education is the necessary precondition for the recognition and implementation of basic rights of life, dignity, committed freedom and equality both in social and individual levels.

The Islamic Declaration

Article 11

I)   As of the moment of birth, every child has rights due from the parents, the society and the state to be accorded proper nursing, education, and material, hygienic and moral care. Both the fetus and the mother must be protected and accorded special care.

II) Parents and those in such like capacity have the right to choose the type of education they desire for their children, provided they take into consideration the interest and future of the children in accordance with ethical values and the principles of the Shari'ah.

---

172 - For further reading on the subject of education, see M. T. Ja'fari, *The Fundamentals of Education*. (Originally in Persian).

III) Both parents are entitled to certain rights regarding their children, and relatives are entitled to rights from their kin, by the tenets of the Shari'ah.

The UN Declaration

Article 25

2- Motherhood and childhood are entitled to special care and assistance. All children, whether born in or out of wedlock, shall enjoy the same social protection.[173]

Shared Characteristics

1- Both declarations are unanimous on the necessity of the observance of children's rights to proper nursing, education and material, hygienic and moral care. It could be said, indeed, that these rights are as fundamental as the right to life that is agreed upon by all nations and peoples around the globe.

Although the moral care of children has not been stipulated in the UN Declaration, regarding the emphasis that has been laid on the necessity of mental health of the society, we could say that both declarations are unanimous on this right.

2- Both the fetus and the mother are entitled to be protected and accorded by special care. Although the UN Declaration has not stipulated the right of fetus to protection, there is evidence in the document that endorses the indispensability of this right.

Differences

The second clause of Article 25 of the UN Declaration states that all children, whether born in or out of wedlock, shall enjoy the same social protection. But Islam has another view on these two groups of children.

Explication: Those children who are born out of wedlock shall enjoy the basic rights of life, dignity and committed freedom, according to Islamic jurisprudence, since they are not participants in the mortal crime that has been committed by their fathers and mothers. However, children born out of wedlock are not entitled to such positions of judgment, leadership and other higher vocations not because of their participation in a mortal sin but as a warning to those men and women who commit the evil act of adultery while they know that how odious is breaking the sanctity of a creature that has been honored by God the Almighty as her vicegerent on the earth. Do the

---

173 - The first clause of this article has already been discussed in our debates on the basic right of life. There are several themes in this article of the UN Declaration and Article 11 of the Islamic Declaration that are disconnected with the basic right to education that we shall, however, not debate on here.

uninformed UN authorities on human rights who have implicitly declared adultery as a legitimate act of their declaration, while all revealed religions have clearly prohibited it as a mortal sin that tramples primordial sanctity of humanity, not really know that by doing so they have made themselves and their so-called human rights the laughing stock of aggressive chasers of power, wealth, and fame? Will a day come when the egotist despots will allow humanity to be relieved from the paradox stating that, "the entering gate of life is open while its existing gate is closed"?

This paradox could be outlined as follows: all legal authorities and experts are unanimous in taking homicide as the ever-grievous crime that can be committed by a criminal. Moreover, this unanimity on the repulsiveness of homicide is also agreed upon by all revealed religion and human schools of thought throughout the history. Thus, the existing gate of life is a closed one to a man, and nobody is allowed to expel someone from life or even expose him to beating and foul language.

Revealed religions and all intellectual schools which are informed, whether consciously or unconsciously, have unanimously forbidden the illegitimate entrance to life, just like the prohibition of illegal existence of life and hold that this divine gate should not be taken as a plaything for the gratification of one's carnal desires. Do those straw thinkers who defend free sexual relations with a philosophical gesture and abuse the divine gate of life as a means for the gratification of their carnal desires while giving fervent speeches on the prohibition of homicide not understand the paradox that has engulfed them? Is this not a direct and plain paradox? And does this paradox not demonstrate the groundlessness of legal, moral and political cultures of human societies? Verily, a culture that is not able to answer this straight paradox is baseless and doomed to disappearance. This is why Islam has deprived the children who are born out of wedlock from some social rights so as to reveal the true repulsiveness of adultery that is the root cause of modern nihilism.

The Islamic Declaration

Article 12

I) The question for knowledge is an obligation, and the provision of education is a duty of society and the State. The State shall ensure the availability of ways and means to acquire education and shall guarantee educational diversity in the interest of the society so as to enable man to be acquainted with the religion of Islam and the facts of the Universe for the benefit of humanity. This right is called "the right to intellectual enlightenment."

II) Every human being has the right to receive both religious and worldly education from various institutions offering education and guidance, including the family, the school, the university, the media, etc., and in such an integrated and balanced manner as to develop his personality, strengthen his faith in God and promote his respect for and his defense of both rights and obligations. This right is called is called "the right to educational enlightenment".

Article 13

I)   Everyone shall have the right to advocate what is right, and propagate what is good, and warn against what is wrong and evil, whether individually or collectively, according to the norms of Islamic Shari'ah. This duty is obligatory upon everyone who has capability and sufficient rational reasons for his own success, including the state and the society. The state is more obligated toward this duty, since it has much more capability. Every human being can cooperate with other individuals and groups in implementing this right, and all of these rights and duties must be carried into execution according to Islamic Shari'ah laws; furthermore, the state and society are obligated to make the ground ready for implementation of these rights and duties."

II)   Information is a vital necessity to society. It may not be exploited or misused in such a way that it may violate sanctities and the dignity of Prophets, undermine moral and ethical values or disintegrate, corrupt or harm society or weaken its faith.

III) It is not permitted to arouse nationalistic or doctrinal hatred or to do anything that may be an incitement to any form or racial discrimination.[174]

The second clause of Article 23 of the Tehran Charter states, "Everyone shall have the right to advocate what is right, and propagate what is good, and warn against what is wrong and evil, whether individually or collectively, according to the norms of Islamic Shari'ah and it is incumbent upon the state and society to afford these rights and duties."

This clause in the Cairo Declaration has been grievously modified; it reads, "Everyone shall have the right to advocate what is right, and propagate what is good, and warn against what is wrong and evil, whether individually or collectively, according to the norms of Islamic Shari'ah." Unfortunately, this immensely significant Islamic duty has sorely been underestimated by removing the words that articulate indispensable roles of the state and society in fulfilling this duty.

The UN Declaration

Article 26

1- Everyone has the right to education. Education shall be free, at least in

---

174 - As the first clause of this article was more relevant with the right to committed freedom, we moved it to its appropriate place.

the elementary and fundamental stages. Elementary education shall be compulsory. Technical and professional education shall be made generally available and higher education shall be equally accessible to all on the basis of merit.

2- Education shall be directed to the full development of the human personality and to the strengthening of respect for human rights and fundamental freedoms. It shall promote understanding, tolerance and friendship among all nations, racial or religious groups, and shall further the activities of the United Nations for the maintenance of peace.

3- Parents have a prior right to choose the kind of education that shall be given to their children.

Shared Characteristics

1- The general principle of education as an inalienable human right is agreed upon by both declarations.

2- Education needs to be directed to achieve the full development of the human personality according to both declarations, although they have different conceptions of human development.

3- Education should promote the highest moral ideals of humanity that Islam introduces as the building blocks of intelligible life, and the UN Declaration takes them as the embodiment of aspirations reflected in human basic rights.

4- Parents have a prior right to choose the kind of education their children will have. Nevertheless, this right is conditioned upon religious and moral observations.

5- Every human being is entitled to receive such an education that prepares him/her for a decent life.

Differences

1- Islam declares education as a duty that needs to be undertaken by everyone who has the ability to take it up. This is a colossal comparative advantage for the Islamic educational system, while the UN Declaration only insists on the general accessibility of elementary education. It should be said that since Islam invites all human beings to a righteous life, and such a life needs necessary epistemic preparations. As a result, education is taken to be an obligation for everyone who is to enjoy dignity and honor.

2- The parents' right to decide the kind of education of their children will have is conditioned upon the chosen educational system's consistency with moral values and primordial principles and provisions of Islam, while there is no such condition in the occidentally-motivated UN Declaration. It might be said that the UN Declaration has sufficed here to an outline of this right and did not articulate the details, but as we know, the more articulated articles are, the better they shall be understood.

3- If a child has lost his parents, his guardian chosen according to provisions of Islamic Shari'ah Law shall decide the kind of education. This has not been stipulated, however, in the UN Declaration. The comparative advantage of this principle is that it reveals the interconnection of relatives as the boughs of *primordial tree of life* that could fill the gaps between human beings and cure the pernicious malady of this century, i.e. the estrangement human individuals suffer from in regard to each other.

4- The priority of *spiritual enlightenment* in education distinguishes the Islamic Declaration from the UN Declaration in a very decisive manner. As we have mentioned earlier, every attempt for the articulation of basic human rights without taking spiritual values into prime consideration shall result in a mechanistic life.

5- The propagation of moral goods and prevention from evils is among the brightest points in the Islamic Declaration that has sorely been neglected in then occidentally-oriented UN Declaration.

6- The vitality of information has clearly been stipulated in the Islamic Declaration, as mass media today cover large numbers of peoples around the world and form the public opinions on various issues. It is due to this very reason that Islam insists that it is an urgent need to make sure that these instruments of mass communications are not managed by aggressive hunters of power who make everything the victims of their greed and carnal desires.

4
The Principle of Committed Freedom

The Lord has created the human being for spiritual and intellectual evolution, and this would not be possible unless man harnesses his animal self, the underlying characteristic of which is egotism, so as to make room for fulfilling this divine task. Otherwise, man shall be a slave of his passions and carnal desires forever.

Intellectual and spiritual evolution is then the *Ultimate Telos* of human life, and this Telos could not be achieved but through true freedom of the human self.

The one who has declared freedom his own ideal in life and says that, "I am ready to sacrifice my life for your freedom of expression although I would be against your opinions!!"[175] has neither understood the meaning of freedom nor the meaning of life; furthermore, has he also been unable to distinguish between the means and the goal.

Freedom Its Various Kinds and the Meaning of Liberty

O freedom, whose word is the happiest of words and whose meaning is the most miserable of meanings! O freedom, what heavy chains have captivated man in your name!

We need to start our discussion on the basic right of freedom by asking a fundamental question in the spirit of our previous debates on basic rights to life and dignity, i.e. what is freedom?

To this day, many theories have been proposed of the nature of freedom, some of which only express elementary conceptual understandings of the nature of freedom, and some others approach its truth. For example, some have stated that "Freedom is my ability to choose or not to choose this task."

It is obviously needless to say that this is a naïve and shallow sensation of freedom that is not able to give an intelligible interpretation of the graded reality of freedom.

Scholars do not usually distinguish between these three stages of "emancipation," "freedom" and "liberty," which is a must for a complete understanding of the nature of freedom. I have previously discussed these

---

175 - This is allegedly ascribed to Voltaire, eighteenth century French writer and philosopher.

three stages of freedom in other works of mine,[176] and here I will suffice to give an outline of these concepts:

1- **Emancipation** involves deliverance from all bondages that block human beings on their road to development, whether these bondages are physical or psychological, obligatory or contractual. For instance, when a person kept captive in a room takes a sigh of relief on his release, his physical captivity was the major concern for him. Similarly, another person, who owes somebody something like debt, feels released from the obligation of full payment. Similar feelings are observed on release from mental tensions and anxieties.

In brief, emancipation involves the removal of confinements from the path toward the free flow of will in a relative fashion. Thus, no form of emancipation can provide an explanation for what the situation will be once confinements have been removed, however.

2- **Freedom:** We need here to distinguish between two significant degrees of freedom:

A) Purely Natural Freedom: Apart from being released from bondages, a person is free to choose his way to act regardless of the point whether the way chosen by him is good or bad, magnificent or despicable, ugly or beautiful. Here, individuals have a better sense of independence and upholding selfhood than in the stage of emancipation, but it cannot be estimated whether the freedom earned will realize best of objectives. There is always a chance that the glorious freedom attained might be spoiled by unrestrained behaviors or will be ruined by a poor choice.

B) Escalated Freedom involves the comprehensive knowledge of the self of both positive and negative outcomes of a choice which assists the subject to enjoy more freedom and its benefits. The greater the supervision and control exercised by the character upon the action, the more freedom man will enjoy in it. It is clearly in this state of supervision that man selects objectives and means from among countless realities and activates them, thus exercising his will in the realization of the objective or means he has selected. Needless to say, this stage of freedom is very different from emancipation, as the human self and his knowledge of the positive and negative consequences of his choice play a major role here.

3- **Liberty** consists of the comprehensive knowledge of the self of both positive and negative outcomes of a choice and using freedom to reach goodness and development and avoiding loss and failure.

The Differences between Freedom and Liberty

I) Liberty is distinguished from freedom by having goodness

176 -See, for instance, Ja'fari, M. T, (2011): *Intelligible Life*, translated by Beytollah Naderlew, pp. 103-106.

(righteousness) as its ultimate goal. Precisely speaking, liberty consists of justifying freedom and applying it in a righteous act that aims at a good purpose.

II) Freedom, which consists of comprehensive knowledge of the self of both positive and negative outcomes of a choice, is pleasant in itself since the sense of freedom is always an effect of two desirable issues. Firstly, it involves the deliverance of human liberty from all bondages. Secondly, it involves feeling that one can choose one's means and goals among numerous existed realities, and this sense is similar to the sense of life, which causes the most pleasant mental state in human beings. This is why we believe that *freedom makes life whole*. While liberty not only does not seek pleasure in natural life, since it aims at righteousness and is associated with a sense of duty, it would nonetheless prove to be even tiresome and annoying. Verily, fulfilling a duty for the sake of goodness without thinking about personal interests causes an intelligible pleasure that is not comparable with natural pleasures at all. This pleasure is not even significant for those enlightened spirits and minds that have achieved to the divine position of **union with reality**.

III) A human being who can do a righteous act or righteously deprive himself of something for a good purpose will surely act within the borders of highly respected values of humanity; on the other hand, if someone does an act or avoids something with based on their pure freedom, they will have only a natural advantage.[177]

The Right to Freedom versus the Right to Liberty

Freedom, whether in its natural or escalated sense, could be one of the magnificent means for man's spiritual and intellectual aspects only if we take the two conditions that we will elaborate on hereunder into serious consideration. Nevertheless, escalated freedom naturally excels over natural freedom.

The First Condition: Freedom both in natural and escalated forms should not block human movement toward liberty and evolutionary "becoming"; that is to say, the pleasant sense of freedom must not shut our eyes to the philosophy of our existence and neglect our duties and goods in

177 - These discussions show in a very clear fashion that the theory that is supported by some Westerners and states that, "the human right to freedom is not founded upon human unities; in fact, it is essentially based on human divides" is grounded on natural freedom, since it is this kind of freedom that brings about human conflicts. In other words, it is freedom in this sense that leads to clashes between human beings and makes people trespass other peoples' rights; in scientific parlance, this is the very kind of freedom that has its *privatio* in itself. Thus, the right to freedom understood according to human natural freedom results in human conflictions and has immense distance from liberty as the source of human unions.

the course of intelligible life.

The Second Condition: Freedom in all degrees should not violate other peoples' natural and escalated freedoms and liberty. Every human being is obliged to make sincere efforts, informed by their knowledge of the indispensable role of freedom in human spiritual and intellectual evolution, for pushing freedom toward its higher stage of escalated freedom and then tiling the way for liberty which could be termed as intelligible freedom in the course of intelligible life.

Regarding our elaborations on "freedom" and "liberty," it seems doubtless that every human being could enjoy freedom and liberty in their highest degrees by means of observing the two conditions mentioned above, and this right, like the right to life and dignity, is a divine bounty that has been conferred upon humanity by God the Almighty. Therefore, straightforwardly speaking, violating the basic rights of life, dignity and freedom are declaring war against Divine Will.

Here, once again we must emphasize this significant issue that if someone abuses human life and dignity to undermine other peoples' life and dignity, one has no longer any right to life and dignity; this is the case when someone misuses freedom to transgress the boundaries of intelligible life.

The Right to Liberty

The right to liberty not only is an irremovable right in the perspective of all divine schools and revealed religions that take freedom as an indispensable precondition of human spiritual and intellectual development, but it is also the main goal of these divine schools and revealed religions to prepare humanity for the exercise of liberty that could lead human beings to an intelligible life with a righteous orientation.

The Right to Freedom in Islam

The right to freedom in Islam could be debated under the following quintuple categories:

1- Freedom of belief

2- Freedom of opinion

3- Freedom of expression and speech

4- Freedom of action

5- Freedom or deliverance from bondages and slaveries

1- Freedom of Belief

The study on this freedom will be carried out in three dimensions:

The First Dimension: The principle of belief, i.e. are human beings free in choosing either a life devoted to a belief or a life void of any belief? In other words, does man have the right to be free in choosing either to live a life devoted to a belief or to live a belief-free life?

It is impossible for human beings to live a belief-free life, as belief in this context means providing an interpretation of "being," and every mentally balanced man willy-nilly has his *attitude* at least in regard to natural life in the sense that either he finds it as desirable or he does not find it in tune with his individual ideals. Even if someone thinks that he is living a belief-free life in this world, he has for sure a reason for his claim and this very reason is itself a belief.

Concisely speaking, since man is not able to prove the necessity and adequacy of general principles of his life, he needs to view them as matters of belief.

The Second Dimension: Are human beings free to spend and wear out their lives in leaving old beliefs and taking new ones? Although this question may, at first sight, seem irrelevant – as the generality of people always lives their life with an irremovable set of beliefs without even reshuffling them, let alone replace them with new ones – it nonetheless seems not to have missed the mark with regard to the possible intellectual and spiritual changes occurring in human beings; if these changes take place in the wake of superior truths, then they will signal spiritual evolution in human beings. However, although the fundamental beliefs that settle human beings in the path of "intelligible life" should be continuously evaluated with sound rationalizations, they are in fact not provisional in their essence.

The Third Dimension: This dimension concerns truths that are chosen as the subjects of belief, and are related to five general categories:

The First Category: This category concerns those truths that reveal parts of the world "as they are." There is a primordial reality of the whole parts of the natural world that is irremovably certain forever. This general truth is that the whole parts of this world are governed by a set of unchanging laws; that is to say, everything in this world functions according to some unexceptionable laws, since it is real and something that is real acts according to a law that reveals itself in an interaction with other realities. There are different opinions on the source of this natural lawfulness. The theory that seems to be less problematic and more explicative to us states that the law is a general theorem that is abstracted according to the *divine order* that governs the whole parts of the world in totality.

The truths that are revealed by these scientific realities are naturally relative due to the epistemic limitations of human empirical knowledge and the essential relativity of scientific experimentations, and this is why science never could claim to have said the last word on something, while the belief does require its believer to submerge himself in it insofar as to see and interpret everything in its light *alone*.

On the other hand, scientific knowledge, regardless of its degree of certainty, is always liable to change with regard to the possible new discoveries on the same subject; and this liability renders it impossible to be a belief. Thus conceived, it does not seem not to be an exact usage of the term to apply "belief" to a scientific knowledge that reveals truths of parts of the world "as they are". As a result, freedom of belief in regard to the "*isness*" of whole parts of the world is totally logical.

The Second Category: pertains to the truths of the world as a whole. These truths reveal the world in its totality as the locus of a creature that has been created to take part in a cosmic movement toward Supreme Perfection. However, even this knowledge of the world as a whole is also liable to change and renewal.

The Third Category: This category concerns truths of human beings "as they are". This category is divided into two basic domains:

1- The domain of the material parts of human beings, within which renewal of belief not only is not interdicted but is in fact among the most significant factors of scientific development from these parts. The massive body of published works on the material dimensions of human existence is itself telling of the necessity of epistemic renewal in this field of human knowledge, as the subject is itself an ever-changing matter. Thus, freedom of belief or freedom of scientific renewal on material dimensions of human beings is a secured right in every human society.

An Outline of Beliefs

I) The scientific and philosophical reasons and also the primordial sensations displayed and expressed by human beings demonstrate the existence of God and also God's essential relation with the world and human beings. The controversies denying this evident existence are either professional verbosities or reflections of egotisms and crude emulations and the baseless belief that, "If there is a God, why has he not created the world in my desired form!" Theism could only provide the most logical and convincing answers for ontological problematics. Without believing in the One Almighty God, no one would be able to justify Creation. Without belief in God, no purpose or philosophy would be conceivable for human beings' worldly life and their system of values and virtues. It was for this very reason that during the long course of history, humanity not only could not dispense with this original sensation, but has even resorted to colossal scientific developments so as to provide more viable reason for divine existence. This is what is it called monotheism – i.e., the belief in the one and only God the Almighty.

II and III) The long course of human history shows that humanity has not succeeded in reaching happiness without the assistance of holy prophets and their true vicegerents. This is an undeniable fact that human beings, despite their epoch-making scientific breakthroughs, have not succeeded in tasting true happiness, and instead of healing a pain they have in fact added to the pain. This is not something that could be covered up with verbal consolations. This deep-rooted belief represents the principle of prophecy and Imamate.

IV) The following line by Naser Khusraw, the renowned eleventh-century Iranian poet, makes the reader free from the pursuit of extra reasons for the demonstration of the belief in "resurrection":

This world, the sky and stars are thoroughly in vain
If this long worldly day does not have a tomorrow…

If one believes that the universe and all of its particles does not originate from a supreme order and is merely a plaything, such a person has in fact fallen into a conflict with his own reason and senses; we have nothing to say to such a person, except for suggesting that he might cure his disease of self-conflict and then delve into supernatural issues. Every mentally balanced human being who takes serious the brilliant divine order reflected in whole parts of universe in its totality shall also believe in the reality of resurrection and the Day of Judgment.

V) The belief in a God Who is simultaneously both omniscient and omnipotent requires one to believe in theodicy, the belief that the Lord always acts upon divine principles of wisdom and justice.

Nevertheless, these primordial principles require continuous reevaluations and interpretations in new lights so as their ever-renewing dimensions may find the opportunity to show themselves. The necessity of such new visions of primordial truths could be better understood in the context of the following quotation from the Holy Prophet (PBUH) that reads:

The paths toward God are as many as the individuals.[178]

The following verse of the Holy Quran eloquently demonstrates the necessity of eternal quest for divine signs reflected in the world:

Say: if the sea were ink for the words of my Lord, the sea would surely be consumed before the words of my Lord are exhausted, though we were to bring the like of that (sea) to add.
(The Cave 18:109)

---

178 - Majlesi, Muhammad Baqir, *Bihar al-Anwar*, Vol. 94, p. 111.

Also, another holy verse in the same spirit reads:

> ***And were every tree that is in the earth (made into) pens and the sea (to supply it with ink), with seven more seas to increase it, the words of Allah would not come to an end; surely Allah is mighty, wise.***   (Luqman 31:27)

The necessity of this unending quest for the knowledge of divine signs has also inspired many great poets, as reflected in the following poems:

> *The services of your throne inhabit in a new world in every moment,*
>
> *the wayfarers of the path of your love experience new moments in new worlds* (Khajouye Kermani)
>
> *Every time I take a look at Him,*
>
> *a more glorious and beautiful face than before will I see…*
>
> *I detest this outdated and old god you have,*
>
> *for my God is new and fresh every moment…*

Needless to say, this eternal quest for new visions of divine realities does not necessarily imply the continuous renewal of Divine Essence as it is beyond all changes and movements; nevertheless, it signifies the unending treasury of meanings indwelling in divine words and signs waiting there to be unearthed by new visions. Obviously, an increase in the knowledge of divine words and signs could result in the escalation and intelligent of beliefs and take them nearer to realities.

2- The domain of the immaterial forces, dispositions and activities of humanity. In this domain, there are subjects that are necessary to be believed in, such as:

> ➤ Belief in the authority of common sense,
>
> ➤ Belief in the purity of moral conscience – which is the basic human propellant for fulfilling man's duties (without expecting any reward),
>
> ➤ Belief in the primordial nature that could be used along with common sense and moral conscience as steps to ascend to higher levels of intellectual and spiritual evolution and perfection; as in the cases of the two forces mentioned above, they are either strengthened and put to use – which will lead to man's development and perfection – or they will be suppressed and ruined.
>
> ➤ Belief in the existence of the "self," which – if in line with sound reason and moral conscience – will guide man toward perfection and development.
>
> ➤ Firm belief in the Holy Quran's statement, "***Surely we are Allah's and to him we shall surely return***" (The Cow 2:156) as the true answer to the quadruple existential questions of: Who am I? Whence have

I come? Whither will I return? Why have I come? These beliefs, which happen to be the most natural form of beliefs which cannot be subject to any other kind of change, are also, however, open to new visions and fresh understandings.

The Fourth Category: This category concerns truths of the totality of human existence "as it is." Man is a progressive and evolutionary being who is able to pace toward intellectual and spiritual perfection through continuous spiritual and moral purification. This progress and evolution could be attained both in individual and social levels. The long course of human history is replete with enlightened minds and spirits like prophets, their disciples and saints that have ascended to the pinnacle of spiritual and intellectual evolution and revolutionized their societies.

Imam Ali, (SAW) as a great anthropologist, states:

> *O' Man! Do you think that you are a small body, while a magnus mondus is hidden inside you?*

A magnificent being in the scale of human beings could thus not have been created as merely a determined part of the natural world; as some anthropologists say, "Such a magnificent being, who has descended from the Heaven, could not be the eternal resident of the earth."

Human beings, who have been honored by the Lord as the noblest of all creations by their mental powers and liberty, cannot be reduced to eating, sleeping, and passions. These two beliefs are not baseless utopian ideals; as a matter of fact, they have their roots in the very reality of human existence. These beliefs are also open to fresh understandings.

The Fifth Category: This category involves truths concerning human *oughts* and *virtues*. The idea that a human being has other obligations to fulfill rather than those compulsive actions that man undertakes for the gratification of his natural and carnal desires like eating, drinking, sleeping, and copulating is a necessary belief. The one who challenges the veracity of this necessary belief intends to align humanity with senseless animals that are captives of their passions. In fact, humanity minus this belief, due to its more complicated kinds of existential equipment, is more fierce and cruel than any other predator. Human beings are the creatures of extremes, as they can be the noblest of all creation; man also has the capability, on the other hand, to be even the undermost of all beasts and cause tragic massacres that are not within the competence of any fiercest predator living on the earth.

The reason for describing a morally uncommitted person as the fiercest of all predators on the globe is that no animal of prey would slaughter its hunt being conscious of the pain it suffers or its fervent enthusiasm for life; an uncommitted man, on the other hand, consciously transgresses other peoples' rights and derives pleasure from inflicting pain on other human beings and surprisingly sees himself as a hero whose name shall be remembered with honor forever in human history! As a result, we can conclude that the oughts and virtues which are taken here are beyond natural compulsive behaviors which are the very divine obligations revealed by Holy Prophets, common sense, and human moral conscience.

If we deliver ourselves from the bondages of carnal desires and egotisms and begin to think only about human interests, we shall acknowledge that divine obligations can only secure man's worldly and otherworldly happiness, and it is merely through the fulfillment of these duties that man could ascend to the highest levels of intellectual and spiritual perfection and transcend beyond the finite boundaries of natural life.

Since human existence could not be interpreted without the above-mentioned beliefs, then the prescription of negligence toward them in the name of freedom of belief is tantamount with the promotion of nihilism as the fundamental philosophy of life.

2- Freedom of Opinion

It shall not be far off the mark to claim that freedom of opinion is one of the fundamental features of Islam. There are several verses in the Holy Quran that, albeit in different words, invite human beings to think and reflecting, which is a clear reason for this claim. If thinking about the realities of external and internal worlds were not free, the Lord would never invite a man to think and reflect without determining the objects of his thought and reflections.

As freedom of opinion should not be restricted to such an extent that deprives human life of any interpretation and justification, by the same token, freedom of opinion must not be prescribed to such a degree that makes the opinion itself null and void; in addition, freedom of opinion needs not to derange other peoples' mental activities.

Are we allowed to promote freedom of opinion to such a degree that it would dig up the very foundations of thought and opinion?! Could we sustain a freedom of opinion that casts serious doubts about self-evident scientific axioms? Is it logical to trample other peoples' inalienable freedoms under the plea of freedom of opinion? Needless to say, opinion in this context does not surely imply baseless, scatter-minded wool-gatherings.

What is needed to be practiced here is a *productive* opinion (thinking) which signifies the positive mental activity that leads the thinker to the discovery of realities. Thus conceived, thinking is the best of all means for the best of all goals, i.e. touching realities, and is not a goal per se; in a similar sense, knowing realities could not be in itself the ultimate goal of science and knowledge, but the known realities must be used for human purposes.

It might be objected that these statements could divest human beings of their basic right of freedom of opinion, and such a task shall be detrimental to humanity. This objection has a clear answer: these statements do not indeed deprive human beings of their intelligible freedom of opinion, but in fact sustain them from idle exhaustion of their precious mental energies for baseless endeavors, since thinking is one of the wonderful intellectual capabilities of the human brain that should be utilized for regulation of "intelligible life." As a result, as the theory of "art for intelligible life" is to uncover the true value of intelligible life not to censure the art, thinking about intelligible life is also an attempt for revealing the status of intelligible life and does not imply intellectual censure; moreover, as conducting serious researchers for the diagnosis of the capability of a medicine signals the value of human life rather than censuring chemistry, pharmacology and medicine.

A Solution for Freedom of Opinion

Freedom of opinion could find its true meaning only in the context of intelligible life in the following manner:

A) Those opinions that address the material issues of the natural world and material aspects of humanity – which are discussed in positive sciences –can enjoy unrestricted freedom only if they have no harmful consequences for humanity.

B) Since those opinions that are proposed about the identity of human beings as creatures of meaning, their obligations and existential potentialities and the world in its totality and man's place within it address subjects and issues that are not essentially objective but at the same time could be easily informed by individual and social ideals and environmental impressions and cause social and individual agitations, they need to be governed by a general law, i.e. aiming at the knowledge and discovery of intelligible life in an intelligible and logocentric world. It is only through observing this law that a thinker could avoid taking human beings into a logo-centric world consisting of his mental chess-men and aligning divine figures such as Moses, Jesus, Muhammad (PBUH) and many other men of God alongside aggressive chasers of power, wealth, fame, and carnal desires.

It is an undeniable fact that reality and the knowledge of reality are two different things and that the former has its rules and the latter is an attempt to uncover these rules; indeed, it is only through a committed frame of thinking that this enterprise could be correctly undertaken.

3- Freedom of Expression and Speech

This form of freedom, like the two, previously discussed freedoms, is highly promoted in the West. This freedom has been well expressed in the following words by Voltaire:

> *I am ready to sacrifice my life for your freedom of expression even though I might not see eye to eye with your opinions.*

I wonder how dearly Voltaire valued his life; had claims been made in contradiction to the right to freedom, would Voltaire still have been ready to sacrifice himself so that he could pour out his volcanic lava upon people's minds and ruin them? As the Persian proverb goes, "he was so greedy that he threw himself into the boiling pot of broth!" Indeed, are such thinkers saying these words out of true sincerity, or is their aim merely to say something and them become a legend? Alas, as Rumi has said: [179]

> *We have drowned ourselves in words;*
> *We have made so many stories that we have become stories and words as well…*

These words represent an uncommitted view on freedom that may result in the outburst of passionate volcanoes of carnal human desires and exterminate human life on earth!! It seems that by this word Voltaire was to clear a space for his views. As the greatest scientist throughout the twentieth century has once eloquently stated:

> *Freedom of speech and expression has usually been promoted during history to make room for some particular ideas that have poor audience.*

The Consequences of Unreasonable Freedom of Speech

We shall now mention some of the grievous consequences of "unintelligible freedom of expression" and then outline Islam's view on the matter:

1- The overindulgence in pointless speeches as a way of mental catharsis.

2- Narcissistic generalizations of personal views.

3- Heedless self-expressions in the sense of showing one's personal thoughts and feelings without thinking about their social relevance.

> *We deceive and show off so as to create astonishment, awe, and deception;*
> *our only desire is for the public to be in awe with us,*
> *and this is indeed our greed regarding the divinity*
> *When you arrive at a glorious garden, however,*
> *you should also guide others to come there and realize the truths as well…*[180]

4- Spreading fear in the society using baseless rumors. However, these baseless rumors could break the monotonous atmosphere of techno toxification societies and awaken them from their dogmatic slumber.

But what is the truth then? In fact, the true remedy for the uncured malady of boredom is spiritual and intellectual renovation; we must

---

179 - Rumi's *Masnavi*, Book 3.
180 - Ibid.

wash our eyes and watch the world in a fresh light. Such baseless rumors are like heedless recitation of the Holy Quran, as Rumi has beautifully expressed in his *Masnavi*:[181]

> *Those who have fallen astray from the true path of life read the Quran, but not to get closer to God or achieve truths, but rather as an attempt to relieve themselves of their pains, sensitivities, and grievances.*
>
> *To quench such meager flames, water, and urine will, in fact, lead to the same results, like wine and sleep, both of which will sedate you temporarily. Nonetheless, if man finally comes to realize the pure water of the truth, it will relieve his heart of all temptations and guide his soul to God's Heaven.*

They are like narcotic drugs, which temporarily dull the senses and relieve the addict from his problems for a while. But this relief is passing; it disappears when the effects of narcotization become extinct.

> *People try to escape the liabilities they have in life; but what is all this rush for?*
>
> *Why do they indulge into their intoxicating amusements to avoid consciousness?*
>
> *Why do they turn to narcotics and liquor and deprive themselves of deserving to be called humanity?*
>
> *With the drunkenness or engagements they indulge in, they lose their "self,"*
>
> *But they ignore the fact that by neglecting God's orders,*
>
> *the chains of their souls pull them back into their natural self once again.*[182]

Unfortunately, these scaremongers in slumbered societies are called "thinkers." While tearing down one's slumber essentially differs from a true awakening that leads the man to the consciousness of principles of life, scaremongers only spread ignorance in the society and ruin the highest principles of humanity. Therefore, nobody is allowed to undermine the spiritual atmosphere of the society under the plea of freedom of expression. Let us now compare the following two statements with each other:

➤ I should express what I have in my mind freely, although it may derange human values and deceive minds.

➤ Here we shall quote Albert Einstein on his meeting with an American diplomat in 1949 that shocked him with his uncommitted words of the future of the world as a practice of freedom of expression:

---

181 - Ibid, Book 4.
182 - Ibid, Book 6.

> *Recently I met with a clever American diplomat who was seemingly a*
> *man of good will. I reminded him that the danger of a new war seriously*
> *threatens humanity and if such a war is triggered, it may annihilate*
> *humanity on the planet, and it is only an institution that is superior to*
> *nations could prevent this disaster. Surprisingly, however, my addressee*
> *shocked me with his answer; he replied, "Why you are so intensely at odds*
> *with the annihilation of humanity?!*[183]

If we read Einstein's reaction to this uncommitted statement on human future, we shall see that what has led Einstein's interlocutor to such shocking indifference about the future of humanity is the mental exhaustion caused by paradoxical nihilistic theories that are developed in the name of absolute freedom of expression and speech. Einstein continues:

> *Such a rash answer bespeaks an explicit misery that is the souvenir of the*
> *contemporary world. This answer is, in my view, the answer stated by*
> *someone who has made serious efforts to reach mental equilibrium but had*
> *failed. This answer is an expression of a painful recluse that all human*
> *beings suffer from today.*

These statements have their origin in the absence of a transcendent ideology which could interpret and justify human identity in both domains of "isness" and "oughtness." This absence is surely an effect of uncommitted paradoxical statements that have been made in both domains. On the other hand, the day shall come that everyone should account for their statements, as the following lines of Rumi eloquently depict:

> *O tongue! You are both the fire and the harvest stack;*
> *how long will you set fire to this harvest stack?*
> *In the darkness of the cotton field,*
> *what is this fire doing among all of the cotton?*
> *How cruel those people are who closed their eyes ignorantly*
> *and set fire to the world with their tongues…*
> *One wrong word can destroy a whole world,*
> *and turn dead foxes into lions…*

When Voltaire was saying to God, "O God of Newton! Do you not envy Newton?" would he have said that had he been aware of what he was saying? It has not been proven to us whether the above statement can be attributed to Voltaire or not. Whoever quoted it either meant to astound his readers or his audience using presenting such baseless nonsense or truly knew neither Newton nor God. Apparently, such shocks only astonish and deceive the simple-minded.

The Freedom of Expression and Speech in Islam

The expression of realities useful for humanity both in material and spiritual

---

183 - Frank, Philipp, *Einstein, His Life and Times*. (Originally in English).

domains not only is free but as a matter of fact, everyone who knows a reality and can express it and yet deprives people from this reality is convicted and shall be reproved both in this world and hereafter. The following verses of the Holy Quran eloquently depict this truth:

> *O followers of the book! Why do you confound the truth with the falsehood and hide the truth while you know?*
> (The Family of Imran 3:71)
> *Surely those who conceal the clear proofs and the guidance that We revealed after we made it clear in the book for men, these it is whom Allah shall curse, and those who curse shall curse them (too).*
>
> (The Cow 2:159)

Although the addresses of the first verse are the followers of book, concerning the generality of the next verse and regarding the meaning of clear proofs and the guidance which lays the foundations for the true life (intelligible life), this injunction is applied to all kinds of concealment and concealers of truth, clear proofs and guidance.

There are numerous quotations from the Holy Prophet (PBUH) on the necessity of expression of practical truths, and here we suffice to some examples of them:

1- *Imam Al-Sadegh (SAW) has stated, "I read in the book of Imam Ali (SAW) that God before making the ignorant promise to seek knowledge, charged the men of knowledge with the duty of the munificence of wisdom and knowledge since knowledge existed before ignorance."* [184]

2- *Imam Al-Sadegh (SAW) was quoted as saying, "Jesus addressed the Israelites and said, 'O' Israelites! Don't share wisdom with those who are ignorant, as it is an injustice to knowledge and wisdom. And do not conceal knowledge from the men of wisdom as it is an injustice to these people.'"* [185]

3- *Anyone who teaches a good shall be awarded to the one who has done that good.* [186]

4- *Verily the knower who hides his knowledge shall be resurrected on the Day of Judgment, while no one could bear his putrid smell.* [187]

5- *All people are members of Allah's family, and their most blessed one with the Lord, is the one who is most beneficial for the members of Allah's family.* [188]

---

184 - Al-Kulayni's *Usul Al-Kafi*, Vol. 1, pp. 41-42.

185 - Ibid.

186 - Ibid, p. 35.

187 - Sheikh al-Hurre al-Ameli, *Wasa'el Al-Shi'ah*, Vol. 6, p. 510.

188 - Ibid.

The following results could be deduced from these transmissions:

I)   The expression of realities and truths is an obligatory practice for those who know them since the Lord has obliged the possessors of knowledge to disseminate their knowledge.

II) These transmissions are equally applied to every kind of knowledge without any exception. According to reason and also the two previously cited verses of the Holy Quran, this knowledge should be both materially and spiritually useful for humanity.

III) As the Lord has made the men of knowledge promise to disseminate their knowledge and teach the ignorant, He has also made the ignorant promise to seek knowledge.

IV) Knowledge and wisdom should not be shared with those who are unfamiliar and unaware of or even the enemies of wisdom since they do not know its value and would stand against it; as Imam Ali (SAW) has eloquently stated:

People are the enemies of what they do not know.[189]

V)   Wisdom should not be concealed from the people of knowledge since this is an unforgivable injustice to enlightened souls. The reason for this injustice lies in the fact that these concealed truths could easily lead people to or at least bring them nearer to wisdom.

VI) Everyone who teaches something to people that are gainful for them shall be benefitted from the advantages of it. The teaching material here includes everything that is of avail for the people.

VII) Those who know some useful truths and hide them from the public shall be punished on the Day of Judgment.

VIII) Social profitability is the criterion of existential excellence in the sense that those who are of more value with the Lord are more beneficial for their society and fellow human beings.

Thus, freedom of expression in Islam is the necessary prerequisite of the dissemination of knowledge, which is of vital significance for social life. Also, those who deprive the public of necessary information should be treated like social agitators. For instance, if one knows that there is a spring of water on the other side of a mountain but does not inform the people around of its whereabouts, he will be regarded as the main factor bringing about any damage cause shortage of water there; if the people in the region die from the lack of water, he will, in fact, have caused their death.

The Principle of the Limitation of Freedom of Expression

The truth is that freedom of expression as an inalienable right or even

---

189 - *Nahj ul-Balaghah*, Aphorisms 172.

ordinance which needs intellectual maturity on both sides, i.e. the speaker and the listener. Do the speakers and the listeners in Eastern countries enjoy the same degree of intellectual maturity that we usually come across in such philosophers and thinkers as Al-Biruni, Avicenna, Al-Farabi, Muhammad Mahdi Naraghi and Sheikh Morteza Ansari? Moreover, do the speakers and the listeners in Western countries enjoy the same degree of intellectual maturity that we find in such philosophers as Kant, Aristotle, Plato, Socrates, Descartes, Augustine, Hegel, Whitehead and Saint Hiller?

We would not be exaggerating if we were to say that there are few people on the planet who enjoy such a degree of spiritual and intellectual maturity that makes them qualify for the right to freedom of expression. As a result, we need to act very intelligently regarding this very delicate right so as not make it the plaything of the aggressive hunters of power, wealth, fame and carnal desires. It is known that Schopenhauer's statements on the degraded nature and humiliated state of women only affect incapable minds, not the minds of the like of Socrates and Kant from the West or Avicenna, Abu Rayhan Biruni, Mirdamad, Mulla Muhammad Mahdi Naraqi and Sheikh Murtaza Ansari from the East.

Absolute versus Intelligible Freedom of Expression

Today we can better understand the true value and importance of intelligible freedom in the light of adversities that humanity has gone through during the last two centuries. These adversities have been mainly caused by absolute freedom of expression and positivism that both have exhausted many precious mental activities and potentialities.

By considering the catastrophe that man has been subjected to as of the mid-nineteenth century, the value and significance of intelligible freedom can be better realized. This catastrophe involved the introduction of absolute freedom of speech in all societies, which led to anyone expressing anything one desired to, whether in speech or writing. Although the consequences did involve cases in which truths were presented, such an immense amount of ridiculous, selfish content was poured onto the minds of people all around the world that, as a result, most human values and virtues faded away; people's minds grew frustrated and exhausted, and became not only unable to receive any more basic truths, but also accustomed to accepting the baseless nonsense as the real truth! The even more unreasonable event was the rise of a school known as positivism, which gathered many "thinkers" stating that "All there are consists of merely what I see." Rumi has thus pointed out the destructive request "I do not need eyes, so please make me blind."

I do not deserve such kindness;
it hurts me, so why should it hurt you?
Kindly take this kindness away from me,
I have no need for eyes; blind me quickly![190]

They indeed failed to realize that if we were to set the statement "Only what is tangibly observable is to be presented" as the basis for knowledge, the first victim of such a limiting siege would be science itself, which has (as a matter of fact, all sciences, without exception, have) been founded upon laws abstracted from origins – i.e., relations and correlations between objects – which have no observable intangibility.

To explain the meaning and value of intelligible freedom, we will need first of all to understand the concrete fact that intelligibility and unintelligibility lie in the very nature of freedom itself since freedom consists of the human ability to do or not do an act. What makes freedom intelligible or unintelligible is the way one puts it into operation; if it is used according to human principles, it is intelligible, and if it is used against human principles, it will be regarded as unintelligible.

Thus conceived, the freedom of expression that is used against the material and spiritual interests of humanity is "unintelligible freedom," that is like "the sword at the hand of a drunken man;" otherwise, it is the intelligible freedom that is surely protected by the rule of law. To put the matter in clear terms, unintelligible freedom is a freedom that helps the natural ego be extremely benefitted from its carnal desires. Is it not logical to prescribe several experiments on different animals to prove the effectiveness of medicine for headaches, whereas it is not to expect an unrestricted freedom to express and discuss the issues of humanities that involve the whole existence of humanity?! While medical experiments would lead to animal fatalities, any negligence regarding extremely significant issues of the humanities could result in the annihilation of all humanity.

We believe that "intelligible freedom of expression" must be practiced in the following manner:

1- The natural sciences that deal with material aspects of inanimate things, vegetables and animals could enjoy of absolute freedom of expression.

That is to say; there is no everlasting principle for developing an epistemic relation with material dimensions of the natural world. For instance, if until not so long ago the natural sense of sight and the naked eye were regarded as the only apparatus used for the study of corporeal beings, today we are witnessing the development of such powerful optical devices as microscopes and telescopes, and tomorrow we may witness other instruments that can more expand the boundaries of our knowledge of the natural world. There is also

190 - Rumi's *Masnavi*, Book 3.

no restriction for the analysis of material subjects in the sense that we need to carry out all possible analyses of the same matter, according to common sense and Islam. However, when our analyses of material subjects crossed the borders of objectivity and entered the realm of fundamental issues that represent the theoretical or philosophical issues of science, it is necessary that the freedom of expression not give rise to paradoxes in Islamic teaching. For example, a biologist has the right to propose a myriad of theories about the material dimensions of nature, but when it comes to the grand issue of the nature of life, the biologist needs to take more intelligent steps and focus upon realities alone.

2- In the field of human sciences and fundamental ontology which directly or indirectly influence our conceptions of human beings both in the realms of "isness" and "oughtness," the supervision and authority of some conscious, proficient and just scholars is needed.

This is what we understand by freedom, and it is surely different from the positions of those who say, "We love freedom for the sake of freedom itself, whether in the field of beliefs or in the domain of opinions or politics," or those excessive hedonists who are the chasers of carnal desires since they are even under most than the quadrupeds.

By the same token, if someone says, "I love the freedom of expression for the sake of expression itself since every word deserved to be heard and defended freely!" the truth is that we have nothing to reply to this person since he is blind-hearted. Once again, let us quote from Rumi, who has said:

> The true man gains pleasure through his endeavors,
> whereas the wrongdoer is only pleased through his libido,
> which has become his only religion and aim.
> How pitiful it is for a man to devote the great human mind to his sexual needs.
> Now matter how much progress such a man may make,
> he has in fact degraded himself to the lowest of the low.
> He may seem to be heading upward, but he is in fact nose-diving.
> You may have seen beggars carrying flags;
> Are they indicators of power and affluence?
> On the contrary, they show that they are beggars...

Likewise, someone might claim that "I love the freedom of expression for the sake of the expression itself; one should be able to express oneself, whoever it may be and about whatever it may be." As a matter of fact, such a person cannot be responded to in any way, for – at the most optimistic level – it can be said that such a person does not know what he is talking about.

To put this long story in a nutshell, in the field of human sciences and fundamental ontology which directly or indirectly influence our conceptions of human beings both in the realms of "isness" and "oughtness," researchers and opinions that are not permeated with egotists are divine services.

Regarding the theoretical nature of most issues discussed in human sciences and fundamental ontology on the one hand, and the necessity of understanding the basic principles of those issues with sincerity on the other, all opinions and researchers in these significant domains are always exposed to paradoxes. Since these two important domains are continuously susceptible to be penetrated with predestined principles, personal views and ideals, the proposed hypotheses, theories and opinions in these fields need to be reevaluated and revised by conscious and just scholars so as not to derange the basic values of human societies. Whereas God always empowers man to get necessary knowledge of the facts, man will need only to fulfill two basic conditions to achieve this aim:

I) incessant efforts without exhaustion and depression, and

II) pure-heartedness that prepares man for the reception of divine illuminations:

> *And (as for) those who strive hard for Us, We will most certainly guide them in Our ways; and Allah is most surely with the doers of good.*
>
> (The Spider 29:69)

We need here to take into serious consideration that, as we have already mentioned, "the newfangled theories in human sciences and fundamental ontology should be assessed by conscious, proficient and just scholars." The reason for the necessity of these three conditions (consciousness, proficiency, and justice) is clear since those who are in charge of the assessment of an idea may also have the right to determine the intellectual and even the spiritual orientation of the society.

Concisely speaking, the condition of "consciousness" certifies that the theory or idea shall not be studied with a limited perspective on the matter at hand. The necessity of this condition becomes even more obvious when we see it in the light of the following principle that has been reiterated by some philosophers:

> *In human sciences, contrary to Euclidian geometry, a beeline may be the longest and most circuitous line between two points, while in Euclidian geometry a straight line is the shortest distance between two points.*

For example, a true scholar may need to deal with some issues of culture, politics, and psychology in his research on a legal principle, while an incompetent, unskilled legal expert would turn a brown eye to these sides of the issue and thus fail to understand the nature of the legal principle at hand.

The necessity of the condition of proficiency is also clear enough and does not need to be more explicated since it is evident that unskilled man is not competent at all to remark on a newly emerged theory.

We come now to the condition of justice, which has its origin in the serious sense of commitment and helps the researcher not to remark on an issue which is not within his competence. This condition secures the basic principle of freedom of expression, for an incompetent statement on a new idea could ruin the whole future of that idea. On the other hand, an uncommitted remark on an idea would deprive the society of its possible benefits and the new horizons that it could open before the society.

It might be asked, "Does this theory not lead to epistemic stagnation?" The answer to this question is negative, and the following reasons can be provided:

Firstly, have medical and pharmacological researches and experimentations conducted for the substantiation of a medicinal prescription inflicted the constructive scientific competitions within academia with stagnation?!

Secondly, this theory merely puts an end to aggressive competitions based on inhuman purposes and replaces them with constructive competitions, since those conscious, proficient and just scholars who are in charge of the reevaluation of newly emerged ideas will engage in an intellectual contest with each other. These continuous intellectual reevaluations could serve as an epistemic alarm for the society and keep it alert and creative so as to be able to face newly emerged challenges.

As we have already stated on more than one occasion, considering the freedom of research and opinion, everyone is in continual intellectual endeavor and competition, for conscious, just experts will keep the society continuously up to speed, claiming, for instance, that, "Dear researchers and seekers of science! If have any opinions or thoughts on this certain issue, please present them, for new theories have arisen about it." Thus, not only will constructive academic and scientific competitions avoid stagnancy, but will also be directed toward intelligible paths.

4- Freedom of Action

It is almost a century since the so-called civilized societies began promoting this right in an unrestricted form and sometimes declare it as a matter of honor for them. This freedom finds its expression in the following maxim: "Provided that you do not violate other people's rights, you are allowed do whatever you want." It is of essential importance to take it into prime consideration that as opposed to this latter inhuman principle, the long course of human history shows that human desires, in general, have hardly ever been in agreement with reason and realities, since those human desires that are totally in accordance with human reason and realities are in the minority and are confined to those who are committed to religion and moral ideals of humanity. A great many crimes, treasons, and villainies that history is replete with have all been committed for the gratification of human desires. Moreover, if there were no liberty (i.e., willful desire), those evil acts would never have been declared as crimes, treasons, and villainies. Thus, it was demonstrated that telling man "You are allowed do whatever you want" is an uncommitted remark that clears the space for aggressive hunters of power to feel free to commit any manipulations or wrongdoing they wish to.

It might be said that all crimes, treasons, and villainies point out indications of violations of other people's rights; in fact, this has been reiterated in the opening words of the sentence as the condition of absolute freedom of action. This objection has a clear answer, since when you allow a man to do whatever he wants to do, you have permitted him to treat his life in an unprincipled manner; as a result, by doing so, you have pushed him to the verge of the crag!

Now this question is raised: could we oblige someone who does not observe his rights to respect other people's rights and freedoms?

Those who claim "As long as you do not violate other peoples' rights, you are allowed to do whatever you want" are similar to someone telling a volcano, "You are free to play with your molten rocks inside yourself as long as you would kindly take care not to destroy the surrounding huts, farms, and people."

These people need to know that if someone is rotten at the core, he will never come to observe his fellow men's basic rights of life, dignity, and freedom. Such a man does not even understand the meanings of "right," "ordinance," "life," "dignity" and "freedom," let alone observe them. In fact, these morally corrupted people are embodiments of violation, transgression, depravity, treason and other possible crimes, and they only need a lean motive to commit all these evil acts.

> I heard from German thinkers that when it was proved that Germany had been defeated in the war and the enemy crossed the borders, some German citizens started to plunder the houses of their fellow countrymen even before the enemy had entered the city.

Moreover, those who suggest "you are free to do whatever you want" not only are in fact activating some inactive volcanoes in the society, but they are also doing injustice to these volcanoes themselves, since with the promotion of absolute freedom of action, they repress reason, conscience, and other evolutionary forces within humanity. As a result, we may easily call this century the "century of insanity," and may there never be a war, for if war were to be triggered, and billions of people lost their lives, everyone would shift off the responsibility to insanity.

As we have mentioned earlier, freedom of expression is divided into

216 Universal Human Rights

two major kinds: "absolute freedom" and "intelligible freedom"; the same division is the case with the freedom of action. That is to say, freedom of action is also divided into two kinds: "intelligible freedom of action" and "absolute freedom of action."

If the action is preceded by principled natural desires, freedom in such an action is an intelligible freedom; otherwise, it would not be intelligible to grant freedom to an action that is not done under rational desires.

It might be said, "What is this obligation you are charging man with, that he must act according to moral principles and the law? When man has no other knocker to knock on, there is no reason for him to commit himself to any principle or law?!"

This question has a clear answer: Is a man not an evolutionary being? All schools of thought have accepted this as self-evident that only by resorting to reason, conscience, and divine messages could man detach himself from animals and ascend to higher existential stages; indeed, this is why man cannot be both an evolutionary being and also turn a blind eye to the principles of morality!!

It is said that once a great thinker made serious efforts to discover and know human nature. One day one of his acquaintances came to his office and asked, "What are you doing, Master?" "Studying the human nature," the master replied. "You are making useless efforts and indeed wasting your time," the acquaintance said, "since people are entertaining themselves in bars, night clubs, coffee shops and other places and nobody cares about your researches." The master stopped writing and said, "Am I not a human being myself? Even a lifelong of thinking is too short for me to explore and know my nature."

Secondly, could we make an iron circle one individual who lives in society? If you have such a concept of man, you will need to make an immediate revision in your anthropology. Those who deny the contagiousness of moral diseases have not even taken the preliminary steps toward knowing human nature. The contagious nature of moral diseases has been eloquently depicted in the following lines by Abul-Ehtayah:

> The people shall not be morally regenerated as long as you are corrupted in soul and mind. If you think that you can remain the same and have a reformed society, you are wholly mistaken.

It seems that the fatal disease of "you can do whatever you want" has its origin in the irrational separation of religion, morality, law and politics, which has inflicted human societies with nihilism and blocked the way for the growth and development of justice, intelligible freedom, conscience, constructive loves and many other human ideals.

Let us now take into consideration the story of this separation in the words of the former U.S. General Attorney Robert Houghwout Jackson:

The existing obstacles discouraged the people to show their interest in Islamic laws. For paying our debts to Arab culture, we contented ourselves with preparing surprising reports on their laws [....] In the eye of an American, law and religion are essentially in conflict with each other. In the West, even in those countries which do not strongly believe in the separation of religious and civil affairs, the legal system is seen as a totally secular phenomenon within which current circumstances play a major role [....] Thus, our law in America does not determine religious duties; rather, it deliberately neglects them indeed. Law in the U.S. has limited contact with moral obligations. In fact, an American citizen could act totally in accordance with the law, while being a morally corrupted person. On the contrary, in Islamic law, it is divine will that forms the source of laws; a will that has revealed itself to the Prophet Muhammad (PBUH). This will regards all individual believers as the members of the same society, although they may come from different tribes and live in various geographic locations. Here, it is religion that unifies the people, and neither nationality nor geography can do so. In this way, the state itself is submissive and amenable to the Holy Quran; thus, there remains no room for any other legislator, let alone any room for controversy and discord. The believer sees this world as a corridor which brings her/him to the other and better world, and the Quran provides a set of divine codes for individual and social conducts, so as to make the transition sounder and easier. It is impossible to separate Prophetic teachings from political and economic theories; these teachings instruct man how to conduct himself in social, economic, political and individual affairs ...[191]

5- Freedom and Deliverance from Slavery

If we take the phenomenon of slavery into precise account, we shall see that this phenomenon has had deep social, cultural and economic roots; thus, it was hard to deal with. It is needless to say that the two pillars of Western civilization (Plato and Aristotle) have clearly declared this phenomenon as an authentic social norm and in fact founded their political philosophy upon it. Of course, we are not here to defend slavery by resorting to Plato and Aristotle; nonetheless, having said this, we shall discuss the historical backgrounds of this phenomenon. To better understand how deeply rooted slavery is, let us consider the following statements by Alfred North Whitehead:

Now, in respect to the political factions of the ancient world, nothing has yet been settled. Every problem which Plato discusses is still alive today. Yet, there is a vast difference between modern and ancient theories, for we differ from the ancients on the one premise on which they were all now. Slavery was the presupposition of political theorists then. Freedom is the

191 - Lisbani, *Herbert J, Islamic Law.* (Originally in English).

presupposition of political theorists now. In those days, it was found difficult to reconcile their doctrine of slavery to certain plain facts of moral feeling and of sociological practice, and in these days our sociological speculations also find difficulty in reconciling our doctrine of freedom to another group of plain facts. Yet, when all such qualifications have been made, freedom and equality constitute an inevitable presupposition for modern political thought with an admixture of subsequent lame qualification, while slavery was a corresponding presupposition for the ancients with their admixture of subsequent lame qualification.[192]

Having said this, it becomes clear that if the Holy Prophet Muhammad (PBUH) had dealt with this phenomenon in haste, he would have dug under the foundations of social and economic life of the time. It was right due to this very reason that the Holy Prophet Muhammad (PBUH) decided to approach this issue in an intelligible pace and gradually uproot it by taking the following steps:

1- He has not shown any partiality in the depiction of moral virtues and vices of humanity in the sense that they are equally applied to freemen and bondmen. Let us take into consideration the following quotation from the Holy Prophet (PBUH) as an example of this impartiality:

> **The Lord has created Heaven for the one who obeys Him, even though he may be an Ethiopian slave, and verily He has created Hell for the one who sins against Him, although he may even be a man of wealth and fame.**

2- In Muslim communities, slaves would succeed in assuming higher positions by showing their individual competencies, while in other communities they were treated like animals.

3- If a bondwoman was impregnated by a Freeman, she was freed as "the mother of the baby."

4- Those bondmen who were able to work for their freedom concluded a contract with their owners so as to work for them instead of their prices. This contract is called *"Mukatebah"* (which translates as "correspondence") in Islamic jurisprudence.

5- There are numerous transmissions related from the Holy Prophet Muhammad (PBUH) on the rewards of freeing slaves. The rewards of big undertakings have usually been compared with the rewards of freeing slaves; for instance, the rewards of saving one's life have been regarded as equal with the rewards of freeing a bondman.

6- The expiration of many sins is freeing slaves.

7- Slavery was mainly the outcome of wars. The Holy Prophet Muhammad (PBUH) targeted this very root of slavery by proclaiming free all residents

---

192 - Whitehead, Alfred North, *Adventures of Ideas.*

of Mecca when he had conquered and taken control of the city. This was the biggest step taken by the Holy Prophet for uprooting the cancerous tumor of slavery. To put the matter otherwise, if we take the economic and social circumstances of the time into serious consideration, we shall soon realize that the Holy Prophet (PBUH) was facing much harder circumstances than the conditions with which Abraham Lincoln had dealt with issuing the Emancipation Proclamation of 1863.

8- The prisoners of war were allowed to be freed by teaching their knowledge to Muslims by Prophet's order. However, it may be asked that if Muhammad uprooted slavery, why has it continued up to present times? This question has a clear answer: the reason is that people are usually careless about crimes and moral values.

Had Islam not issued strong ordinances on the regulation and reformation of economic issues? Had Islam not underlined the significance of excellent virtues in human societies? Insofar as the Holy Prophet (PBUH) stated:

> *I was delegated as prophet to make whole the moral virtues.*

All of these human ordinances of Islam have been revealed as eternal truths issued by God the Almighty, but sadly, they have not taken into serious consideration by Muslims, who were too preoccupied with carnal desires and their autocrat despots. Slavery should have been uprooted very long ago according to the divine logic of Islam, but the aggressive chasers of wealth, fame and power blocked the road for this ideal to be realized. The best reason for the necessity of the abolition of slavery, at the very least from Muslim countries due to the Prophets' incessant efforts, is that we see that during the time of Omar ibn Abdul Aziz, the public treasury had lost its purpose since, as it has been written in history books, poverty was uprooted in the Muslim community. When Yahiya ibn Saeed was delegated by Omar to go to Africa and collect their shares of the Muslim state treasury, on his return to distribute the money to poor people, he found no one to give money to; Omar, the Muslim Caliph, had already made them all free of want. Thus, Yahiya Ibn Saeed decided to use the treasury for freeing the slaves, both Muslim and non-Muslim.[193]

Omar Ibn Abdul Aziz had died by 101 Hijri. If we presume that Yahiya Ibn Saeed had done the task one year before Omar's death, it means that poverty had been eradicated from the Muslim community, since it is evident that if there had indeed been slaves in Muslim countries, the Treasury would not have been used for freeing the slaves of non-Muslim countries.

9- There are several reasons that show the marginal nature of slavery in social life in the sense that it is not a natural phenomenon and thus needs

---

193 - Abi Muhammad Abdullah ibn Abdulhakam, *The Life of Omar Ibn Abdul Aziz as Narrated by Malek ibn Anas*, p. 59.

to be uprooted from human societies by adhering to the ideal of equity of human beings. In this spirit, Fayz Kashani quotes Imam Ali (SAW) as saying:

> *O' people! Adam has fathered neither a bondman nor a bondwoman, since all human beings are equal with the Lord; however, God has assigned the affairs of some to be looked after by some others.*[194]

This transmission clearly shows that slavery is a baseless phenomenon that has its origin in human abuses of laws; that is to say, the reality of social life was so that some people could undertake the management of some others by virtue of their spiritual and intellectual competencies; gradually, however, this divine mission became overshadowed with human egotisms and those who were in charge of looking after people's social affairs saw them as their own slaves. This is, in my view, the best social analysis that has ever been given to the phenomenon of slavery.

10- One of the important steps taken for the eradication of slavery in Muslim communities is the Holy Prophet Muhammad's order about those Africans that had been kidnapped and trafficked to Asian countries as slaves:

> *These people are not slaves; they are free men like other free people.*[195]

The Outcome of Emancipation from Slavery

By studying Islamic texts, one can easily concede that freedom is a vital issue (i.e., related to life) for human beings rather than being a secondary, decorative quality. The serious efforts made by Holy Prophets for the deliverance of humanity from the bondages of atrocities and cruelties are themselves obvious reasons for the claim that Islam, which contains the original messages of all previous revealed religions, is strongly against slavery in all its forms and tries to deliver the servants of God from bondages.

If we pay enough attention to the wonderful persistence displayed by Holy Prophets for the deliverance of the oppressed people from the Hawks of aggressive hunters of power, we can easily understand the vehemence of the hostility of revealed religions with slavery as the most despicable form of oppression. There are numerous verses in the Holy Quran on the necessity of the defense of the oppressed and the repulsiveness of surrendering to oppression while having the ability to rise against it, thus pointing out Islam's capacity for taking the lead in the global movement for deliverance from all bondages and eradication of slavery. God the Almighty states:

> *Surely (as for) those whom the angels cause to die while they are unjust to their souls, they shall say: in what state were you? They*

---

194 - Fayz Kashani, *Al-Wafi*, Vol. 14, p. 20.

195 - This *hadith* reveals the jurisprudential principle that reads: a freeman shall not be sold as a slave.

> *shall say: We were weak in the earth. They shall say: Was not*
> *Allah's earth spacious, so that you should have migrated therein?*
> *So these it is whose abode is hell, and it is an evil resort.*
>
> (The Women 4:97)

There are several verses in the Holy Quran on the necessity of uprising against oppression and defence of the oppressed and even fighting for delivering them from oppression. We will here suffice to point out a few instances of them:

> *And what reason have you that you should not fight in the*
> *way of Allah and of the weak among the men and the women*
> *and the children, (of) those who say: Our Lord! Cause us to go*
> *forth from this town, whose people are oppressors, and give*
> *us from Thee a guardian and give us from Thee a helper.*
>
> (The Women 4:75)

Oppression in this context implies both physical and mental bondages; indeed, the Lord has proscribed His messenger from deceiving his peoples, as eloquently depicted in the following verses of the Holy Quran:

> *And it is not attributable to a prophet that he should act*
> *unfaithfully, and he who acts unfaithfully shall bring that*
> *in respect of which he has acted unfaithfully on the day of*
> *resurrection; then shall every soul be paid back fully what*
> *it has earned, and they shall not be dealt with unjustly.*
>
> (The Family of Imran 3:161)

> *Those who follow the Messenger-prophet, the Ummi, whom they*
> *find written down with them in the Taurat and the Injeel (who)*
> *enjoins them good and forbids them evil, and makes lawful*
> *to them the good things and makes unlawful to them impure*
> *things, and removes from them their burden and the shackles*
> *which were upon them; so (as for) those who believe in him*
> *and honor him and help him, and follow the light which has*
> *been sent down with him, these it is that are the successful.*
>
> (The Elevated Places 7:157)

Indeed, there must have been no load heavier than the absolute wills of the slaves' owners that made the slaves feel that they had no right to life at all.

The Islamic Declaration

Article 14

I) Human beings are born free, and no one has the right to enslave, humiliate, oppress or exploit them, and there can be no subjugation but to God the Most-High.

II) Colonialism of all types, being one of the evilest forms of enslavement, is totally prohibited. Peoples suffering from colonialism have the full right to freedom and self-determination. It is the duty of all states and peoples to support the struggle of colonized peoples for the liquidation of all forms of colonialism and occupation, and all states and peoples have the right to preserve their independent identity and exercise control over their wealth and natural resources.

The UN Declaration

Article 1
All human beings are born free and equal in dignity and rights. They are endowed with reason and conscience and should act towards one another in a spirit of brotherhood.

Article 4
No one shall be held in slavery or servitude; slavery and the slave trade shall be prohibited in all their forms.

Article 8
Everyone has the right to an effective remedy by the competent national tribunals for acts violating the fundamental rights granted him by the constitution or by law.

Shared Characteristics

1- All human beings are born free, and nobody is allowed to make them his slaves.[196]
2- All human beings are equal in dignity and rights.[197]
3- All human beings are endowed with reason and conscience. These divine forces are the sources of inherent human dignity which qualify him to enjoy particular rights and obligations.
4- All human beings should act toward each other in the spirit of brotherhood and fraternity. Both declarations are unanimously agreed upon this article.

   We must have in mind that the spirit of brotherhood shall be preserved as long as the utilitarian voracities, egotisms and selfishness have not separated souls and minds from each other.
5- As we have mentioned earlier in our debates on the right to dignity, no one is allowed to humiliate human beings.

---

196 - We have already discussed the origins of this ordinance in our philosophical debates on freedom.
197 - This shall be discussed in the section dealing with the principle of equality.

Differences

1- Nobody is allowed to enslave any other human being, and this is a general principle that is agreed upon by all human cultures and legal systems. This principle has found its clearest form of stipulation ever in the Islamic Declaration, which proscribes all forms of subjugation.

   The second clause of Article 14 of the Islamic Declaration reads: "Colonialism [in the ordinary sense of the term[198]] of all types, being one of the evilest forms of enslavement, is totally prohibited." The Islamic Declaration proclaims that it is the duty of all states and peoples to support the struggle of colonized peoples for the liquidation of all forms of colonialism and occupation and all states and peoples have the right to preserve their independent identity and exercise control over their wealth and natural resources.

2- The fact that all human beings are the servants of God, and nobody is allowed to enslave other people for his evil purposes – and slavery in its ancient form as a social institution was an unnatural phenomenon – reveals a highly relevant truth for humanity, and this indicates why Islam has gradually uprooted this anti-freedom phenomenon.

The Islamic Declaration

Article 15

Everyone shall have the right to express his opinion freely in such manner as would not be contrary to the principles of the Shari'ah.

Article 16

Everyone shall have the right to enjoy the fruits of his scientific, literary, artistic or technical production and the right to protect the moral and material interests stemming from that place, provided that such production is not contrary to the principles of Shari'ah.

The UN Declaration

Article 18

Everyone has the right to freedom of thought, conscience, and religion; this right includes the freedom to change one's religion or belief, and also the freedom, either alone or in community with others and in public or private, to manifest his religion or belief in teaching, practice, worship and observance.

---

198 - By "ordinary sense of the term" in this context we mean that colonialism is only proscribed in the sense of mere territorial expansions which aim at the exploitation of other peoples as it can also be used for the deliverance of people from bondages of ignorance and imposed slaveries.

Article 19

Everyone has the right to freedom of opinion and expression; this right includes freedom to hold opinions without interference and to seek, receive and impart information and ideas through any media and regardless of frontiers.

Article 27

1- Everyone has the right to freely participate in the cultural life of the community, to enjoy the arts and to have a share in scientific advancement and its benefits.

2- Everyone has the right to the protection of the moral and material interests resulting from any scientific, literary or artistic production of which he is the author.

Shared Characteristics

1- Both declarations have declared freedom of opinion, expression, and speech as a basic right of every human being. The arguments[199] held between non-Muslim nations and Muslim intellectuals including Imams are themselves witnesses to the significance of committed freedom in Islam.

2- Intellectual property right has been stipulated in both declarations as one of the inalienable rights of humanity. That is to say; everyone is entitled to enjoy the fruits of his scientific, literary, artistic or technical production.

3- Freedom of belief has been declared by both declarations as a basic human right. Nevertheless, there is still a divide on the matter in the sense that the Islamic Declaration has conditioned it upon the provisions of Shari'ah Law, but the occidentally-oriented UN Declaration takes it as an absolute right.

4- Everyone shall have the right to express his opinion freely in such manner as would not be against the interests of the society.

Differences

1- Whereas human beings are, in addition to their divinely-ordained obligations toward their personal evolutionary destinations, also according to Islam as responsible in regard to the social norms governing their societies, nobody is allowed to disturb the ideal life of the society by absolute freedom of opinion, expression, and speech.

As we have already mentioned in our debates on the philosophy of freedom, freedom is not a goal in itself, but it is the quality of enjoying the creative forces of life through which the man can arrive at intelligible life.

---

199 - These arguments have been collected in a book entitled *The Arguments of Sheikh Tabarsi*.

Freedom in its absolute sense could be used for fulfilling evil purposes like suicide. On the other hand, the unrestricted prescription of freedom for every subject and action could bring about the elimination of all laws, punishments, and rewards from the society.

Thus conceived, freedom is not an absolute goal and ideal, but it is the best means for a creative life. Freedom in this sense has an essential relationship with "good;" this is why the codifiers of the UN Declaration need to address the paradox existing between "the right to inherent dignity" and "the right to absolute freedom of expression and speech." That is to say, to secure the inalienable and primordial right to inherent dignity, we have to make the freedom of expression intelligible. It is for this very reason that Islam has conditioned freedom of expression upon the principles of the Shari'ah in the sense that nobody is allowed to derange the society by overindulgence in freedom of expression.

It is not fair to align these intelligible restrictions regarding freedom of expression with medieval inquisitions since nobody would enter any protest when told that the approval of medical authorities is needed even for prescription pills to relieve a headache. If the human "soul", "spirit", "character", and "self" are not as significant as a tablet for a headache, why do some thinkers defend absolute freedom of expression and claim that it would be abused by the aggressive chasers of power, wealth, fame, and name for reaching their evil purposes?!

2- The freedom of belief needs intellectual maturity whether as a social quality or as a personal practice as its unintelligible application could bring grievous havocs upon human societies.

According to Islam, human individuals could spend an intelligible period for intellectual and pure-hearted research and study of religion. The Holy Quran states:

> There is no compulsion in religion; truly the right way has become clearly distinct from error [through the Holy Quran and the Messenger]. (The Cow 2:256)

Needless to say, it is not intelligible to give an absolute freedom of belief to an individual and society for whom the right way has not become distinct from the wrong; in fact, they need to be instructed and truly justified. This verse reminds us of a wholly obvious reality in the sense that when the right way becomes distinct from the wrong, every enlightened mind and soul shall accept the divinely revealed religion without compulsion.

Having said this, we could deal with the dilemma of the banning of conversion in Islam, which some believe to be evidently in conflict with Islam's claim to be a pro-freedom religion. Since Islam is the total sum of all human advantages of previous revealed religions and the most secure of all committed rights and freedoms, conversion from Islam not only does not have any advantage for the converter but it also sorely deprives him of intelligible life, which is the basic goal of Islam. Islam indeed means "Abraham's religion," which is the total sum of all revealed religions.

3- Both declarations are unanimous on intellectual property rights, and it is needless to say that intellectual productions need not be contrary to the social norms. Nevertheless, intellectual productions should be by the principles of Shari'ah that secure the moral health of the society as seen in the Islamic Declaration. Thus, no artist, for example, is allowed to use his art for the arousal of sexual instincts in the society.

Generally speaking, one of the underlying differences between the UN and the Islamic Declarations on human rights is that the former only imposes restrictions where the stipulated individual freedoms transgress other peoples' rights while the Islamic Declaration is generally concerned with morality in the sense that freedoms never should endanger the moral ideals of the society.

Does the Conditionality of Freedoms Imply Their Non-existence?

Here we need to answer a serious question: does restricting freedoms for social and individual interests imply their non-existence?

As we have mentioned earlier, this question could be answered by paying earnest attention to the following realities:

I) Laxity and escaping from the laws of society and nature cannot be called "freedom," as they are the very enemies of freedom and human selfhood.

Epicureanism in the sense of seeing pleasure as the highest good in the world has always been criticized by many moral scholars as a false philosophy since the ancient times. Moreover, devoting one's life to the gratification of animal desires in a careless manner leads him to nihilism.

II) When we say "freedom, not laxity," we do not mean to deprive people of the pleasure of freedom and artistic and intellectual creativity, but we are to acquaint them with true pleasures that help man to develop his selfhood.

III) In a society, if some institutions are established to undertake the supervision of intellectual and artistic activities, this does not necessarily imply the nullification of individual freedoms; in fact, these institutions are to distinguish basic realities from vain imaginations. They are indeed to save human minds from the tornado of paradoxes that have stuck them in the swamp of nihilism and deprived them of intelligible and constructive ideas. This is such an enterprise that seems impossible in the face of a universally-followed logic supported by aggressive hunters of power and carnal desires and states that all people are equally entitled to have freedoms even if these people are different regarding the basics of primordial human nature.

The Islamic Declaration

Article 17
Every human being is eligible to be benefited from her/his right to citizenship and no one shall be deprived of her/his citizenship.[200]

The UN Declaration

Article 15
1- Everyone has the right to a nationality.

2- No one shall be arbitrarily deprived of his nationality nor denied the right to change his nationality.

Shared Characteristics

Both declarations are univocal in this article providing citizenship and nationality in this context imply the right of residency.

Differences

Muslims are not permitted to take residence in countries that do not believe in Islamic beliefs and morals, according to Islamic jurisprudence.

The Islamic Declaration

Article 18
Every human being has the right to enjoy his legal capacity regarding both obligation and commitment, should this capacity be lost or impaired, he shall be represented by his guardian.

The UN Declaration

Article 6
Everyone has the right to recognition everywhere as a person before the law.

Shared Characteristics

This article is unanimously agreed upon by both declarations; however,

---

200 - The eighth article of the Tehran Charter; however, this article has been removed from the Cairo Declaration, since there is no such concept as "citizenship in Islam." We have delineated the Islamic sense of this term in Article 20 of this declaration.

there may be some nuances in civil laws prevailing in Muslim countries regarding this matter.

The Islamic Declaration

Article 19

I)   Islam is the religion of unspoiled nature. It is prohibited to exercise any form of compulsion on man or to exploit his poverty or ignorance to convert him to another religion or atheism.

II) It is incumbent upon the state and society to obliterate heresies and the baseless ideas from Muslim societies, and also if possible, from non-Muslim communities through intellectual debates and rational advice. This duty, if fulfilled, could result in the spiritual and intellectual evolution of the society.

III) The coexistence of believers of unorthodox views with the Muslims is a matter that shall be decided by the Islamic Judge who is the guardian of Islamic Shari'ah Law according to the exigencies of time and emerging issues.

The UN Declaration

Article 19 of the UN Declaration is closely related to two other articles in the same declaration, i.e. Articles 15 and 16, which have already been discussed and compared with Articles 18 and 19 in the UN Declaration.

The Islamic Declaration

Article 20

I)   Every man shall have the right, within the framework of Shari'ah, to free movement and to select his place of residence whether inside or outside his country and if persecuted, is entitled to seek asylum in another country. The country of refuge shall ensure his protection until he reaches safety unless asylum is motivated by an act which Shari'ah regards as a crime.

II) No non-Muslim is permitted to cross the Sacred Shrine of Mecca unless with the permission of Leader of Believers.

III) Non-Muslims are not permitted to dwell in Mecca.

The UN Declaration

Article 13

1- Everyone has the right to freedom of movement and residence within the borders of each State.

2- Everyone has the right to leave any country, including his own, and to return to his country.

Article 14

1- Everyone has the right to seek and to enjoy in other countries asylum from persecution.

2- This right may not be invoked in the case of prosecutions genuinely arising from non-political crimes or acts contrary to the purposes and principles of the United Nations.

Shared Characteristics

1- Both declarations are univocal on the freedom of movement and residence within the borders of each state. Moreover, everyone has the right to leave any country, including his own, and to return to his country.

2- Everyone has the right to seek and to enjoy in other countries asylum from persecution and oppression.

3- One cannot seek asylum in any country for non-political crimes.

Differences

1- No Muslim is permitted to choose a country as his residence that is the land of blasphemy and infidelity.

2- That UN Declaration states that the right to seek asylum upon may not be invoked in the case of prosecutions genuinely arising from non-political crimes that could be prosecuted in national courts and according to the civil laws of the society. This right cannot be invoked, according to the Islamic Declaration, even in the case of prosecutions that arise from political crimes when the asylum seeker lives in a country that is governed by Islamic Shari'ah Law.

3- No non-Muslim is permitted to cross the Sacred Shrine of Mecca unless with the permission of Leader of Believers.

The Islamic Declaration

Article 21

Work is a right guaranteed by the state and the society for each person able to work. Everyone shall be free to choose the work that suits him best and which serves his interests and also those of the society. The employee shall have the right to safety and security as well as all other social guarantees. He may neither be assigned work beyond his capacity nor be subjected to compulsion or exploited or harmed in any way – without any discrimination between males and females – except for Shari'ah-prescribed reasons.

Article 22

I)   Every employee shall be entitled to fair wages for his work without delay even if the employee has been unaware of his service's just value either due to his ignorance or because of compulsion. As the Holy Quran states:

> *Therefore give full measure and weight and do not diminish to men their things.* [201]
>
> (The Elevated Places 7:85)

The necessity of paying just value applies to both services and goods; moreover, it also applies to all cases in which the employee or the owner of goods is either aware or unaware of the just value of their services and goods.

II) All workers are entitled to demand fair wages for their works and services, and it is incumbent upon the state to help them attain their right. The employee shall have the right to the holidays' allowances and promotions which he deserves. For his part, he shall be required to be dedicated and meticulous in his work. Should workers and employers disagree on any matter, the state shall intervene to settle the dispute and have the grievances redressed, the rights confirmed and justice enforced without bias.

III) The employee shall be entitled to be provided with his expenses by his employer at the time of disability, senility, and gestation (for female employees) and should the employer prove to be unable to assure this right, the state shall be obliged to undertake the duty.

The UN Declaration

Article 23

1- Everyone has the right to work, to free choice of employment, to just and favorable conditions of work and to protection against unemployment.

2- Everyone, without any discrimination, has the right to equal pay for equal work.

3- Everyone who works has the right to just and favorable remuneration ensuring for himself and his family an existence worthy of human dignity, and supplemented, if necessary, by other means of social protection.

Article 24

Everyone has the right to rest and leisure, including reasonable limitation of working hours and periodic holidays with pay.

Article 25

1- Everyone has the right to a standard of living adequate for the health and

---

201 - Also Huud (11:85) and The Poets (26:183).

well-being of himself and of his family, including food, clothing, housing and medical care and necessary social services, and the right to security in the event of unemployment, sickness, disability, widowhood, old age or other lack of livelihood in circumstances beyond his control.

Shared Characteristics

1- Work is a right guaranteed by the state and the society for each person able to work.

2- Everyone has the right to work, as well as to the free choice of employment.

3- The employee shall have the right to safety and security as well as to all other social guarantees. This right in the Islamic Declaration is conditioned upon something that shall be discussed in differences.

4- No employee may be assigned work beyond his capacity. This right has not been stipulated independently in the UN Declaration, but the articles of this Declaration on the right to work show that it is also concerned about this issue.

5- It is not permitted to subject the employee to compulsion or to exploit him.

6- All employees are equally entitled to work rights without any discrimination between males and females, white and black or eastern and western. The UN Declaration has stipulated this in a more general fashion by saying that "Everyone, without any discrimination, has the right to equal pay for equal work." As we shall tend to be more articulate on differences, this is only about equal pay and does not address other rights.

7- Everyone, without any discrimination, has the right to equal pay for equal work.

8- The employee shall be entitled to be provided with his expenses by his employer at the time of disability, senility, and gestation (for female employees) and should the employer prove to be unable to assure this right, the state shall be obliged to undertake the duty.

Note: Although all citizens are equally entitled to having a decent life and it is incumbent upon the society and the state to provide the conditions of a decent life for all citizens, employees are of greater priority to other citizens in this regard as they exhaust a high amount of energy for the welfare of the society.

Differences

1- Free choice of employment needs only not to be harmful to the individual and the society.

2- No employee may be assigned work beyond his capacity. This right has not been stipulated independently in the UN Declaration, but the articles of this Declaration on the right to work show that it is also concerned about this issue.

3- Although the necessity of avoiding any discrimination between sexes, races, colors and nationalities about the equal rights of work has been implicitly stipulated in the second clause of Article 23 of the UN Declaration, as we have already mentioned, we nonetheless need to be more articulated and stipulated in rights as suitable articulation and clear stipulation help the rights to be easily put into operation.

4- The issue of a fair wage is a point on which the two declarations are explicitly divided. This issue had even sorely been neglected in the Tehran Charter on Human Rights in Islam, and we addressed this issue in our discussions on the right to work. There is no doubt that any negligence in this regard is not tolerable for Islamic jurisprudence concerning the following verse of the Holy Quran that reads,

> *"Therefore give full measure and weight and do not diminish to men their things.* (The Elevated Places 7:85)[202]

The UN Declaration has used two words of "just" and "favourable" in this regard where it reads, "Everyone who works has the right to just and favorable remuneration" and this verbal imprecision has no place in the law.

Note: These two words have three possible implications:

I)   They are complementary in the sense that the wage must be both favorable and just at the same time.

II) The wage has to be just, but necessarily favorable.

III) The wage has to be favorable, but not necessarily just.

The UN Declaration, however, needs to elaborate on this verbal lapse.

According to Islam, wage must be "just," as Justice has more legal burden than fairness. Moreover, if the wage is not favourable for the employee, he could refuse to accept it by his right to free choice of employment, but he cannot call upon legal authorities for his case, since it is taken for granted that the wage has been paid justly, and if the wage is favourable but is not just in the sense that the employee is pleased with his pay but the wage is not just, we need to see whether the employee is informed of the true value of his work or not. If the employee is cognizant of the true value of his service, we need to see why he resigns himself to an unjust pay, and if this resignation signifies ineluctability, then the employer is obliged to pay the just value of his employee's work; otherwise, the employee has the right to call upon legal authorities for his case and it is incumbent upon the society and the state to help him to reach his right. If

---

202 - Also in Poets (26:183) and Huud (11:85).

the employee is uninformed to the just value of his work and is pleased is with the wage that is paid to him by the employer, then according to the previously-cited verse of the Holy Quran that reads:

> *"Therefore give full measure and weight and do not diminish to men their things"* (The Elevated Places 7:85)

The employer is an oppressor, and it is incumbent upon the society and the state to remove the oppression from the employee.

5- According to the Islamic Declaration, all workers are entitled to demand fair wages for their works and services, and it is incumbent upon the state to help them attain their right. Although this right has not been independently stipulated in the UN Declaration, it seems that both declarations are univocal on this matter.

6- The Islamic Declaration binds the employee to be dedicated and meticulous in his work. This duty has not been stipulated in the UN Declaration, while this seems to be a necessary obligation regarding the justice-based relationship between the employer and the employee.

The Islamic Declaration

Article 23

    a) Liability is, in essence, personal.

    b) There shall be no crime or punishment except as provided for in the Shari'ah.

    c) A defendant is innocent until his guilt is proven in a fair trial in which he shall be given all the guarantees of defense.

The UN Declaration

Article 11

1- Everyone charged with a penal offense has the right to be presumed innocent until proved guilty according to the law in a public trial at which he has had all the guarantees necessary for his defense.

2- No one shall be held guilty of any penal offense on account of any act or omission which did not constitute a penal offense, under the national or international law, at the time when it was committed. Nor shall a heavier penalty be imposed than the one that was applicable at the time the penal offense was committed.

Shared Characteristics

1- The presumption of innocence is agreed upon by both Declarations in the sense that a defendant is innocent until his guilt is proven in a fair trial.

2- Liability is, in essence, personal. Although this has not been independently stipulated in the UN Declaration, it is nonetheless deductible from both of the articles mentioned above.

3- No one shall be held guilty of any penal offense on account of any act or omission which did not constitute a penal offense, under the national or international law, at the time when it was committed.

4- Nor shall a heavier penalty be imposed than the one that was applicable at the time the penal offense was committed.

Differences

1- There is no article in the UN Declaration that stipulates the personal essence of liability. Nevertheless, since this is a rational principle agreed upon by all legal systems around the globe we can take it for granted that the UN Declaration has it as a presumed principle as well.

2- One of the underlying differences between the two declarations on human rights is that in Islamic jurisprudence, knowledge is counted among the rational and general conditions of an obligation and as long as the defendant is uninformed of an obligation, no one could punish him on account of an omission or a penal offense. Of course, personal dereliction regarding getting enough knowledge of the duty shall make the defendant liable regarding his negligence.

The Islamic Declaration

Article 24

I) Everyone shall have the right to own property acquired in a legitimate way, and shall be entitled to the rights of ownership without prejudice to oneself, others or to society in general. Expropriation is not permissible except for the requirements of public interest and upon payment of immediate and fair compensation.

II) Confiscation and seizure of property are prohibited except for a necessity dictated by law.

Article 25

I) Everyone shall have the right to legitimate gains without monopolization, deceit or harm to oneself or others.

II) Usury (riba) is absolutely prohibited.

The UN Declaration

Article 17

1- Everyone has the right to own property alone as well as in association with others.

2- No one shall be arbitrarily deprived of his property.

Shared Characteristics

1) Both declarations are univocal on the arbitrary prohibition of confiscation and seizure of property.

2) Although the prohibition of socially harmful ownerships has not been clearly stipulated in the UN Declaration, it is also agreed upon by the UN Declaration as a rational presumption.

3) Although the prohibition of ownerships that may lead to harm in the society has not been explicitly stated in the Universal Declaration of Human Rights as seen in the West, it can be claimed that the proven rights of people living in the society followed by all peoples and nations of the world, Western human rights also regard ownerships that may lead to harm in the society as prohibited. The word "arbitrarily" in the second clause of Article 17 of the Western human rights also points this out.

Differences

1- The inviolability of individual rights is univocally agreed upon by both the Islamic and the occidentally-oriented UN Declarations of human rights. All the same, wherever individual rights imperil public interests, both declarations prefer to side with the society in the wake of reason, or precisely speaking, in keeping with a natural ordinance. But in the case of possible physical or spiritual harms, the UN Declaration gives priority to individual rights, while the Islamic Declaration uses an injunctive language. As a result, nobody is allowed to harm oneself, neither physically nor spiritually, by way of exerting one's right of ownership on something, as indicated by the Islamic Declaration.

2- Usury is prohibited in Islam, and everyone shall have the right to legitimate gains without monopolization, deceit or harm to oneself or others.

The Islamic Declaration

Article 26
Taking hostages under any form or for any purpose is expressly forbidden.

The UN Declaration

Article 3
Everyone has the right to life, liberty, and security of person.

Article 9

No one shall be subjected to arbitrary arrest, detention or exile.

This article includes kidnapping as well. Though the prohibition of kidnapping has not been stipulated in the UN Declaration, one could still infer it upon other articles such as the indicated ones.

The Islamic Declaration

Article 27

I) Authority is a trust, and the abuse or malicious exploitation thereof is prohibited, so that fundamental human rights may be guaranteed.

If Muslim authority is at the hands of Holy Prophets and Immaculate Imams, they shall not be interpellated due to their Divine Immaculateness; otherwise, the interpellation shall necessarily be done according to the provisions of Islamic Shari'ah Law. Interpellation is not a   penal device, but it serves as means of transparency in a democratic sense.

If authority is directly delegated by people – as is believed by Sunnites that God and the Holy Prophet (PBUH) have delegated issues regarding governance to the people to choose, and also in so-called democratic systems – it would be even more significant to ask the ruler to answer for mistakes he has made, for a ruler elected by people may prove to be not only unjust but also guilty of political or non-political crimes.

In any case, since authority is a *dignitate homenis,* it shall be conferred upon those who are just and more adherent to the principles of conscience.

II) Everyone shall have the right to participate, directly or indirectly in the administration of his country's public affairs. All people shall also have the right to assume public office by the provisions of Shari'ah.

The UN Declaration

Article 21

1- Everyone has the right to take part in the government of his country, directly or through freely chosen representatives.

2- Everyone has the right of equal access to public service in his country.

3- The will of the people shall be the basis of the authority of government; this will shall be expressed in periodic and genuine elections which shall be by universal and equal suffrage and shall be held by secret vote or by equivalent free voting procedures.

Shared Characteristics

1- The prohibition of autocracy is agreed upon by both declarations.

2- Everyone has the right to take part in the government of his country, directly or through freely chosen representatives. This participation is merely restricted to public and individual affairs as primary prescripts, and principal rules have been revealed by God the Almighty to the Holy Prophet Muhammad (Peace Be Upon Him).

3- It is univocally agreed upon by both declarations that the will of the people shall be the basis of the authority of government.

4- Both declarations proclaim that all citizens have an equal right to assume public office.

Differences

1- Authority is a highly significant issue in Islam, and according to the principles of Shi'ism, it is a divine affair; as a result, abuse or malicious exploitation thereof is prohibited. Thus conceived, authority is an exclusive right of the Prophet and his impeccable household, in the absence of whom it needs to be passed on to those who are the most in knowledge and piety and wholly purified of carnal desires and passions. This position is wherefrom human duties, and rights both in physical and spiritual domains are revealed.[203]

2- God is the true source of authority and power, as all of His servants are under His administration. Consultation is prescribed in all public affairs except principal rules revealed by God the Almighty.

---

203 - For more detailed discussions on authority from an Islamic point of view, see *The Principles of Politics in Islam: An Interpretation of Imam Ali's Order to Malek Ashtar*, by M. T. Ja'fari. (Originally in Persian).

5
Equalities and Unities

We need to begin by discussing what "equality" and "unity" mean.

The Principle of Equality

It is needless to say that equality in this context does not refer to a complete similarity or homogeneity between human individuals. By the same token, it does not mean that human individuals have the same characteristics, since it is basically a false impression of reality, and even no two inanimate things would be similar in such way, let alone animals or human beings who are the most complicated creatures on the planet when it comes to free will and numerous capacities, forces and possibilities. Thus, human differences are not merely accidental phenomena, but rather genuine in the sense that they are essential prerequisites of human existence, as it is reflected in the general principle that reads:

> As long as a thing has not been individuated by its individual characteristics, it could not exist.[204]

Then what do fraternity and equality mean in this context? To explain this issue, we need to mention that equality here does not refer to a comprehensive issue in all human respects, but rather three equalities about each other:

1- Equality about the supreme source and principles of existence.

2- Equality in the essence and essential qualities.

3- Covenantal equality before natural and positive laws and other rules, which are necessary for the regulation of natural and intelligible life.

These three equalities are divided into twelve principal kinds. Human unities, which are above the equalities, can be categorized into three major kinds. We shall now discuss them here.

The natural equality of human beings can be divided into two kinds:

1- Physical similarity and homogeneity, which is also visible even in other natural bodies; nevertheless, the similarity in this respect could not be a thorough homogeneity. As Rumi says in Book 2 of his *Masnavi*:

> *Incomplete examples and similes serve to relieve man of his confusion and awe; for indeed, no two beings in this world are the same.*

204 - Avicenna, *Al-Isharat wa Al-Tanbihat ("Theorems and Remarks")*, Vol. 2, p. 119.

Moreover, this has also eloquently been depicted in the following mystic rule:

No repetition is possible in physical manifestations of deity.

2- Equality in intangible truths like intellection, imagination, wills, associations of concepts, pleasures, pains and so on and so forth. This is a higher equality than physical equality, as the intangible is essentially more valuable. Therefore, there is truth within human beings that, it perceived, can also lead to the perception of them in others as well.

Unity

Unity in this context does not refer to an absolute unity that could not be manifested but in a supra-quantitative one; rather, it consists of the state of the union in a reality that human individuals can conceive themselves as the parts of the same reality. Thus conceived, human individuals are the closely interwoven constitutive parts of a whole. This shared reality, which represents a whole, can be divided into three kinds:

I) A reality that is as a whole – but not a genuine whole – that is the total sum of its parts, such as a society.

II) The similarity that unites all human individuals with each other like the waves of the same sea. The following verses of the Holy Quran indicates this unity:

> *For this reason, did We prescribe to the children of Israel that whoever slays a soul, unless it is for manslaughter or mischief in the land, it is as though he slew all men; and whoever keeps it alive, it is as though he kept alive all men; and certainly Our messengers came to them with clear arguments, but even after that many of them certainly act extravagantly in the land.*
>
> (The Dinner Table 5:32)

> *And He it is Who has brought you into being from a single soul, then there is (for you) a resting-place and a depository; indeed We have made plain the communications for people who understand.*
>
> (The Cattle 6:98)

III) Acquired unity that could be achieved through acting upon the moral principles and self-purification of evils and carnal passions. This, in fact, is the time when human beings can understand the pleasures and pains felt by each other and experience the divine state of the union.

Thus, human similarities are of two kinds:

1- Equalities

2- Unities

Unities can be categorized into three cases:

A) Unity in the sense of parts of an arbitrary whole, such as the human society that consists of real individuals.

B) A unity above all natural unities and multiplicities, which is not acquired.

C) Unity based on acquired dignity, which exposes human individuals to the eternal sparks of divine majesty.

The Twelvefold Equalities

The unities and equalities discussed here have been driven from authentic Islamic texts; not only do they demonstrate that the idea of human rights has its roots in Islam, but they also show that the universal idea of human rights presumes human evolutionary movement. There are numerous indications in human sciences and cultures about the unity that can be taken as the basis for a just and peaceful coexistence. But no other school of thought has addressed this serious issue better than Islam. According to Islam, there are twelve kinds of equalities and three kinds of unities between human beings:[205]

The First Kind: Equality about the Creator

All human beings have been created by a transcendental being who is the Creator of all creatures:

> *Allah is He who created you, then gave you sustenance, then He causes you to die, then brings you to life. Is there any of your associate-gods who does aught of it? Glory be to Him and exalted be He above what they associate (with Him).* (The Romans 30:40)

The existence of the Divine Being has already been demonstrated by several reasons and His being the Creator of all creatures is a self-evident reality. By understanding this equality, all human individuals could recognize that they all are equally subjected to Divine Love unless they have deprived themselves of this divine bounty by committing evil acts.

The Second Kind: Equality in the Wisdom of the Ultimate Telos

We mean here the Divine Wisdom that has created human individuals

---

205 - Some thinkers suffice to the indication of the indispensability of equality and unity and thus do not give any indication of its reasons and kinds. In his magnum opus *De L' Esprit de Lois*, Montesquieu has stated:

"Human rights are civil laws of the world; that is to say, as in every country the citizens enjoy their civil laws, in the world every nation shall enjoy universal human rights, and before these rights every nation is like an individual in the human society."

Nonetheless, the revealed religions can only meaningfully address the issue of universal equalities and unities of human beings and have the claim for a global family of human beings.

and put them in the course of ultimate telos they are equally equipped to reach using making sincere efforts. The divine wisdom that has rendered the creation of human beings in this possible world consists of illuminative domination of "the human self" over the world through being exposed to absolute perfection which could lead human being to *visio Dei* by sincere efforts in the course of intelligible life. This is the true meaning of Divine Service that has been described as the philosophy of the creation of jinn and man in the Holy Quran:

> *And I have not created jinn and man except that they should serve Me.*
> (The Scatterers 51:56)

The Third Kind: Equality in the Divine Spirit

> *Then He made him complete and breathed into him of His spirit, and made for you the ears and the eyes and the hearts; little is it that you give thanks.*
> (The Adoration 32:9)

The Fourth Kind: Equality in the Planting of the Seeds of Divine Knowledge within Man

> *And He taught Adam all the names, then presented them to the angels; then He said: Tell me the names of those if you are right.*
> (The Cow 2:31)

This verse has surely been revealed as a response from God to the angels regarding the creation of Adam and his children rather than Adam himself, for the question asked by the angels did not pertain to the creation of Adam himself, for he had not shed blood; it was about Adam's children, who had each other's blood on their hands.

The Fifth Kind: Equality in the Factor of the Perfection of the Context of the Divine Message

It is needless to say that all true religions have been revealed for humanity by the Lord, and regarding their primordial unity, the Divine Message of revealed religions is one – and it is Abraham's Religion:

> *The messenger believes in what has been revealed to him from his Lord, and (so do) the believers; they all believe in Allah and his angels and his books and his messengers; we make no difference between any of his messengers; and they say: we hear and obey, our Lord! Thy forgiveness (do we crave), and to Thee is the eventual course.*
> (The Cow 2:285)

> *He has made plain to you of the religion what he enjoined upon Noah and that which we have revealed to you and that which we enjoined upon Abraham and Moses and Jesus that keep to obedience and be not divided therein; hard to the unbelievers is that which you call them to; Allah chooses for himself whom he pleases, and guides to Himself him who turns (to him), frequently.*

(The Counsel 42:13)

It is a demonstrable reality that the Holy Quran has revealed Abraham's message without any distortion.

The Sixth Kind: Equality in Inherent Dignity

This is the very primordial dignity that God has bestowed to all human beings:

> *And surely We have honored the children of Adam, and We carry them in the land and the sea, and We have given them of the good things, and We have made them excel by an appropriate excellence over most of those whom We have created.*
>
> (The Children of Israel 17:70)

The Seventh Kind: Equality in Acquired Dignity

> *O you men! Surely we have created you of a male and a female, and made you tribes and families that you may know each other; surely the most honorable of you with Allah is the one among you most careful (of his duty); surely Allah is knowing, aware.*
>
> (The Chambers 49:13)

The Eighth Kind: Equality in General Orientation

The goals that human beings seek in their life are either related to their natural life or related with their ideal life; moreover, both forms of life are oriented by a primordial sense of self-preservation.

The Ninth Kind: Equality in the Origin of Creation of Human Beings

All human beings have been created from one spirit.

> *O, people! Be careful of (your duty to) your Lord, who created you from a single being and created its mate of the same (kind) and spread from these two, many men and women; and be careful of (your duty to) Allah, by Whom you demand one of another (your rights), and (to) the ties of relationship; surely Allah ever watches over you.*
>
> (The Cow 4:1)

Sa'adi has eloquently poeticized these equalities (the eighth and ninth) in the following renowned lines:

> *Human beings are members of a whole,*
> *in the creation of one essence and soul.*
> *If one member is afflicted with pain,*
> *other members uneasy will remain.*
> *If you've no sympathy for human pain,*
> *the name "human" you cannot retain!*

Rumi, on the other hand, gives a deeper account of this transcendent equality of humanity:

If you see great men of God together,
even if there may be hundreds of thousands of them,
do not think that they are arrogant or wrongdoing;
in fact, they are all like one, like an ocean of water,
their large numbers like the waves of the ocean.
To the simple mind, this will seem like multiplicity,
whereas it is nothing but unity indeed.
One who is aware of what water and the wind are like,
knows only too well that these plentiful waves are caused by the wind upon
the sea,
and will never contradict the unity of the ocean.
Have you not seen sunlight passing through many different holes at the same
time?
Does that imply that the sunlight is not one but many? By no means!
Likewise, men of God have each contained the Holy Divine Spirit within
themselves; indeed, those who feel doubtful about this are in fact captive of
the layers of their physical being.
Such divisions and multiplicities exist in fact only in animal spirits; human
spirits, on the other hand, are one. [206]

The Tenth Kind: Equality in the Matter of Creation

There are several verses in the Holy Quran that introduce the soil as the matter of human creation:

> **And certainly, We created man of clay that gives forth sound, of**
> **black mud fashioned in shape.**   (The Rock 15:26)

The Lord has commissioned the sperm undergoing development within mothers' wombs to sustain human generations:

> **He created man from a small seed and lo! He is an open**
> **contender.**   (The Bee 16:4)

The Eleventh Kind: Equality in Human Essence

All human individuals have different physical and mental peculiarities. That is to say, although all human individuals have been created from a single spirit breathed by the Lord into them all; nonetheless, they enjoy different physical and mental peculiarities that make their individuality. However, God the Almighty has reminded His servants of these shared realities. We shall now cite hereunder three verses of the Holy Quran which indicate these shared realities:

1- The fact that all human beings are equal in their being endowed with the

---

206 - Rumi's *Masnavi*, Book 2.

Divine Spirit:[207]

> So when I have made him complete and breathed into him of My
> spirit, then fall down making obeisance to him.
>
> (Saad 38:72)

2- Reason: there are at least forty verses in the Holy Quran that directly
refer to human reason and its capabilities:

> Know that Allah gives life to the earth after its death; indeed,
> We have made the communications clear to you that you may
> understand.   (The Iron 57:17)

3- Conscience: The following verse is an example:

> Though he puts forth his excuses, do not move
> your tongue with it to make haste with it.
>
> (The Resurrection 75:14-15)

> Nay! I swear by the self-accusing soul.
>
> (The Resurrection 75:2)

The Twelfth Kind: Equality in Laws

Laws in this context include natural and positive laws that have been
legislated for regulating natural and intelligible life.

The Three Kinds of Unities

The First Kind: The Unity beyond All Unities and Differences

This unity exclusively belongs to revealed religions alone. As God Almighty
has stated in the Holy Quran:

> For this reason did We prescribe to the children of Israel that
> whoever slays a soul, unless it is for manslaughter or mischief
> in the land, it is as though he slew all men; and whoever keeps
> it alive, it is as though he kept alive all men; and certainly our
> messengers came to them with clear arguments, but even after
> that many of them certainly act extravagantly in the land.
> (The Dinner Table 5: 32)

There are two points in this verse that are worth to be noted:

1- This holy verse could be summarized in a mathematical formula: all=1
and 1=all. This is the true remedy for all human pains.

2- This unity is a supra-natural reality that could be used as the basis of all
universal rights for humanity.

---

207 - Another example is, "And I created him and breathed into him a Spirit from My
Presence" (The Rocky Tract 15:29)

The Second Unity: Unity by Acquired Dignity

> *The believers are but brethren, therefore make peace between your brethren and be careful of (your duty to) Allah that mercy may be had on you.*
>
> (The Chambers 49: 10)

> *Surely (as for) those who believe and do good deeds for them will Allah bring about love.*
>
> (Marium 19: 96)

Moreover, Abu Basir has quoted Imam Al-Sadegh (SAW) as saying:

> *The believer is the brother of his fellow believers like the organs of the same body; if one organ is afflicted with pain, he feels the pain of that organ. The spirits of believers come from the same Divine Spirit.*[208]

This form of unity is the highest of all unities since it originates from the divine attraction between enlightened spirits. This unity is acquired and is thus more valuable on account of the efforts which should be made by human individuals.

The Third Unity: Social Unity

All human individuals together form the society, and the whole constitution of the society is dependent upon all human individuals. Thus conceived, the individuals' destinies are interwoven. The Holy Prophet Muhammad (Peace Be Upon Him) has been quoted as saying:

> *A group of people got on a ship, and everyone took his seat. One of them started to make a hole in his seat. "What are you doing?" the other passengers asked. "It is my seat, and I am boring into my place." If the passengers try to stop him, they could save their lives and the ship; otherwise, they are all doomed to death.*

Thus, Muhammad (PBUH) is the messenger of true unity and equality between human beings, which is far from the compulsory and sentimental unions that have existed throughout history.

It shall be very useful here to quote Iqbal Lahori, who has argued that:

> *The source of unity of humanity, the Holy Quran, states: "O people! Be careful of (your duty to) your Lord, who created you from a single being" (The Women 4:1). But seeing the life as a general and organized unity is a task carried out at a slow pace, and its development depends on a nation's participation in global equations. Islam has brought man the message of unity, whereas the Roman Empire was not successful in doing so. Flenit has rightly mentioned that no thinker in the Roman Empire had an objective concept of human unity.*[209]

---

208 - Al-Kulayni, *Usul Al-Kafi*, Vol. 2, p. 166.
209 - Mobasheri, Asadullah, *Human Rights*, p. 21. (Originally in Persion).

Lahori continues by quoting a historian of civilization:

> *It seemed that a civilization that has taken four millennia to emerge was in the fall and humanity was on the verge of new barbarism.... Thus, the world was in need of a fresh culture so to be replaced with despotism and autocracy and it was astonishing that this new culture emerged in Arabia.*

Such an astonishment would only be overcome when man realizes that a true form of unity – rather than efforts rising out of pure imaginations, emotions, and fatalistic emergencies – will necessitate a supernatural factor beyond human thoughts and perceptions and that divine tradition have not determined a specific place for the activation of such a factor which can establish a true civilization.

The Islamic Declaration

Article 28

I) All individuals are equal before the law, without distinction between the ruler and the ruled.
II) The right to resort to justice is guaranteed to everyone.
III) Everyone who lives in the Islamic society is not to cause turmoil in the society, and everyone who lives in a non-Islamic society is also obliged not to corrupt the society, regardless of his race, color, language, religion – providing that it is not based on heresies and unprincipled beliefs – nationality and social class shall be entitled to be benefitted from all freedoms and rights stipulated in Universal Declaration of Human Rights in Islam.

Article 29

Every human being has an equal right to establish societies for charity activities, and all individuals are entitled to found associations for social and political consultations, providing they do not trample on the constitution and governing provisions of the society. Should there be any legal deficiencies, they shall need to consult and cooperate with the authorities in a peaceful manner.

The UN Declaration

Article 10

Everyone is entitled in full equality to a fair and public hearing by an independent and impartial tribunal in the determination of his rights and obligations and any criminal charge against him.

Article 7

All are equal before the law and are entitled without any discrimination to equal protection of the law. All are entitled to equal protection against any discrimination in violation of this Declaration and any incitement to such discrimination.

Article 2

1- Everyone is entitled to all the rights and freedoms outlined in this Declaration, without distinction of any kind, such as race, color, sex, language, religion, political or another opinion, national or social origin, property, birth or another status.

2- Furthermore, no distinction shall be made on the political, jurisdictional or international status of the country or territory to which a person belongs, whether independent, trust, non-self-governing or under any other limitation of sovereignty.

Article 20

1- Everyone has the right to freedom of peaceful assembly and association.

2- No one may be compelled to belong to an association.

Article 28

Everyone is entitled to a social and international order in which the rights and freedoms outlined in this Declaration can be fully realised.

Article 29

1- Everyone has duties to the community in which alone the free and full development of his personality is possible.

2- In the exercise of his rights and freedoms, everyone shall be subject only to such limitations as are determined by the solely for the purpose of securing due recognition and respect for the rights and freedoms of others and of meeting the just requirements of morality, public order and the general welfare in a democratic society.

Shared Characteristics

1- Both declarations are univocal on the essentiality of the equality of all human individuals, groups and organizations before the law. Moreover, all individuals, groups, and organizations are to enjoy equal rights. Although this is a universally approved judicial principle, and has been accepted by people of various societies who had perceived the concept of respect for and the greatness of the law in regard to one another in all aspects of their life, it has always been violated by the aggressive hunters of power, whose lone logic is "I am the goal and the others are my means," and believe that all human laws, even the strongest, should all be regarded as feeble as a spider's web so that they can do as they please.

2- Both declarations regard the resort to justice as a global right guaranteed for all human individuals.

3- Everyone who lives in the Islamic society is not to cause social turmoil, and everyone who lives in a non-Islamic society is also obliged not to corrupt the society, regardless of his race, color, language, religion – providing that it is not based on heresies and unprincipled beliefs – nationality, and social class shall be entitled to be benefitted from all freedoms and rights stipulated in the Universal Declaration of Human Rights in Islam.

4- Every human being has an equal right to establish societies for charity activities and all individuals are entitled to found associations for social and political consultations, providing they do not trample on the constitution and governing provisions of the society. Should legal deficiencies arise, they shall need to consult and cooperate with the authorities in a peaceful manner.

5- Everyone is entitled in full equality to a fair and public hearing by an independent and impartial tribunal, in the determination of his rights and obligations and any criminal charge against him. Both declarations are univocal on the essentiality of this right.

6- All are equal before the law and are entitled, without any discrimination, to equal protection of the law. All are entitled to equal protection against any discrimination in violation of this Declaration and any incitement to such discrimination.

7- Everyone is entitled to all the rights and freedoms outlined in this Declaration, without distinction of any kind, such as race, color, sex, language, religion, political or another opinion, national or social origin, property, birth or another status. This basic right has always been violated both in the past and in the present by the aggressive chasers of power, wealth, fame, and name. Unfortunately, today many of those so-called protagonists of human rights are themselves the real discriminators. Even many natural disasters can be regarded as divine reactions to these discriminations.

8- Everyone is entitled to a social and international order in which the rights and freedoms outlined in both Declarations can be fully realized. Article 28 of the Western human rights is in line with the common points between the two legal systems this book has discussed.

9- Everyone has duties to the community in which alone the free and full development of his personality is possible. If one lives in a society that does not have the necessary conditions for the realization of this ideal, one will have to move to another society.

10- In the exercise of their rights and freedoms, as indicated by the common points seen in the two declarations, three issues are seen as prohibited in Islam:

a) When these rights and freedoms interfere with secondary laws or decrees issued by officials of Islamic societies.

b) When these rights and freedoms interfere with the rights of other individuals; in such cases, judiciaries and other relevant officials will take action based on the principle "the more important has priority over the important."

c) If the execution of the rights and freedoms indicated in the common points in the two declarations necessitate distortions and disturbances in other moral issues of the society and leads to corruption, they shall be limited to safeguard moral standards and eliminate corruption.

Differences

1- If someone's presence in a society is needed, he is obliged to enter that society to fulfill a duty according to the provisions of the Shari'ah Law; otherwise, he or she shall be punished.

2- Both declarations are univocal in their insistence upon the essence of morality, public order and general welfare in a democratic society in the exercise of rights and freedoms; nonetheless, it should be taken into consideration that these conditions are different in an Islamic society. Concisely speaking, freedom, as understood by Westerners, is not compatible with the articulated meaning of freedom as seen by an Islamic society. The rights and freedoms stipulated in Islamic Declaration are all morally and religiously oriented, and it is, in fact, this orientation that makes their full realization possible.

3- The UN Declaration's second article has pointed out that people of all ethnic groups, races, genders, nationalities, languages and social ranks are entitled to all rights and freedoms – both legal systems are univocal on this point. However, it has not addressed the issue of religious beliefs in a meaningful fashion; as we have previously seen in our discussion on Article 6 of the Declaration of Islamic Human Rights as well as the issue f illegitimate children in our study of Article 11, the two systems do not see eye to eye here.

The Islamic Declaration

Article 30

I) All of the rights and freedoms stipulated in this Declaration are subject to the Islamic Shari'ah.

II) In non-Islamic societies, people shall need to commit themselves to their native rights and duties. This is the commitment maxim which reads:

> Commit all those who are not co-religionist with you to what they are committed to themselves.[210]

---

210 - See Shahidi Tabrizi, Fattah, *Tahzib-ul-kalam fi Qa'idat ul-Ilzam.*(Originally in

Article 31

The Islamic Shari'ah is the only source of reference for the explanation or clarification of any of the articles of this Declaration.

Note 1. Whereas some of the articles stipulated in this Declaration may be matters of dispute between jurisprudents, Muslim states shall be obliged to establish an organization for the proximity of Islamic schools of jurisprudence.

Note 2.Continuous comparisons shall be made between Islamic and Western concepts of human rights.

Article 32

Islamic states – whether member states of the Organization of Islamic Conference or independent states – shall be obliged to afford all rights and duties stipulated in this Declaration.

Note:

I) It shall be obligatory upon member states to establish an organization to observe the process of the implementation of the articles of the declaration in Islamic societies, and each member shall have at least one representative of that organization. Every member state shall need to have a national organization to observe the process of the execution of the articles in the corresponding country.

II) The articles stipulated in this Declaration shall be, having undergone research and articulation by jurists and ratified by just jurisprudents and authorities of Islamic countries, regarded as "Limits Ordained by God" and nobody shall be allowed to transgress them.

> *These are the limits of Allah, so do not exceed them and whoever exceeds the limits of Allah these it is that are the unjust.*

(The Cow 2: 229)

The UN Declaration

Article 30

Nothing in this Declaration may be interpreted as implying for any state, group or person any right to engage in any activity or to perform any act aimed at the destruction of any of the rights and freedoms set forth herein.

Shared Characteristics

1- Both declarations have strongly prohibited possible abuses of stipulated rights and freedoms.

2- Nothing in these Declarations may be interpreted as implying for any state, group or person any right to engage in any activity or to perform any act aimed at the destruction of any of the rights and freedoms set

Arabic).

forth herein.

Differences

1- It has not been determined in the UN Declaration who is in charge of the interpretation of stipulated articles and rights. The Islamic Declaration is, on the other hand, very clear on this matter: "The Islamic Shari'ah is the only source of reference for the explanation or clarification of any of the articles of this Declaration."

2- Islamic Shari'ah is the only source of legitimacy of rights and freedoms stipulated in the Islamic Declaration.

3- In non-Islamic societies, people shall need to commit themselves to their native rights and duties. This is the commitment maxim which reads: *Commit all those who are not co-religionist with you to what they are committed to themselves.* There is no such stipulation in the occidentally-motivated UN Declaration, which obliges all people around the globe to adhere to the articles stipulated in the declaration.

4- In the first clause of Article 31 as some of the articles stipulated in this Declaration may be matters of dispute between jurisprudents, Muslim states shall be obliged to establish an organization for the proximity of Islamic schools of jurisprudence. Moreover, continuous comparisons shall be made between Islamic and Western concepts of human rights. These notes reveal the inherent dynamicity and tolerance within the Islamic Declaration.

5- The second note of Article 31 of the Islamic Declaration shows the necessity of a mutual discourse between the East and the West for the full development of human aspirations regarding man's global rights and freedoms.

6- One of the major differences between Islamic and the occidentally-oriented UN Declaration lies in the issue of practical sanctions. Although many nations around the globe have ratified the UN Declaration as a universal covenant and committed themselves to its execution, there are nonetheless countless cases in which the articles and clauses of the human rights are not in line with the laws, beliefs and moral ethics of various countries, such as Islamic countries and many Oriental and also third-world countries. Therefore, those in charge of the execution of these rights will fall into difficulties, in particular when discriminations arise – which frequently occurs. On the other hand, the factor guaranteeing the execution of human rights from Islam's point of view pertains to Islamic sources. As mentioned in the second clause of Article 32, all of these articles and their corresponding clauses are regarded as "God's Limits," the execution of which has been guaranteed by the context of the religion of Islam.

About the Author

Muhammad Taghi Ja'fari (1923-1998) was born in a religious family in Tabriz, Iran. His parents were pious and greatly respected by the community. The Allameh started formal schooling from the 4th grade, as he had already been taught reading and writing by his mother at home. The Allameh's formal religious education began at the Talebieh seminary in Tabriz, where he became an outstanding student of Ayatollah Shahidi's. He had also studied under the celebrated teachers of his time in Tehran and Qom for a while, but his real mentor advised him to attend the Najaf School of Theology, where he stayed for 11 years. He made remarkable progress and was awarded the highest degree of jurisprudence – *Ijthad* – at the young age of 23. After completing his education, he began teaching at Najaf.

Ja'fari is a contemporary sage who has expounded his theory about the sociology of Islam. His domain of interest includes practical issues and problems faced by people in their social lives. He is an original and innovative thinker in providing genuine solutions being well versed in Islamic *fiqh*, methods of Western philosophy, and knowledge as it is advanced by social sciences. He has continued the tradition of great masters like Allameh Tabatabaei, the martyr Ayatollah Seyed Muhammad Bagher Sadr, and the martyr Ayatollah Motahhari to bring classical Islamic knowledge in modern diction to quench the thirst of youth with the eternal spring of original knowledge. To realize the mission, the honorable master Allameh Muhammad Taghi Ja'fari has made innovative use of knowledge extracted from modern disciplines like psychology, sociology, anthropology and political science by rationalizing it in the context of classic Muslim Philosophy and ethics as coded in Nahj-al-balaqeh, Rumi's *Masnavi* and other great works.

His voluminous work speaks unconditionally of the rejuvenation of rational thought in Islam. He offers us a broad range of topics and issues related to human needs and basic rights discussed in various paradigms, such as the arts, the humanities, philosophy, aesthetics, literature, mysticism, psychology, and pedagogy. In spite of being a devoted scholar of Muslim philosophy and also a master of *fiqh* (jurisprudence), he did not ignore the invaluable wealth of wisdom replete in Islamic mysticism. The Allameh had fully realized the powerful impact of classical Greek thoughts in the renaissance of the European World. He knew how to dive deep for pearls of wisdom in the works of ancient philosophers such as Socrates, Plato, and

Aristotle as well as modern, e.g. Descartes, Leibniz, Hume, Kant, and Hegel. His great appetite for knowledge also relished the taste of world literature such as Balzac, Dostoevsky, Tolstoy, Hugo, and modern-day physicists including Max Planck and Einstein. He says:

> *"The true intellectual should always maintain his contact with the vast sea of knowledge in the flow of time, and make use of current logics, known cause-and-effects and their impacts tactfully to make intelligible life in his society a reality. It is mandatory to feel a personal obligation and do one's duty by taking any number of suitable measures to realize one's mission."*

His contemporaries remember him as a man who "never rejected anyone; Allameh Ja'fari was a teacher, not a judge!" His passion was to unveil the unknown about the phenomenon of human life. "Life," he believed, "should always be inspired by the original and must follow originality, or it would be merely a burden on man's shoulders." He can be called the philosopher of life, for most of his intellectual pursuits involved knowing about the relationship between man and society. He believed that "Beyond their appearance, all human cultures have a lot in common, and are inseparably associated." He was in search of that unitary element that devises "common human culture" and was able to present it in uniform styles of life that are observed in all societies and cultures: the 'natural' lifestyle and the 'intelligible' one.

Allameh Ja'fari shared a long and intimate friendship with his contemporaries Muhammad Reza Muzaffar, the great philosopher, and Ahmad Amin, the renowned mathematician of Baghdad University and author of the book *At-takamol fil-Islam ("Evolution in Islam")*. The Allameh also had a great taste for modern social sciences and began his research work with open-minded skepticism. Allameh Ja'fari strongly believed in originality and discussion. Those who knew him well and had witnessed his long years of study and research would admit that nothing was more important to him than asking and answering questions. He often shifted from one field of science to another in search of answers to questions and spent most of his time reading books that contained new scientific material and ideas, which provided him with new questions. He said:

> *"Questions mean that the questioner is saying that he has encountered a dark point on his path toward knowledge, and is eager to overcome it. Thus, passing the bridges and turns of doubt that are the necessity of the phenomenon we call asking, is quite natural. In fact, we can say that on the long road to knowledge, the more bridges and turns we pass with certainty, the better. That means facing many questions."*

The Allameh's epistemic geometry comprises of the knowledge of the mind, the revelation of the heart, tradition and modernity, physics and metaphysics, and law and aesthetics. While the first three sources were the main pillars of his thinking, still the expressions of his thoughts were the result of a dialogue among the different basis of this epistemic geometry, which for its up-to-date research and dialogue, made his works novel and attentive to the debates on the issues and problems faced by the "modern human" in the "modern life".

His first book, *The Relationship between Man and the Universe*, shows the enthusiasm of a young scholar in pursuit of knowledge as well as his firm faith and fortitude in the principles of Islam. The Allameh strongly believed that man and the universe have objectives and attainable goals and these goals are far higher than man's material pleasures and worldly desires. He has explained his theories based upon "the four relationships" and "the six questions." His six basic questions are: Who am I? Where have I come from? Where have I come to? Who am I with? Why am I here? And where do I go from here? The Allameh would never leave mankind to drown in his "what there is;" he always called a man to "what there should be." Looking for moral excellence, he seeks his ideal values and behaviors in Imam Ali (PBUH), regarding him as the best proof of the four relationships (1- man-himself, 2-man-God, 3-man-the universe, 4- man-his fellow humans).

A Commentary, Review, and Analysis of Rumi's Masnawi in fifteen volumes and *A Translation and Interpretation of the Nahj-al-balaqeh* in twenty-seven volumes have a distinct place in the Allameh's body of work. Referring to the former, Professor Nasr has noted in the foreword he wrote for "The Structure of Rumi's Mathnawi" written by Professor Safavi (Safavi, S. G., 2006), "it allowed for the tradition of writing commentaries on *Masnawi*, from Mulla Hadi Sabzevari to Allameh Ja'fari, to endure." Moreover, when the Allameh took the challenge of writing commentaries on these two noble texts, one of which is rendered "the Quran in Persian" by Jami and the other is the immortal work of the Master of Masters, Imam Ali (PBUH), both of these texts were considered obsolete in intellectual circles of seminaries as well as universities. Clergies would hesitate to talk about the *Masnawi* in fear of heresy, and writing commentaries on the *Nahj-al-Balagheh* was considered a virtue, not a science. The scholarship was and still, is seen as footnoting on important books of *fiqh* (jurisprudence). It was in such an environment that the honorable master unveiled the beauty of the *Masnawi*, restoring its worth and esteem in the creative minds of students and scholars.

By comparing Rumi's sublime and amorous assertions with those of French and Russian thinkers and scholars, with whom modern Iranian intellectuals are more familiar, he reintroduced the *Masnawi* to Iranians who were acquainted with the Western thought and culture only. Afterward, by writing an exegesis on the *Nahj-al-balaqeh*, "A Manifesto on Wisdom, Mysticism, and Politics," he familiarized the younger generation with Islam as a religion which is devoid of superstition, factionalism, and backwardness, an Islam based on the appropriation of the mind, revelation, justice and love. We deem the Allameh as the revivalist of the spirit of the *Ummah* by role playing the vanguard of spiritual assets of Islam, the *Masnawi*, and the *Nahj-al-balageh*. Not only will contemporary scholars benefit from this beacon of light, but the future generations will also continue seeking illumination through this valuable resource.

According to Allameh Ja'fari, the spirit of love and creativity of the mind are the two wings that make humans fly towards the absolute truth. The mind and revelation, science and religion, the mind and Shari'a (Islamic law) are all compatible and do not contradict one another. Of course, the mind is the solid pillar of knowing (episteme). His political vision renders justice, compassion, mercy, tolerance, serving the people, reliance on consultation (*Shura*) and shared decision-making as the founding pillars of Islamic governance.

Ja'fari was genuinely a humble and modest person, sound in character, and gentle in mannerism. Despite his high stature, he always kept a low profile, neither exaggerating nor exhibiting traces of arrogance and contemptuousness for others. He completely devoted himself to the cultivation of rational thought in Muslims, preparing them to get into intelligible life. The book *Intelligible Life* has been authored by the ideas that Allameh Ja'fari has dealt with in the 8th volume of his 27-volume translation and interpretation of the *Nahj-al-Balagheh*. These ideas mainly belong to the fifth decade of the Allameh's intellectual life.

He passed away on 15 November 1998 suffering from a cancer disease in London. He was buried in Dar-Al-Zohd, by Imam Reza's Holy Shrine in Mashhad.

The Allameh Ja'fari Institute

Translator's Note

I have a dream that one day on the red hills of Georgia the sons of former slaves and the sons of former slave owners will be able to sit down together at the table of brotherhood... I have a dream that my four little children will one day live in a nation where they will not be judged by the color of their skin but by the content of their character.[211]

Imagine a Bangladeshi rural girl sleeping every night with the nightmare that she would lose her life tomorrow morning when she is swimming with her classmates through the lake while carrying their books and clothes in copper cauldrons so as to get to their school. Our South Asian rural girl and her friends are not alone in being deprived of their basic right to have free and easy access to education. There are millions of children around the globe who are suffering from such tragic deprivation. Surprisingly, such tragedies keep occurring at the moment in history prescribed as the age of rights. Although we are no longer witness to old racial disputes and slavery, this does not mean that we live in a just world. Not only have slavery, discrimination, and injustice not been uprooted from human societies, but they have in fact been restructured in a much more intricate fashion and transplanted into organizations and institutions around the globe.

The present work on Human Universal Rights by Allameh Muhammad Taghi Ja'fari has addressed this sore condition of basic human rights in the modern world. Ja'fari believes that the struggle for human rights began with the creation of man; it is spread across the leaves of history book reminiscent of life-long movements initiated by conscious minds and concerned hearts. M. T. Ja'fari very well explains his point of view is substantiating his claim through historical exemplifications. He subtly draws our attention towards the Universal Declaration of Human Rights having occidental orientation and the Cairo Declaration on Universal Human Rights as an allegedly Islamic approach to the problem. Ja'fari's stance here is not to create an opposition; as a matter of fact, he invites the scholars and codifiers to confront the problem of human rights with open-mindedness and a comparative spirit to reach the best solution. Ja'fari finds both declarations insufficient in addressing the

---

211 - Martin Luther King, Speech at Civil Rights March in Washington, 28 August 1963, in *New York Times*, 29 August, 1963, p. 21

fundamental question of human rights as they have both been issued from a partial and non-primordial perspective. Instead, Ja'fari contends, we need more natural views grounded in Primordial Law that may provide us with enough integration before dealing with practical issues of the problem. He seeks unity in Abrahamic Faith and proposes that representatives of major Abrahamic Religions (Judaism, Christianity, and Islam) must sit together to seek the true path that could lead humanity to the threshold of justice and equity. This book is an interdisciplinary meta-theoretical encounter with a theoretically disciplinarian issue. Ja'fari does not argue in favor or against a theory, but he carefully evaluates each point in an attempt to reach the truth. The reader will undergo an enlightening experience, as Ja'fari slowly and gradually unfolds the myths and realities about various movements for human rights, their agenda and their achievements regarding coding of rights in a charter. The experience adds value as we encounter an enlightened conscience and honest spirit dedicated to seeking Truth.

This work would have never seen the light of day if some people had not helped me during its translation process. Ali Ja'fari, the director of The Allameh Ja'fari Institute, informed me of the importance of this work and the necessity of its translation and publication for a global audience. I am sincerely grateful for his incessant supports and sympathies. Mr. Shahriar Fassih generously accepted to edit my translation. Verily, what the reader finds of eloquence in my translation is his. I am also indebted to my friend Dr. Hossein Nabilou from Erasmus University Rotterdam, who greatly inspired me with the peripatetic debates we had with each other on the alternative perspectives on human rights. The last but not the least, this work has been possible through sympathetic associations and sincere accompaniments of my lifelong Socratic company Dr. Sedigheh Moosazadeh Nalband, whose presence has always encouraged me to enter the wonderlands of knowledge. I express my wholehearted gratitude and humbly dedicate this work to her as a small compensation for the hard times she has undergone with me.

Beytollah Naderlew
Nov. 2012

Epilogue

It is indeed a pleasure to review a book from M. T. Ja'fari on the most interesting and hotly debated topic: Human Rights. The rise of capitalism has enthralled the whole world with its promise of liberal economy. There is rat race going on for a better style of life and status. The education is an industry which is assembling a huge number of graduates with enough technical knowledge to serve the aims of industry and corporation. Getting a good job and earning money is enough. The wisdom of seeking a purposeful life is no more the goal of life. Many educationists and thinkers blame the modern education system for its failure to develop proper morals and character.

Allameh Ja'fari, with his thoughtful concern for humanity, expresses his doubts about the intended fruitful outcomes of the Universal Declaration of Human Rights, where advocacy for democracy has, in fact, become advocacy for capitalism and secularism. The emerging tendencies of powerful governments do not offer any egalitarian worldview offering equality and equity, the promise of Islam to humanity. By taking an Islamic stance, Ja'fari has not opposed to basic rights for food, shelter, and safety, or scope to earn a decent living for oneself; in fact, Ja'fari's concern is with relatively serious issues faced by knowledge society, self-esteem, ethics, character building, family bonding, etc. Ja'fari is of the view that the Universal Declaration of Human Rights has presented only one side of the picture, and balance of human relationships, especially between the genders has become lopsided. Ja'fari envisions the world in which rights are balanced with duties and accountability to authority.

M. T. Ja'fari forewarns that the prevalent atmosphere of the countries does not reflect any possibility of real freedom and liberty as discussed in Intelligible Life previously or as identified in the 4th part of this book. Allameh Ja'fari renders the Universal Declaration of Human Rights as a deceptive, masking effort. When this charter was offered, the Western capitalist influence was declining on the international community as communism was readily becoming popular; therefore, the West had desperately wanted to sustain its influence. Moreover, in-house antagonism against war was also increasing. Autocracy (ruling others by force) exhibited in wars and democracy (empowering people) propagated at home are two opposing ideas and people around the world were becoming mindful of this conflict. Therefore, international face-saving had become vital. Thus, it was decided to give a sweet pill to worldwide community in shape of the

Universal Declaration of Human Rights to awaken in their consciousness more want for freedom. They were given the impression that this human rights charter will emancipate them of their current problems. This way they were able to entice the world into an idea of wayward freedom: fight for the rights and forget about the duties and responsibilities. The oppressed communities around the world readily accepted this idea as a quick fix, and they were deceived into another ideological slavery. The main challenge of restoring world peace or human dignity remained as it is and human beings' status could only be lifted from "social animal" to "social machine."

Ja'fari does not oppose the UN Charter of Human Rights for its content; in fact, he has hinted upon its lack of application in real terms. Even after a hundred years, the Charter has failed to take effect. Therefore, he feels obliged to question its moral base; how sincere were its codifiers in its real time application? Did they want to use it as an excuse to hunt the weak and opposing nations or did they plan to use it as a weapon to alienate some upcoming threatening nations? Since the intentions remain misty covered under a cloud of skepticism, and the charter itself does not seem to do intended good anywhere in the world until today, the Allameh appears very strong in his criticism.

Allameh Ja'fari recommends that the human rights charter must acknowledge first of all the foundation of human existence, which is not only biological or social but psychological and moral as well. Then it should be well versed in the course of human social and moral development as well. Most of the conditions, violating human rights emerge from a misinterpretation of laws and cultural customs. In *Intelligible Life*, Ja'fari has gifted us with a deep insight into major styles of living; this book offers us the scope of implications of following these styles that may lead to increase in narcissism and despotism all around the world. Ja'fari warns us clearly that just saving natural ecology would not ensure the sustainability of life; as a matter of fact, what is needed is to pay attention to basic human dilemma, i.e., to define human identity and dignity, which must be distinctive from animals and other lower forms of life. Unless human beings are recognized as moral and conscientious beings, the purpose of human rights will not be realized. Ja'fari is hopeful and thinks that knowledge society is ready to bear such a responsibility, only a declaration is needed, and Ja'fari's principles of equalities and unities do the needful.

Seema Arif

Lahore. Pakistan

Index

A

Abbas Mahmud Al-Aghad 67
Abdulaziz Fahmi 24
Abdulhalim Najjar 18, 266
Abi Muhammad Abdullah ibn Abdul-hakam 219
Abortion 112, 116, 122, 145, 154, 156
Abraham 170, 219, 226, 241, 242, 257
Abrahamic Religions 60, 62, 170, 257
Abrahamism 102, 103
Abstract culture 40
Abu Basir 245
Abul-Ehtayah 216
Abu Muhammad al-Hassan Ibn al-Hussein Ibn Shu'ba al-Harrani 63, 116
Abusa'idi, Mahdi 23, 24, 28, 266
Academy of International law 36
Acquired dignity 162, 163, 171, 176, 240
Acquired Dignity 163, 242, 245
Adam 46, 104, 125, 163, 164, 168, 169, 174, 176, 220, 241, 242, 252
Afghanistan 41
Al-Biruni 183, 210
Al-Farabi 210
al-fetra 16
Al-Isharat wa Al-Tanbihat 238, 266
Al-Kulayni, Muhammad Ibn Yaqoub 65
Al-Wafi 220
al-wathighah 118
American Declaration of Independence 25
Antigone 20
Antisthenes 20
Applied ethics 19
Aquinas Thomas 25
Argentina 41
Aristotle 210, 217, 253

Attila 83
Avicenna 183, 210, 238

B

Basic laws 26
Beier, Ullie 16, 266
Belarus 41
Belgium 41
Bihar Al-Anwar 171
Bolivia 41
Bondsman 21
Bouden 36
Brazil 41
Bréhier, Émile 18, 266
Burma 41

C

Cairo 118, 119, 120, 121, 122, 123, 125, 129, 132, 156
Cambodia 41
Canada 41, 87
Carrel, Alexis 183
Catherine 34
Cesare Borgia 52
Charmont 36
Chili 41
China, People's Republic of 41, 42, 74
Christianity 62, 66, 126, 170, 185, 257
Cicero 23
Civilized man's Eight Deadly
Claude, Inis L.
  27
Civil law 20, 23, 228, 229, 240
Civil rights 27, 29, 256
Colonialism 128, 221, 223
Columbia 41
Committed freedom 71, 95, 98, 105, 107, 124, 128, 154, 189, 191, 194, 224
Compartmentalization 50
Costa Rica 41
Cuba 41
Cyrus 22
Czechoslovakia 41

Bibliography

➤ Abi Muhammad Abdullah ibn Abdulhakam, *The Life of Omar Ibn Abdul Aziz as Narrated by Malek ibn Anas.*

➤ Abu Muhammad al-Hassan Ibn Ali Ibn al-Hussein Ibn Shu'ba al-Harrani, *Tuhaf ul-Ughul.*

➤ Abusa'idi, Mahdi, *Human Rights and Its Evolutionary Course in the West.*

➤ Avicenna, *Al-Isharat wa Al-Tanbihat ("Theorems and Remarks").*

➤ Beier, Ullie, *The Origin of Life and Death: African Creation Myths*, translated by Z.A. Sadighi.

➤ Bréhier, Émile, *The Religious and Philosophical Ideas of Philo of Alexandria* (*Études de philosophie antique*), 1955, translated by Muhammad Yusef Musa and Abdulhalim Najjar, (Arabic translation).

➤ Claude, Inis L. Jr., *Swords into Plowshares: The Problems and Progress of International Organization*, New York: Random House, 1956.

➤ Del Vecchio, Giorgio, *Philosophie de Driot*, Persian translation by Javad Wahedi.

➤ Dougherty, James E., Pfaltzgraff , Robert L., *Contending Theories of International Relations.*

➤ Du Pasquier, Claude, *A la Philosophie du droit introduction a la Theorie*, Persian translation by Muhammad Ali Tabatabaei.

➤ Fahmi, Abdulaziz, *On Justinian Codes*, (originally in Arabic).

➤ Ferdowsi's *Shahnameh.*

➤ Frank, Philipp, *Einstein, His Life and Times*, Persian translation by H. Saffari.

➤ Gaddis, John Lewis, *The United States and the Origins of Cold War*, 1972.

➤ Ghasemzadeh, Murteza, *The French Constitution.*

➤ Shahidi Tabrizi, Fattah, *Tahzib-ul-kalam fi Qa'idat ul-Ilzam.*

➤ Hassan al-Hassan, *al-Qanun al-Dastouri wal-Dastour fi Lobnan.*

➤ Ja'fari, Muhammad Taghi, *Positive Mysticism*, the Allameh Ja'fari Institute, Tehran, 2008.

➤ Ja'fari, Muhammad Taghi, *The Principles of Politics in Islam: An Interpretation of Imam Ali's Order to Malek Ashtar*, the Allameh Ja'fari Institute, Tehran, 2009.

➤ Ja'fari, Muhammad Taghi, *Science and Religion in Intelligible Life*, the Allameh Ja'fari Institute, Tehran 2001.

➤ Ja'fari, Muhammad Taghi, *The Fundamentals of Education*, the Allameh Ja'fari

Institute, Tehran, 2009.

➢ Ja'fari, Muhammad Taghi, *Legal Inquiries* the Allameh Jafari Institute, Tehran 2014.

➢ Ja'fari, Muhammad Taghi, *A Translation and Interpretation of the Nahj ul-Balaghah.*

➢ Ja'fari, Muhammad Taghi, *The Message of Wisdom*, the Allameh Ja'fari Institute, Tehran, 2000.

➢ Ja'fari, Muhammad Taghi, *The Human Genome Project*, the Allameh Ja'fari Institute, Tehran, 2014.

➢ Ja'fari, Muhammad Taghi, *Intelligible Life*, translated into English by Beytollah Naderlew and edited by Seema Arif, 2000.

➢ Javan, Mousa, *Fundamentals of Laws.*

➢ *Keyhan*, No. 6627, September 7, 1965.

➢ Khaje Nasir-e Tusi, *Akhlaq-e Naseri (Naserian Ethics).*

➢ Lisbani, Herbert J., *Law in Islam*, translation by Z. Rahnema.

➢ Mobasheri, Asadullah, *Human Rights.*

➢ Moghtader, Hooshang, *The Developments of United Nations.*

➢ Montesquieu, Charles Louis de Secondat, *De L' esprit de Lois*, Persian translation by Ali Akbar Mohtadi.

➢ Muhammad Ibn Yaqoub Koleyni,

➢ Fayz Kashani, Mullah Mohsen, *Al-Wafy.*

➢ Motahhari, Morteza, *Women's Rights in Islam.*

➢ *The Nahj ul-Balagha.*

➢ Pirnia, Hassan, *Ancient Persia.*

➢ *The Holy Quran.*

➢ Rumi, *Divan-e Shams.*

➢ Rumi, *Masnavi.*

➢ Sa'adi, *Gulistan.*

➢ Sabien, George, *History of Political Philosophy*, Persian translation by Baha'oddin Pazargad.

➢ Sarton, George, , *The History of Science*, Persian translated by Ahmad Aram.

➢ Sheikh Abbas Qomi, *Safinat Al-Bihar.*

➢ Sheikh al-Horre al-Ameli, *Wasa'el al-Shi'ah.*

➢ Tabatabaee, Allameh Seyyed Muhammad Hussein, *Almizan* ("The Balance", A Commentary of the Holy Quran).

➢ Whitehead, Alfred North, *Adventures of Ideas.*

➢ *Yearbook on Human Rights*, 1949.

www.ingramcontent.com/pod-product-compliance
Lightning Source LLC
Chambersburg PA
CBHW052015030426
42335CB00026B/3163